Child Abuse Errors

Child Abuse Errors
When Good Intentions Go Wrong

DENNIS HOWITT

 Rutgers University Press
New Brunswick, New Jersey

First published in cloth and paperback in the United States of America
by Rutgers University Press, 1993

First published in cloth and paperback in the United Kingdom by
Harvester Wheatsheaf, a division of Simon & Schuster International
Group, 1992

Copyright © 1992 by Dennis Howitt

Typeset in 10/12 pt Times and Optima by Keyboard Services, Luton
Printed and bound in Great Britain by
BPCC Wheatons Ltd, Exeter

Library of Congress Cataloging in Publication Data
are available from the publisher.

ISBN 0–8135–1915–2 (cloth)   0–8135–1916–0 (pbk.)

CONTENTS

ACKNOWLEDGEMENTS

The help of Sue Amphlett, Peter Beaman and Alison Stevens was invaluable in contacting the 'abused' families and in a number of other ways. The interviews were transcribed very well by Lorraine Jones. Many families made the research possible by retelling their stories to me, often reliving their distress visibly. I am grateful to each one and to Tessie Ferlita.

I pinched an idea or two from Rex Stainton Rogers and Farrell Burnett and was given a grant by Loughborough University's Research Committee. The British Association of Social Workers gave me permission to reproduce some of their copyright material at length.

The original case studies reported in Chapters 6 to 8 were obtained with the co-operation of a local parents' group dealing with families who had been involved with social workers over allegations of abuse. All individuals on the mailing list of this group were sent a letter by the organiser requesting participation in the research. Approximately forty letters were sent. Seventeen families volunteered to be interviewed. The remaining three case studies were provided by Parents Against Injustice (PAIN), a national organisation. They were selected because of their geographical closeness to my university. The geographical locations involved at least five different local authority social work departments. Everyone participated on the understanding that their identities were protected, although the majority felt that they did not want such protection. They tended to be more concerned about any possible professional relationship I had with social services departments. They were told that the research did not involve any such links. All of the interviews were transcribed verbatim, although these transcriptions were substantially shortened and the texts which appear were slightly edited to remove speech errors, false starts and the like. Some reorganisation of the order of some texts was undertaken to clarify comments.

All of the names appearing in the case studies are fictitious and some detail has been omitted to enhance anonymity.

INTRODUCTION

Susie was abducted from the street outside her home by a man driving an orange car. The alarm was raised within minutes because her 4-year old brother had witnessed the abduction in which the man said, 'Take off your pants and get in the car.' She did. Her brother ran inside their home to inform his father. Susie was found by two birdwatchers 70 hours later inside a mountain outhouse. She had been dropped through the toilet ring and into the fluid material six feet below. She survived because the cesspit was slightly leaking and only contained one foot of sewage, and because she had gathered sticks which were down the pit and made them into a platform to escape some of the fluid. When her rescuers asked her what she was doing inside the pit, she replied, 'I live here,' and then cried for her mother. (Jones and Krugman, 1986, pp. 253–4)

Rarely does research shadow public events at all closely. I did not predict that my concern with the adequacy of child protection investigations was to be mirrored in national events when I began my research. While my worry was about the hidden tragedies of families who felt threatened and damaged by interventionist child abuse policies, the British public was repeatedly given chapter after chapter of public scandals and crises concerning similar kinds of events in their daily newspapers and on television. Britain had become a world leader in child protection disasters. Headlines followed each other in rapid succession, many demanding that the public must believe the unbelievable about child protection. After concerns over deaths of children under the supervision of social workers, many cases of false allegations of child sexual abuse made by social workers and other professionals came to light. An epidemic of buggery in Cleveland (Jervis, 1988a); satanic abuse in Nottingham, then in Rochdale, and then in the Orkney Islands away from mainland Scotland (Eaton, 1991). Then came the uncovering of scandalously harsh treatment of youngsters using pindown control regimes in some children's homes (Community Care, 1991; Ivory, 1991). Professionals – social workers, doctors, teachers, psychologists, police and others – seemed not to be on top of the job. Many reasons were cited, from poor training to feminism to poor communication between professionals to the conflicting demands of the general public. For the professions involved it was one damned thing after another.

But these were the front-page news of child protection, notorious cases of private tragedies writ large, the visible tip of the iceberg – whether one-tenth or nine-tenths under water one can only guess. My concern was with individual families feeling hurt and harmed by allegations of child abuse, parents and children innocently embroiled in bad or overzealous child protection work. Or so I thought. Now it seems too glib a formulation. Many of the families I met did fit this view, but not all. In a few cases something had happened but the consequences for the family seemed excessive. Sometimes the most dreadful things had occurred, such as when children had been taken away permanently; while other families suffered little more than the initial traumata of false accusations and an investigation. All expressed strong anger, though, about their experiences with professionals. Many directed their feelings towards the professionals who had intervened disastrously in their lives, or turned their anger upon themselves and suffered depression. Intervention was no neutral event in the lives of these families, nor an easy event to shrug off. My wish to understand such private grief and experiences led inevitably into consideration of certain well-publicised and notorious public 'disasters'.

Over the last two decades or so, different types of concern about the practice of child protection have gradually unfolded. The stages involved can be summarised as follows:

1. Concern about under-involvement: leaving children to suffer abuse through a reluctance to intervene.
2. Concern about over-involvement: essentially finding abuse where none exists.
3. Concern about the quality of care: just how free of abuse are facilities such as homes for children taken into care?

There are key events which reflect this sequential passage of concern: the Maria Colwell case of 1973 (Department of Health and Social Security, 1974), in which a child was battered to death by her stepfather despite the signs of serious abuse being reported to social workers (and related concerns in the cases of Jasmine Beckford (Parton, 1986) and Kimberley Carlisle, who died in 1986 (Eaton, 1987)); the Cleveland sexual abuse scandal of 1987, in which many tens of children were taken into care largely due to false diagnoses using a flawed test of anal abuse (Butler-Sloss, 1988); and the Staffordshire pindown regimes (Anon., 1991), which involved cruel and humiliating methods of controlling children in public care. Each of these is both a product of its time and symptomatic of a range of broader issues.

Collectively, they reveal major problems of state intervention to prevent abuse. The fundamental problem, of course, is just what are we doing when we intervene? This is not a simple matter of stopping abuse, since there may be undesirable consequences stemming from the intervention itself which need looking at. There is a dearth of knowledge about key aspects of intervention's effects and a comparative surfeit of information about the consequences of abuse itself. In other words, I am asking here: is the price of most interventions worth paying? This is not a simple question to answer, since even evidence about what these costs might be is sketchy at best.

This book is about getting child protection wrong – making errors that lead to injustice and harm. As such, it is right to raise the question of the value of intervention. The lack of clear answers is the failing of the child protection system and the researchers who provide support for many aspects of child protection work. That the problem of getting things wrong is hardly researched is in itself significant. There are numerous arguments coming from research which suggest how harmful abuse is, but by comparison virtually nothing is to be found on the harm caused by child protection interventions. It is not intended to imply that child abuse is morally, emotionally or intellectually tolerable or to be dismissed. After all, while we would all no doubt agree that in general crime is wrong and unacceptable, this is a rather different matter from accepting that the state's means of dealing with the problem is beyond scrutiny. Yes, we would like to stop abuse and punish abusers, but how best is this to be done?

There is nothing exclusively British about the issue, of course. A glance at the following 'paid opinion advertisement' from an American newspaper reveals something of the international dimension to the debate. The sentiment rather that the factual basis of the claims is the major consideration:

> Can You Pass HRS' Child Abuse Test?
> Have you ever paddled your child?
> Has your house ever been messy?
> Have you ever scolded your child verbally? Has your child ever had an unexplained bruise?
> If you answer yes to any of these questions you could be confirmed as a child abuser by HRS under absurd vague Florida laws.
> And if you think your rights are protected by Florida law, think again.
> HRS can take custody of your child at any time, for any reason, without any due process of law. (*The Tampa Tribune*, 24 April 1991, metro-3)

The force of the view expressed is very apparent. At the end of the advertisement the child protection service is described as 'Florida's Gestapo'. A similar description of social workers was used by some of my

British families. Inevitably, it seems likely that child protection errors will undermine child protection services through the creation of defensiveness within organisations and a decrease in public confidence in the value of the services. Thus, the question of error is as important to those primarily interested in the interests of the child as it is to those who are intolerant of injustice.

Finally, as I was writing this introduction, yet another 'scandal' broke into the headlines. This time it concerned the local authority where many of my case studies were collected. The claims were that senior management in the social services had failed to act properly on information alleging the sexual abuse of children by social workers in local authority children's homes (*Mail on Sunday*, 8 September 1991). One case related to these events is described in Chapter 7. The research and the public concern had converged totally.

CHAPTER 1

THE LONG HISTORY OF PROFESSIONAL ERROR IN CHILD ABUSE

The competence of social workers has been put into question by the media, the Chairpersons of Inquiries, other professions and people of standing within social work. Central to many of the indictments made is the assumption that the ultimate measure of competence is that of particular outcomes, and that the responsibility for such outcomes can be traced back to individuals . . . Accordingly, a bad outcome is presumed to indicate a bad decision or negligent action. (MacDonald, 1990, p. 525)

Ultimately, this book is about professional failure. Although many different issues have to be raised before the final paragraphs, what is written leads to just one substantial conclusion – the need to consider error as an important feature of child protection work. This should not be construed as a despairing testament. Nevertheless, our understanding of child abuse needs re-examining in ways which allow the problem of errors to be integral to our thinking. Few have written extensively about the failures of professionals involved in child protection. This is not to ignore the dozens of public inquiries which have investigated individual 'catastrophes' but they were never intended to deal with errors in general. Most cases where things go wrong are unlikely to attract much public concern.

There is little social scientific research on the matter. This absence is no accident or oversight. It reflects as much as anything the characteristics of professions in modern society and the position of research in the social structure (Howitt, 1991a). Research is not funded by victims of mistakes, bad practice and errors. That the protection of children has become such a major concern among many professionals was similarly no inevitable outcome of broad historical trends in ideas about children and childhood (James and Prout, 1990; Sommerville, 1982). Indeed, the most significant feature of professional involvement in child protection is this very historical recency. More a 'blip' than a gradual trend, the bulk of the history of professional child protection has been little more than current affairs. This contrasts markedly with the extensive role that the professions have

1

played in a gamut of social-cum-moral issues – drugs, marriage, sexuality, abortion, education, crime, and so forth. Each of these includes ideological components not totally dissimilar to those involved in abuse. The argument should not be misinterpreted. It is well known that historically there were attempts to protect children from the worst excesses of the labour market – the nineteenth-century exclusion of children from mines, protection from long working hours, prostitution and the like cannot and should not be forgotten (Pinchbeck and Hewitt, 1969; 1973). Nor should it be overlooked that child abuse legislation is far older than the current heightened interest (Pfohl, 1976). However, none of this was particularly redolent of the major social issue of child protection established over the last thirty or forty years. Here the debate has moved substantially from that of standards governing employment, education and so on to the issue of protecting the child from its own immediate family. This is a remarkable change in the conceptualisation of the relationship between the family and the state. Whereas, perhaps, the family was once construed to be *the* major social institution protecting children from harm, that belief has been eroded somewhat. Turned on its head by some, the (patriarchal) family is now seen as a major source of anti-child activities. Coincidentally or not, these changes were achieved during the period of rapid professionalisation and expansion of child protection. However, this is not to assume naively that the state's involvement in the family has just the briefest of histories; that would be untrue. One consequence of the rapid increase in child protection work is that developments have probably outstripped social scientific understanding of professional activity. There is nothing unusual about this, although, of course, medicine is a major significant exception to this 'rule' in so far as it has been extensively researched (e.g. Foster and Anderson, 1978; Gerhardt, 1989; Tuckett, 1976).

Whether one regards the professions as appropriate institutions of child protection depends to a degree upon which matters are considered appropriate for the agenda. Typically, only certain limited aspects of the child abuse problem are subject to examination. At the same time, other significant matters are neglected or regarded even with hostility. It is one thing to make the broken and battered bodies of abused children the chief focus of concern, but this cannot justify avoiding potentially embarrassing questions for professionals. Similarly, catalogues of torn genitals may sometimes legitimately precipitate urgent intervention to stop further abuse, but are there no other considerations? The following are among the other items worthy of inclusion on the agenda but usually missing:

1. What harm is done to children and families by intervention?
2. What harm is done by inappropriate intervention?

3. Do the changes in relationships between professionals and clients caused by reporting requirements inhibit families in need of help from obtaining it?
4. What are the consequences of the pressures on professionals to be demonstrably 'doing something' about child abuse?
5. What are fair and equitable procedures and practices in child abuse work?
6. What child abuse warrants intervention?
7. What are the consequences of interventionist policies compared to other projects which might benefit children and families but which currently cannot be resourced?
8. What 'skills' are demonstrably important in child protection work?

Other questions could be raised and added to the list, no doubt. But most of the items on this alternative agenda are, at best, merely noted by professionals and publications in the field.

Less tangible matters also warrant raising. What about, for example, the nature of female and male sexuality, masculinity and femininity, the family, discipline, male violence, female violence, state intervention, the legitimate needs and rights of children, childhood sexuality, mental and emotional illness, and most of all the professions and professionalisation? These should not be issues peripheral to our understanding of professional work in child protection. Their abstract quality solely reflects how far they are removed from the everyday thinking of professionals. At virtually every other level, they are major determinants of thought and action. To understand how child protection has developed, the impact of all of these issues needs to be absorbed.

Our primary concern is why things go wrong – if one likes, what causes the errors that occur in child protection work. Already words are beginning to fail us. This is not simply a matter that the major child protection scandals seem beyond belief to the general public. But words fail us in another important sense which will require repeated consideration. Language lacks adequate terms to describe what we mean by errors. To use the term 'error' is to accept that there is a way of doing things which otherwise would be perfectly proper and satisfactory. One can only conceive of errors if the notion of an error-free process means anything. However, in child protection the term is sometimes misleading, since 'normal' and 'error' processes may be virtually indistinguishable. In other words, an 'error' is but an aberrent 'success'. Indeed, one response to public inquiry judgements that errors or other forms of bad practice have occurred is to dismiss the claim that anything has gone wrong. We will see examples of this in later chapters. In some ways this may be merely exculpatory rhetoric, a failure to come to terms with reality, or it may have any one of a number of 'commonsense' explanations. Nevertheless it may also be a manifestation of another feature of errors. In child abuse work, an 'error' may be something quite different from our everyday understanding of the word. Regarding errors as aspects of regular child protection activity changes the nature of the explanation. Errors receive much the same ideological support from research and theory as does 'successful' child protection work. That there are child protection cases which will be labelled 'crazy' by the media or 'misguided' by courts of inquiry may have little bearing on the degree of similarity between 'proper' practice and 'errors'.

No such entities as 'child abuse', 'child sexual abuse' and 'child neglect' exist. These notions cannot transcend the social processes which have constructed them. Virtually no characteristic of abuse as seen through modern Western eyes holds up in historical or cultural comparison as a clear sign of child abuse. The obvious contenders are quickly eliminated. For example, it might be assumed that to kill one's own infants would be the epitome of child physical abuse. Not only has this been common in history, but it has even held the status of a legal parental right (cf. Merrick, 1986). But surely, a parent having penetrative sexual intercourse with his or her child must be classified as abuse? It violates the universal taboo against incest, does it not? While one would not wish to argue that such incestuous relationships have been commonly accepted, even the incest taboo has not been a universal one.

Activities which from a modern Western perspective are sexual abuse were seen differently in other places and at other times (de Mause, 1976, contains many stomach-churning examples). Witness the early life of Louis XIII of France during the seventeenth century:

> Louis XIII was not yet one year old: 'He laughed uproariously when his nanny waggled his cock with her fingers.' An amusing trick which the child soon copied. Calling a page, 'He shouted "Hey, there!" and pulled up his robe, showing him his cock . . . He was one year old: In high spirits . . . he made everybody kiss his cock.' This amused them all . . . During his first three years nobody showed any reluctance or saw any harm in jokingly touching the child's sexual parts. 'The Marquise [de Verneuil] often put her hand under his coat; he got his nanny to lay him on her bed where she played with him, putting her hand under his coat.' . . . On another occasion, 'after playing with Mlle Mercier, . . . he told me that Mercier had a private as big as that (showing me his two fists) and that there was water inside.' (Miller, 1985, pp. 130–2)

The casualness of acts which now seem to be little other than the sexualisation of a young boy is the most notable feature of this passage. Doubtless, the physical actions involved are by all accounts common enough in modern society. However, we do not regard them as 'innocent fun' but would label them as sexual abuse warranting intervention.

The important point is not the cultural and historical relativism of abuse as such. More importantly, these examples indicate that 'child abuse' has no meaning outside of the society which construes it as such. The problem of errors becomes compounded by our inability to establish abuse independently of the social mechanisms and institutions involved in child protection, which will serve to impose their own definitions. This is radically different from suggesting that there are no principles which can be brought to apply to child rearing or even that there is little point in child protection. The clear message emerging from the lack of absolutist definitions of 'child abuse' concerns the impossibility of separating abuse from the social system which identifies it, regulates it and polices it. There are numerous cases in which the definition of abuse ultimately resides in the professionalisation of child protection. For example, many organisations regard 'overchastisement' as abuse despite the justification or legitimacy of physical punishment in the eyes of many parents. Such considerations lead to the lack of clear-cut errors in child protection. The social construction of child abuse is as much about the *ways* in which child protection is carried out as about the beliefs and ideologies concerning childhood and child protection which accompany such activities (cf. Parton, 1985).

Inevitably, any investigation of child abuse errors must deliberately distance itself from relying solely on the perspective of professions in the field for a variety of reasons. Least important, but nevertheless significant, is that professional publications on child abuse are mountainous but overwhelmingly unquestioning of the actions of professionals. There is a cosiness in this which undermines any practitioner scepticism. A second reason is in a sense more pragmatic but nevertheless related. My research was carried out entirely from the viewpoint of parents and families who were or had been involved in disputed interventions about alleged incidents of abuse – physical, sexual or involving neglect. That they would see things differently from the professionals is perhaps axiomatic. They, however, did not have a public voice. Not surprisingly, their only mouthpieces were solicitors and parents' support groups. At the time of carrying out my fieldwork, I would have zealously written about 'social work errors' without any qualms about my choice of language. But the marked disparity between the views of the families and what appears in the professional literature does not prove that anyone was wrong. It is more indicative of the way in which ideas about abuse are created within the context of professional activity.

For these families there were different questions of right and wrong. All of them expressed very strongly held, predominantly anti-socialworker attitudes. I chose in this research to explore the issues from their point of view. Consequent on this decision, no attempt was made to contact child protection workers about the cases. In other words, the data gathering was from the viewpoint of the 'victims' of the practices of professionals. Naturally, many of the families were more than a little suspicious of a researcher whose allegiances might be closer to their hated social services than to the families themselves. Escaping the professional ties that bind researchers to practitioners contributed to the questioning orientation of this book. The perspective was, in other words, what I (Howitt, 1991b) describe as 'bottom up'.

In retrospect the decision to include the vantage-point of families rather than just that of professionals was wise. It brought a somewhat different flavour to the research but, more importantly, it brings a competing perspective on child protection interventions. Most vital of all, it was a stimulus to understanding the ways in which child protection activities are part of a wider social construction of child abuse. The question 'How do you know the parents are telling the truth?' was constantly in mind when trying to justify this approach. It took a while before the question 'How would you know that child protection workers were telling the truth?' came to me as the appropriate reply. Much more time elapsed before I realised that probably neither question is worthy of much consideration. Both questions rely on events which have meaning only in terms of the interplay of the ideas of professionalism and parenthood.

The ancient history of professional involvement in child abuse

Professionals as abusers

It is no easy matter to decide where to begin any account of professional involvement in child abuse. Just what exactly constitutes professional work in this sphere? Clearly one needs to identify the likely contenders from among various professions. Religion could be justifiably taken as a starting point, being one of the longest established professions by almost any reckoning. It provided a livelihood for paid employees of the Church as well as a social organisation promoting their interests and specifying rules of conduct for them. Moreover, religious texts have provided legitimation and support for a wide range of social structures and attitudes. It is no surprise then that Christianity provided a framework of appropriate child-rearing practices. These, inevitably, framed views of what constitutes abuse.

Walters (1975) is adamant about the influence of biblical tracts on Western child-rearing practices:

One of the biblical 'justifications' that has resulted in much abuse is in Proverbs. This book tells us, 'He that spareth the rod hateth his son: but he that loveth him chasteneth him betimes,' and 'Chasten thy son while there is hope, and let not thy soul spare for his crying.' . . . 'Withhold not correction from the child; for if thou beatest him with the rod, he shall not die. Thou shalt beat him with a rod, and shalt deliver his soul from Hell.' These and many other Old Testament injunctions support parental harm to children. (p. 11)

Further, Walters suggests that some of the long-held myths about sexual abuse also have part of their origins in the Bible:

In the area of sexual abuse, incest and incest taboo are discussed a great deal in the Old Testament. In Genesis, Lot's two daughters get him intoxicated and seduce him. Both become pregnant as a result. This drama of father and daughter having sexual relations has been repeated time and again. From the story of Lot and his daughters, we inherit the cultural belief that, in many instances, the daughter seduces the father and that the father is intoxicated and the 'innocent victim' of the seduction. (pp. 11–12)

Walters argues that the roots of many child-rearing practices lie in the Bible and the pulpit. Possibly as a result of secularisation, such biblical texts now seem outrageous. However, this does not account for modern ideas about abuse. The question of what is seen as appropriate in modern child rearing cannot be dealt with merely in terms of older practices and ideologies. One should not forget that conceptions of childhood have a bearing on this and have been reconstructed many times in history even within the context of a profession (Woodhead, 1990).

It is far easier to document the nature of professional involvement in child rearing during the nineteenth century. There are, of course, several reasons for this. Primary among them is the process of professionalisation which led to the establishment of the formal and powerful institutional basis for many modern professions, especially medicine and the law (Abbott, 1988; Friedson, 1972; Halmos, 1973). Haller and Haller (1974) describe numerous ways in which nineteenth-century American doctors strayed into matters of morality – while justifying their views as objectively based in the 'science' of medicine. Haller and Haller are primarily concerned with the contribution made by the medical profession to reinforcing ideologies of sexuality. Inevitably, they also deal with childhood and sexuality. A distressing portrayal emerges of the abuse of children by professionals. Although substantially and primarily concerned with the control of sexuality, the remedies and potions proposed by such physicians to achieve this are difficult to conceive as anything other than severe physical and sexual abuse.

Their cataloguing of the medicalised repression of sexuality in Victorian

America deserves close attention. Physicians repeatedly counselled the control of masturbation through virtually any means. That it had to be inhibited for significant ideological reasons is well illustrated by the matter of masturbation and the bicycle. Nowadays the bicycle is not considered ideologically or morally dangerous. More likely it is seen as a fairly mundane machine with largely positive virtues – especially and tellingly in terms of its contribution to our ideology of planetary conservation. The bicycle is dangerous only because of modern traffic conditions. In contrast, for these Victorian medics bicycles were a threat to the family and morality in many unexpected ways. A degree of emancipation was brought to females by them:

> There were some skeptics and moralists both in and out of the medical profession who lamented the fact that woman had found yet another avenue through which she could escape the home circle. In Atlanta, for example, one Reverend Hawthorne spoke out vindictively against the wheel, charging the female cyclist with immodesty, indecency, and mannishness. (Haller and Haller, 1974, p. 179).

There were all sorts of moral implications over and above the direct control of women. Modesty was one, of course, given that women cyclists could not wear long dresses and other restricting garments. Worse still were the 'horrors' of the bicycle seat's contact with the female rider's genitals. This may not worry the minds of modern parents and still less modern doctors, but it certainly did distress some Victorian physicians. One wrote, anxiously, of a 15-year-old girl whose saddle was fixed at an upward angle! This 'nervous and emaciated' girl was regarded with great suspicion by the doctor:

> The saddle can be tilted in every bicycle as desired, and the springs of the saddle can be so adjusted as to stiffen or relax the leather triangle. In this way a girl . . . by carrying the front peak or pommel high, or by relaxing the stretched leather in order to let it form a deep, hammock-like concavity which would fit itself snugly over the entire vulva and reach up in front, could bring about constant friction over the clitoris and labia. This pressure would be much increased by stooping forward, and the warmth generated from vigorous exercise might further increase the feeling. (Haller and Haller, 1974, p. 185; see also Edwards, 1981).

While this seems to tell us more about the male doctor involved than the girl on the bicycle, one should not hurriedly assume that we are raking over historical bones. For one reason, today some women claim to have received similar comments about bicycle saddles from their parents. Myths about masturbation do tend to persist within a community. But more importantly, the passage illustrates how medical science could reflect moral issues very precisely, virtually without challenge. As a side-note to those disposed to the study of early ergonomics, 'doctors advised manufacturers to remedy the saddle problem by taking a plaster or wax cast of the woman's seat and designing a proper saddle with that as its model' (Haller and Haller, 1974, p. 186).

Male masturbators were offered medical interventions which solved the 'problem' in the following ways:

> Other doctors treated the habit by blood-letting, or applying leeches and cups around the sexual parts to remove 'congestion.' Still others perforated the foreskin of the penis and inserted a ring, or cut the foreskin with jagged scissors. Drugs included applications of red iron, tartar emetic ointment, or a Spanish fly-blister to make the genitals tender to the touch. (pp. 208–9)

One wonders the consequences for any modern family applying any of the above 'remedies' for masturbation if brought to the attention of child protection workers.

Engelhardt (1974) explores a similar theme very effectively. He points to a wide variety of illnesses which, during the nineteenth century, were held to be a consequence of masturbation. This list includes dyspepsia, epilepsy, blindness, vertigo, hearing loss, impotency, rickets, nympho-mania (especially in blondes as opposed to brunettes), elongation of the clitoris, reddening and congestion of the labia, elongation of the labia minoria, thinning and decrease in size of the penis, moist and clammy hands, stooped shoulders and insanity. These Engelhardt summarises as 'a broad and heterogeneous class of signs and symptoms [which] were recognized in the 19th century as part of what was tantamount to a syndrome, if not a disease: masturbation' (p. 237).

Masturbation was variously described under the medical headings of 'male diseases of the generative system', 'disease of the nervous system', 'cerebral-spinal disease' and 'genito-urinary system, diseases of'. Given that masturbation was seen as a disease with such personally (and socially) damaging consequences, the full panoply of medical and surgical treatments was available for prescription. Apart from the more obvious restraining devices, infibulation, a ring in the prepuce, circumcision, acid burns or thermoelectro cauterisation could be used to make masturbation too painful; and castration, vasectomy and opium potions employed to eliminate some of its most damaging effects. Striking closer to modern concerns about female circumcision (e.g. Dareer, 1982):

> The classic monograph recommending clitoridectomy, written by the British surgeon Baker Brown, advocated the procedure to terminate the 'long continued peripheral excitement, causing frequent and increasing losses of nerve force . . .' Brown recommended that 'the patient having been placed completely under the influence of chloroform, the clitoris [be] freely excised either by scissors or knife – I always prefer the scissors.' (p. 244)

Furthermore, such surgical procedures were claimed to have the advantage that they could cure sterility, paresis, hysteria, dysmenorrhoea, idiocy and insanity!

But, of course, these treatments were not merely or primarily for adults; they were for children. There is a wide range of issues that these examples bring to the fore, over and above the disfiguring surgery and the drastic medicine that they propose – particularly the view of sexuality which underlies them. It is far from adequate to suggest that the control of embarrassing public masturbation was all that was desired. For one reason, the remedies and fears expressed were designed to encourage families to inhibit masturbation in all children. It was intended to control adult sexuality, particularly in order to ensure the continuation of the then conventional womanhood through marriage. Over-sexual children threatened such a social structure. The involvement of science (through medicine) ensured the legitimation of some of the grossest and crudest child abuse.

That this situation is redolent of much which follows should not go ignored. Indeed, one must dwell quite extensively on the contribution that the institution of science has made to the inadequacies of child protection work. It is worth noting that, according to Schultz (1982): 'As late as 1936 a common American medical textbook recommended that masturbation be controlled by circumcision of children' (p. 24). Before moving on, it is worthwhile reading the following case report carefully so as to dispel any idea that what was done to children was something 'surgical' (in the sense of medical and detached). The extract describes part of the 'treatment' of a frequent masturbator:

> September 11: In order to frighten her as much as possible, I prepared a display of red-hot coals; I placed an enormous iron ax on top of it; I blew on it until it turned red. She trembled at the sight of this infernal scene. 'You did not keep your promise, so now I will show you that you were wrong – by keeping my promise!' I told her. Then I picked up the enormous red-hot ax, but I only cauterized her clitoris with a tiny stylet, three millimeters in diameter, that had been heated red-hot by an alcohol lamp. 'If you do it again,' I told her, 'I will burn you with the large iron ax, and I will show no mercy.'
>
> September 16: A new cauterization. I burned her three times on both labia majora, and once on the clitoris, and to punish her for her disobedience I cauterized her buttocks and loins with the dreaded large iron. (Zambaco, 1882, pp. 81–2)

See no evil

Another theme emerges from the history of professional involvement in the field of child protection – that of professional purblindness to the abuse of children. This is most profoundly highlighted by the case of

Sigmund Freud and his early seduction theory of hysteria. Many feminists, in particular, have pointed to this legacy and its impact (e.g. Bayer and Conners, 1988; but also see Masson, 1985). There is every reason to regard Freudian psychoanalytic theory as emanating from nineteenth-century medical science – it carries a great many of its features and characteristics. Particularly, it presents a 'disease' account of psychological problems. In some respects, much of the debate about Freud's ideas concerning the role of 'sexual assault' in the development of hysteria misses the point substantially. The basic details, however, are clear enough. It was Freud's view, early in his explorations of the human psyche, that hysteria was the consequence of the sexual seduction of the child by an adult. Freud did not simply theorise this relationship – it emerged from his observations during therapeutic interviews. In many respects this could be held to be a remarkable achievement. Not only did Freud postulate an effect of sexual abuse which persisted into adulthood, but he was virtually alone among professional persons in noting that intrafamilial sexual abuse took place. Froula (1986) puts the sequence of events as follows:

> Freud's conversations with hysterical patients began in the 1880s. At first, Freud . . . was able to hear patients' stories, and he found that in every case, analysis elicited an account of sexual abuse suffered in childhood at the hands of a member of the patient's own family – almost always the father, as he belatedly reported. On this evidence, Freud developed his 'seduction theory' – the theory that hysterical symptoms have their origin in sexual abuse suffered in childhood, which is repressed and eventually assimilated in later sexual experience. Freud first formulated the seduction theory in a letter to his colleague and confidant Wilhelm Fliess in October 1895, and he presented it to the Vienna psychiatric establishment on April 21, 1896 . . . The paper, Freud wrote to Fliess, 'met with an icy reception . . .' (p. 629)

The fact of sexual abuse was replaced in Freud's theory by the fantasy of 'seduction' – a term which carries additional baggage of meaning and assumptions. The child was no longer seen as suffering from the victimisation of an assaulting adult but was essentially making up the events. Miller describes this as 'the "guilty" victim' (Miller, 1985, p. 145). One remarkable assertion is sometimes made about Freud's reasons for abandoning the seduction theory, although it is supported by very little evidence. Freud was undergoing self-analysis when his father died during 1886. Given that his own siblings demonstrated some of the symptoms of hysteria, Freud was faced with the possibility that his own father was an abuser!

Freud's own explanation was that 'it was hardly credible that perverted acts against children were so general' (Miller, 1985). The idea was that, since abuse did not always lead to hysteria, sexual abuse would have to be much more common than hysteria. Given that hysteria was common in Freud's experience, this implies that abuse was extremely frequent. While nowadays it is generally held that sexual abuse is common (see Chapter 3), apparently no modern studies have been carried out which link abuse specifically with hysteria rather than with a vast range of other possibilities (cf. Eysenck, 1985; Eysenck and Wilson, 1973). Without such evidence it is difficult to argue that Freud was wrong to abandon his theory. It is worthwhile quoting Freud on his ideas about the effects of abuse:

> Just think: among other things I am on the scent of the following strict condition for hysteria, namely, that a primary sexual experience (before puberty), accompanied by revulsion and fright, must have taken place; for obsessional neuroses, that it must have happened, accompanied by *pleasure* . . . But I am not succeeding with the mechanical elucidation; rather, I am inclined to listen to the quiet voice which tells me that my explanations are not adequate. (Masson, 1985, p. 141)

The notion is of a *primary* sexual experience which has to be seen in the context of the close family. Just any sexual act does not fit into the theory. Furthermore, it should be noted how Freud sometimes allows the experience to be pleasurable, in which case obsessionality may be the outcome. This would contrast markedly with those modern views of sexual abuse as being inevitably traumatic.

Attempts to make sense of Freud's change of heart seem painstakingly to avoid the obvious. The problem is presented as if it were a matter of an individual's whim which fails to take into account relevant matters. Why was Freud a lone voice when he offered the real abuse thesis? Why did Freud continue to articulate the real seduction thesis having repudiated it? (Gallop, 1982). Among the many implications of this set of events is that there was nothing irrevocably hidden about sexual abuse. The emergence of Freud's original thesis clearly demonstrates this. But, at the same time, his decision to repudiate the thesis demonstrates as much the powerful influence of professional groupings on members as Freud's personal lack of moral courage. More than anything, then, Freud's change of mind is a case study of intra-professional pressure bringing a member into line, as well as a study of how broader ideologies are maintained in the professional context. There is nothing remarkable about what happened to Freud in this light. His ideas were rubbished because of their basis in the notion of real seduction in childhood. Dropping the reality of the seduction allowed Freud's ideas to become much more acceptable. The Oedipus complex, with its basic notion of childhood sexuality and the attachment of this sexuality to a parent in fantasy, ensured that the ideological problems disappeared. Notice how this, like the concerns about masturbation, assumes the 'problem' to lie with the sexual child.

That Freud could respond to peer pressure is not surprising, although it hardly enhances his heroic stature. There is no doubt that the peer pressure was severely felt:

A lecture on the etiology of hysteria at the psychiatric society was given an icy reception by the asses and a strange evaluation by Krafft-Ebing: 'It sounds like a scientific fairy tale.' And this, after one has demonstrated to them the solution of a more-than-thousand-year-old problem . . . They can go to hell, euphemistically expressed. (Masson, 1985, p. 184)

Ultimately, Freud was forced by peer pressure to operate within the ideology of his professional group. That this ideology, despite the intellectual and somewhat radical nature of this circle, was the product of the wider community is only to be expected. The lesson, though, is of the extent to which a profession can imbue a false ideology throughout its membership which is also harmful to the profession's clientele. Freud's patients fed him with material which was forced or distorted into the notion of the Oedipus complex. Thus the reconstruction of their experiences as fantasy can scarcely be seen as the basis of sound therapeutic work but rather should be viewed as the imposition of an ideology. But it is wrong to see the events solely in terms of the 'great man' view of history. They reflect better a social view.

Freud's fleeting identification of what we call sexual abuse was just a significant but isolated case. Baartman (1990) reviews a series of cases in which the abuse of children was consistently and regularly ignored or denied by professionals. One of the issues he raises is venereal disease in children. If a child *develops* a sexually transmitted disease, it seems reasonable to regard this as at least possibly a consequence of sexual contact. However, this would appear to be a perception based on modern assumptions:

In 1909 the Swedish physician Welander described the transfer of gonorrhoea and syphilis by parents to their children. It is only very rarely in our society that gonorrhoea is passed on to young girls through sexual contact, he wrote. In an exceptional case, which involved a little boy, the nursemaid turned out to be the source of evil. In cases where both parents suffer from a sexually transmitted disease, it is, according to Welander, nearly always the mother who is the child's source of infection because mothers have more physical contact with their children than fathers. (p. 2)

In contrast, there have been very recent cases involving childhood syphilis which appear to have dismissed the probability of sexual abuse prematurely (Horowitz and Chadwick, 1990).

Moving on to physical abuse, it is also demonstrably clear that the sort of medical data which eventually led one radiologist to diagnose physical abuse of children did not in itself immediately allow the development of the idea of abuse:

> The radiologist Caffey was, in 1946, the first to write about 'the frequent association of chronic subdural hematoma and fractures of the long bone'. In the early 1950s publications on the same phenomenon appeared in Canada, France and the United States. Five publications in all, none of which related these data to the possibility of physical violence on the parents' side. In Great Britain, Astley wrote about the subject in 1953, and he too did not suggest this possibility. 'This despite the coincidental presence of retinal separation, easy bruising, black eyes, compressed vertebrae and the more usual types of fractures.' (Woolley and Evans, 1955, p. 539). The traumas that could be made visible through X-ray diagnostics were attributed to 'metaphyseal fragility of the bones'. (Baartman, 1990, p. 4)

While it is tempting to regard such failures as amusing anecdotes documenting the ludicrous utterances of myopic buffoons of bygone ages, this may itself be foolish. They also demonstrate something not to be taken too lightly. So long as individualised conceptions of history are taken, a manner of thinking is drifted into which allows disparagement of such people. To refuse such an intellectual short-cut necessitates the consideration of these individuals in the contexts of their professions and wider society. Almost inevitably, a lesson relevant to modern times is highlighted. The trappings of professional judgement, science and theory do not in themselves lead to an adequate understanding of events or the discovery of important social facts. In fact, quite the reverse may be true. In themselves they may well encourage those actions, activities and beliefs which retrospectively appear bizarre.

There would seem to have been no convenient disjunction between professionals of fifty or more years ago and current ones. Have things changed in crucial ways such that modern professionals display a cool independence of thought unsullied by wider society? The well-known and controversial cases of child protection failure provide good reason to think otherwise. It is not merely in historical perspective that the views and activities of professionals appear odd or downright stupid – contemporary interventions may sometimes bear the hallmarks of such historical 'lunacies'. The intense and persistent criticisms that have accompanied modern child protection work suggest that modern errors cannot be regarded automatically as substantially different from older follies. They may differ in content but they may well be created by similar or identical social processes. The errors may have changed over the course of time, perhaps becoming errors more of commission than of omission, but that in itself need have little bearing on the nature of the processes leading to both types of error.

Exculpatory history

Accepting that there are no historical facts, only constructions of historical facts, histories are always from a viewpoint and serve a purpose. The very act of deciding what are the significant historical events gives a meaning to those events selected. There are a number of historical accounts of the development of child protection which have to be considered in this light. There are, on the other hand, no histories of child abuse and child protection from the point of view of the child, the parent or the family involved. By and large the histories take as their point of focus institutions which controlled child protection activities, including voluntary organisations or charities, government institutions, legal institutions and statutory child protection agencies as well as the medical profession, the legal profession and the police. By and large, in these histories, the problem of central concern is the family in which the abuse takes place. Rarely, if ever, is the questionable work of the institutions in such matters the crux of the issue, let alone a matter of critical concern. This is an organisation-centred focus which should not surprise anyone given the privileged access to communication resources enjoyed by members of professions. This for the most part means that the authors of historical accounts of child protection will be professionals writing for professionals.

Gordon's 'Child abuse, gender, and the myth of family independence: a historical critique' (1985) is a good example of a theme which is crucial to attempts to understand the role of child protection services. The title needs to be noted carefully as it appears to debunk the idea that families were ever independent of the state and state intervention. However, this historian's article is about something rather different. Gordon asks why cruelty to children rather than spouse abuse was chosen as the focus of attention in the nineteenth century. The Society for the Prevention of Cruelty to Women never existed, as Gordon points out. But societies for the protection of children were increasing and spreading quite substantially at this time:

> Child abuse was 'discovered' in the urban industrial world about 110 years ago. Of course, cruel treatment of children had existed previously, and was controlled through community sanctions. In the 1870s, however, this crime became defined as a widespread social problem; by 1880, 33 Societies for the Prevention of Cruelty to Children . . . had been established in the United States, and 15 elsewhere. (p. 1)

While the early societies were voluntary in nature, the ideology which underlay their activities was anything but child and mother centred. It is better described as an expression of the values of a particular sector of society. These values held up as a model of motherhood the woman who

was exclusively domestic and maternal. The children of such families
were educated full time and contributed nothing to family finances:

> [In the view of the voluntary society] . . . cruelty to children was caused . . .
> by children's labor; . . . boys and girls working in shops, peddling on the
> streets; boys working for organ grinders or lying about their ages to enlist in
> the Navy . . . To immigrants from peasant backgrounds it seemed irrational
> and blasphemous that adult women should work and able-bodied children
> should be idle. (Gordon, 1985, p. 215)

A vital part of Gordon's argument is the notion of an 'autonomous'
family free from social control. This is a sort of pure situation unsullied by
outside intervention. In contrast, the involvement of the new breed of
charitable workers was anything but benign. It largely aimed at imposing
dominant values on dissident value systems. But Gordon rejects this view
of the independent family as merely 'a norm of family autonomy that was
both romanticized and also, to some extent, oppositional, expressing
simultaneously the new sense of home as a private and caring space, in
contrast to that of the increasingly instrumental relations of the public,
commercial, and political arena' (p. 218).

Unfortunately, the evidence on which Gordon bases her views is scant
and relies on instances of *extended family* involvement in dealing with a
case of spouse beating. She renamed the family as the Amatos:

> Yet even the violent and defensive Mr Amato did not question the right of
> his father, relatives, and friends to intervene forcibly, nor did Mrs Amato
> appear shocked that her husband's relatives tried, perhaps successfully, to
> hold her forcibly in her marriage. (p. 218)

This seems remarkably little on which to base an argument about family
autonomy from outside intervention. It can work only to the extent that
the family is conceived of as the so-called nuclear family, consisting of
biological parents and their joint offspring. This is a conception which
may not have met the expectations of the family members themselves and
which seems very different from the notion of state intervention for child
protection purposes.

As a history of the declining autonomy of the family, Gordon's article
seems defensive of the interests of child care professionals rather than
setting out a case for the abandonment of family autonomy. In other
words, it is a self-serving history of family autonomy which adopts a viewpoint convenient to modern professionals and greatly in their interests.
Had Gordon used her material to make a case for the involvement of
the extended family in child protection activities (such as inviting grandparents into case conferences or other means of enabling concerned
family members to help protect the children of the family) then the thrust
of her argument might have been more in tune with the evidence she

presents. Furthermore, there are cases of grandparents, for example, who fiercely try to persuade social workers to intervene to stop the abuse of their grandchildren but who are nevertheless ignored.

Gordon could have found far more convincing historical evidence for the view of the 'myth of family independence'. Some of this demonstrates a reason for the control of families rather different from protecting children from abusive parents. For example, in pre-Norman England, as far back as the time of Alfred the Great, there was an office known as *tithingman*. This was essentially a 'community policeman' centred around the family. A tithing was an area within which ten families resided. The tithingman had responsibility to scrutinise the activities of family members within this tithing to ensure they were within the law. The same office was to be found in parts of the USA as early as the seventeenth century. According to Giovanni and Becerra (1979), tithingmen were:

> chosen from 'among the most prudent and discrete inhabitants' and had to 'diligently inspect' the families under their supervision. The statute listed all types of people and behaviors that were not to be tolerated. Not the least of these were stubborn and disorderly children. (p. 39)

Dipping back so far into history reveals an interpretation of the lack of family autonomy radically different from Gordon's. Intervention was to protect the state from the errant behaviour of family members, not to protect children from the cruelty or abuse of their parents. Revealingly, the control of the family served the interests of the state rather than the interests of the child. In this context, one should not forget the modern concern with 'cycles of deprivation' (Parton, 1985), which politicians were keen to eliminate because of the potential benefits to the state. Similarly, Pfohl (1976) comments about US child abuse legislation in the early part of the twentieth century serving primarily to protect the state rather than the child.

The main consequence of treating family autonomy as a myth is that a particular sort of intervention then seems less problematic. That it might *seem* unproblematic, however, does not mean that it is so. Indeed, Gordon's equation of the family with the nuclear family underscores a very different formulation of the family from that used in most discussions of child abuse (as we shall see in Chapter 3). Gordon carefully establishes a distinction between the nuclear family and the extended family which is contrived and sociologically false (Uzoka, 1979), though common. But implicit in such a formulation is a further false dichotomy – an opposition of intervention and non-intervention, which is graphically demonstrated in the following. La Fontaine (1990) contrasts what she describes as 'freedom' with state intervention:

A related issue is the question of the autonomy of 'the family' and its freedom from interference by agents of the state. There is an irreconcilable conflict here: if children are to be protected, then the agency which protects them on behalf of society must have the power to intervene against any threat to them. If there is no power of intervention, then there is no means of protecting children. If the possibility of children being damaged by the people normally responsible for them, their parents, is admitted, the protection of children and the complete autonomy of the family are incompatible objectives. (p. 8)

The conception of protection as being synonymous with intervention is itself a peculiar notion. It is a very focused definition which sees the problem as residing within the individual family and the solution in dealing with that family directly and individually. Broader strategies for protecting children by eliminating the social factors (perhaps unemployment, family breakdown or poverty) which may lead to abuse can thereby go ignored. It also involves a view of the family versus the state as opposed forces and in conflict. This is a viewpoint perfectly in keeping with the controversial practice of excluding the family from involvement in social work decision-making processes which has not altogether ended (PAIN, 1990).

Although most discussions of the history of modern child protection systems freely acknowledge their origins in the nineteenth-century voluntary sector, the literature is relatively mute about the first half or so of the twentieth century – this being, of course, the initial period of the professionalisation of social work. So silent is this period on abuse that authors are able to write about the 'rediscovery of child abuse' in the latter part of the twentieth century. Somehow professionalised social work, which replaced earlier charitable work, by implication effectively buried the topic. How this came about seems not to be a matter of particular concern in the literature. But very much the same professions which ignored the topic for so long are now at the forefront of anti-abuse work.

In examining any self-serving history, it is important to note who are regarded as its key figures. Not only can such individuals provide a personality which animates more abstract processes, but their characteristics may say a great deal about the functions of that history. It is interesting, then, to examine some of the accounts of the *re*discovery of child abuse in the second half of the twentieth century. The typical chronological history of this, as we have seen, places the initial responsibility with the medical profession – in particular with medical radiologists. Nelson (1984) illustrates the construction of the seminal events as follows:

[I]t was the work of radiologists . . . which alerted pediatricians to the specific problem of abuse. In 1946 Caffey first reported a number of cases in which infants had multiple long bone fractures and subdural hematomas. He did not, however, speculate on the causes of trauma. In 1953, Woolley and Evans suggested that similar injuries might be caused by the children's caretakers. In 1957, Caffey reexamined his original data and concluded that the trauma might well have been willfully perpetrated by parents. It took almost a decade for physicians to conclude that some parents were violently assaulting their children, a delay caused by professional cautiousness and a profound psychological resistance to recognizing that some parental behavior departed from the ideal . . . This research, as well as the early work done by social workers, was well known to pediatricians like C. Henry Kempe and his colleagues, who were investigating the causes as well as the appropriate responses to physical abuse. In 1962 they published their famous article 'The Battered-Child Syndrome' in the prestigious *Journal of the American Medical Association*. Within weeks of its publication, stories on child abuse were featured in popular magazines like *Time* and the *Saturday Evening Post*. (pp. 12–13)

This is a remarkable passage in many ways, except for the fact that it is a version of history which is echoed routinely elsewhere. Kempe's work quickly led to government action and legislation, encouraged further by the popular interest created by press reporting and comment. Most striking is the impression created of 'veils' being removed from the eyes – just as they fell from Caffey's eyes in 1957, they were also a feature of the broader societal response in the early 1960s. The nature of the work justifying the 'rediscovery' claim resulted in a radical change in the profile of child abuse. There was developing in the USA a profound concern about violence at this time. Not only was there the question of urban rioting and the threat posed to society by that, but there were other concerns, including the influence of violent media on young people. That such concern was felt at government level is evidenced by the inquiries, commissions and other initiatives launched into violence during this period. Notice how social work research into abuse is relegated to a short phrase in Nelson's account. Why should this be?

The answer, as Nelson is well aware, is the promise by medicine alone of a quick, clean solution to at least one issue to do with violence. Kempe conceived of child abuse as a clinical syndrome in which the problem dwelt in the character of a 'psychologically diseased' parent. Not only was child abuse thereby defined as a medical-cum-psychiatric issue to do with the parent, but it was further seen as a contagious disease since the battering parents often repeated a pattern of violence perpetrated against them by their own parents – though the evidence for this is of a weak trend (Kaufman and Zigler, 1987). By defining abuse as a clear medical problem with 'public health' implications due to its contagiousness, the US government was handed on a plate a matter which was on first appearances easy to translate into public policy: 'The individually centered psychological construction of the problem made it seem very self-contained. Government response to a self-contained, serious, but noncontroversial issue ought to be easy to obtain. And easy it was' (Nelson, 1984, p. 13).

Certainly, the construction of the issue as medical placed the fault with the parents and effectively distanced abuse from all issues related to social structure, such as poverty, divorce and unemployment. Such non-individual factors are, inevitably, a threat to governments and unwelcome. By comparison, it is interesting to note that a similar imperative to action did not follow Caffey's later identification of the whiplash shaken infant syndrome (shaken baby syndrome) (Dykes, 1986). Presumably the political gains from implementing regular screening for this would be slight. Furthermore, the medical model, by putting the onus on the 'diseased' individual, provides simple solutions – cut out the diseased parts of society. The process becomes the relatively simple one of detecting the signs of abuse and imposing the appropriate social 'cure'. It is notable that a major initial political response in the USA was to improve diagnosticity by making it mandatory for professionals to report their suspicions concerning the abuse of children. This is very much like the mandatory reporting of 'other' contagious diseases.

That these events are indeed a curiosity is highlighted by a review of Kempe's research (Montgomery, 1982a; 1982b). Kempe's work is seen as being seriously misleading, a major error being claims of extremely high rates of success in predicting future abuse using 'diagnostic' criteria. Kempe claims 76.5 per cent accuracy in predicting abuse in 100 families in an original sample of 350 families. The criteria of abuse frequently seem somewhat curious:

(a) 22 (of these one hundred cases) had exhibited 'indications of "abnormal parenting practices"' of an undescribed nature;
(b) 22 children had 'had at least one accident' requiring medical attention;
(c) 10 children had shown 'clear failures' on the Denver Developmental Screening Test;
(d) 8 children were no longer in their 'biologic homes';
(e) 8 children had been reported to the Central Child Abuse Registry;
(f) 5 children had shown signs of failure to thrive.

Montgomery (1982b) points out that:

it is remarkable how little of this relates directly to common conceptions of child abuse. In particular, the relationship between accidental injury and deliberate abuse is by no means made clear in the published results. By strict criteria, indeed, it could be argued that only those eight cases where abuse had been reported to the Central Child Abuse Registry should have been treated as index cases. From this point of view it makes sense to conclude that the 'predictive instrument' used by the researchers was not 76.5 but 8% accurate. Put differently, it was 92% wrong. (p. 192) (See also the further comments of Helfer, 1982; Montgomery, 1982b.)

The idea of 'abusive tendencies' struck Montgomery as faintly ridiculous, very much as nineteenth-century criminology with its notions of the 'criminal mind' or a 'criminogenic personality' are from our modern perspective:

> if – like crime – child abuse is socially defined, then it is defined as a 'bad thing' by reference to values, to notions of what children should and should not experience, and *not*, I would argue, by reference to the discipline of medicine (whatever its contribution to everyday case management) . . . From this point of view, what . . . Kempe . . . embarked upon has the features not of a scientific disclosure of truth, but rather of a political campaign or moral crusade. (p. 194)

Montgomery (1982b) accepts that this campaigning is the prerogative of anyone, but adds that 'it is important to make this point and to be clear about the precise nature of their endeavour, for only then can we know by what criteria to judge it' (p. 194).

Irrespective of how unsatisfactory the 'science' may have been, the underlying medicalisation of child abuse is lauded by the key roles given to medics like Caffey and Kempe. While medicine was the major formative influence on the rediscovery of child abuse, what it promised made it the focus of many of the problems of child protection. This is nothing new or unusual. There are many issues which have been medicalised despite appearing to be more moral or social than medical in character – drug abuse (Bean, 1974; Berridge, 1984; Howitt, 1991a), homosexuality and suicide (Szasz, 1986; 1990) being obvious examples. Although superficially abuse (physical or sexual) may have a lot to do with medicine – detecting long-broken bones or penetrated genitals – the bulk of physical and sexual abuse investigations probably benefit little from the medical involvement (de Jong and Rose, 1989; Bradshaw and Marks, 1990). A fondled genital or trivial bruise gains nothing from the information that a doctor can provide. Nevertheless, the medical profession is central to or at least a co-partner in, the child protection system. This is a radically different matter from the amateur social workers of the nineteenth century with their clear independence on values rather than an allegiance to 'science'.

There is an inheritance from this process of medicalisation for the child protection system. That is the choice between treatment or punishment, which is precisely the same mix as emerged from the medicalisation of drug abuse. Pushing deeper into the argument of this book, the consequences of the medicalisation of child abuse can easily be seen in the

Cleveland child sexual abuse affair in Britain, where an elementary but fundamentally flawed medical test led to a major inquiry into the conduct of the associated interventions. In addition, in my own research complaints about false allegations were repeatedly based on questionable medical diagnoses. It is no accident, of course, that medicine is presented as the science which revealed physical abuse to the world. A simple notion of individual pathology discovered via scientific research lends itself to interventionist remedies focused on the individual and is a powerful tool for policy. The interplay between research and practice in child abuse is also strongly highlighted by the origins of modern child abuse in medical science. The identification of pathogenic characteristics, highly likely to be characteristic of abusers, even if totally mistaken nevertheless defined the child abuse agenda. However, the seemingly rapid response in the United States (a society which was already alerted to and concerned about violence and which had been presented with a straightforward solution to an apparently containable problem) might not necessarily be paralleled elsewhere. (That concern about abuse seems extensive throughout the world is evidence by Farinatti *et al.* (1991), and Ming Yuan (1990); though MacPherson (1987) explains why it cannot be a major priority in some Third World countries and Korbin (1981) gives cross-cultural perspectives.)

In Britain, for example, it was not until the 1970s that a radical upheaval significantly changed child protection activities to something closer to the new interventionist American model. That it did not immediately cross the Atlantic perhaps reflects the fact that concerns about violence in society lagged behind elsewhere. In Britain the key event commonly held to have led to a radical shift in the nature of child protection activities was the Maria Colwell case of 1973. The facts of this case are well known (Parton, 1985). Briefly she was a social work 'scandal'. Having spent a number of years in the care of her aunt, she was returned to her 'family' (consisting of her mother and stepfather) by social workers. Despite a number of reports from anxious neighbours and teachers about her physical well-being, social workers essentially did little to protect the child. Maria was murdered in a final flurry of violence by her stepfather when she was 7 years of age.

It cannot be stressed too much what the nature of the concern about this case was. While there may well be a general societal abhorrence at the cruel and extreme abuse of children as shown in the Maria Colwell case, there is no reason to believe that the anti-social-work sentiment aroused was to do with anything more than the failure to take minimal steps to ensure her safety. These would be as basic as questioning whether the family was the best place for her after she had spent the bulk of her life in the care of her aunt, or investigating thoroughly the worries of those who were aware that she was at risk. In itself, to talk of clashes of ideology between the social work profession and the public seems over-intellectualisation. Despite being a relatively radical voice in social work, Parton (1981) falls into this trap:

> The [Maria Colwell] case also provided an excellent battleground for a clash between the doctrines and ideologies of the traditional and social democratic positions . . . On the one hand young 'namby-pamby, pussy-footing' social workers were seen by the traditional middle class groups as the worst representatives of the 'soft liberalism' which had heralded in the era of permissiveness. Not only were they prepared to let the 'innocent' suffer, they were prepared to excuse the guilty of their wrong doings. It was felt that such workers were now having misguided effects on the most vulnerable and deviant families in society. (p. 405)

Fox (1982) describes the clash of ideologies as between the 'kinship defenders' and the 'society-as-parent protagonists'.

It might be perfectly reasonable to suggest that child protection workers may have difficult decisions to make. Whether or not to intervene and whether to believe parents rather than other evidence are not comfortable choices in practice. However, one should be cautious about elevating such difficulties to the status of an ideological dilemma (Billig *et al.*, 1988). Which of the ideologies Parton describes would defend what happened to Maria Colwell? It is not easy to accept that the various child protection ideologies differ in terms of how a social worker who ignored warning of harm to a child in his or her care would be viewed. To raise ideology as the key factor is to understate the need to explain why professionals can act improperly, insensitively, illegally or impetuously in relatively clear-cut cases. Certain cases will inevitably pose dilemmas. The risks of over- or under-intervention remain irrespective of broader principles. That matters of competence continue to be raised about the child protection system despite changes in ideology must undermine the idea that incompetence and competing ideologies have anything in common. Differences in ideology may explain why child protection activities are sometimes challenged by parents, politicians, the media and others. But that is a matter of how a social issue comes into being.

In this context, Parton's insistence on using the idea of moral panics to explain why something had to be done about the quality of child protection work seems substantially overblown. It also risks hinting that the problem lies in the irrationality of the general public. The notion of moral panic (Cohen, 1972) carries such a connotation of irrationality – the public's response being stronger than the 'facts' justify. Whether this is a reasonable interpretation of the response to the Maria Colwell case is conjecture. That similar crises in confidence in the child protection services occurred in later years when totally different ideologies underlay child protection strategies suggests that Parton states his case too strongly. This is not to suggest that it is wrong to highlight the broader context in which child protection occurs, but Parton (1981) is perhaps wrong in his diagnosis of the nature of the public's response:

> I have argued that the moral panic concerning child abuse in Britain should not be seen in isolation from the social, cultural and economic changes that were evident at the time. The social reaction was very much both a symptom and a cause of the sense of crisis that was so apparent in the early 1970s. We can see the panic as part of a broader moral and political reaction to re-establish the traditional virtues and it provided the ideological battleground where certain representatives of 'soft liberalism' could be more readily harnessed to the traditional virtues and the increased emphasis on 'law and order'. In doing so I hope to have unravelled some of the elements that have been crucial in establishing the issue as such an important one for social workers, and to have demonstrated that their own individual perceptions of role conflict and tension are reflections of much wider historical and cultural confusions and contradictions. (p. 409)

History has overtaken Parton, writing in advance of the several scandals over child sexual abuse which emerged in the late 1980s and early 1990s. The question has become much more clearly one of competence in the public's mind rather than an ideological conflict played out in the child abuse arena. The question, though, has to be that of how professional 'errors' come about – Parton's relegation of the answer to outside the professions is only partially sustainable, and certainly not to the extent that the professions can stand back and blame society itself.

There is a danger in assuming that there is something particularly modern about concern over the ill-treatment of children. While there is little doubt that the treatment of children in the past frequently did not meet modern ideals, this is not the same thing as saying that attitudes towards the abuse of children were totally dissimilar in the past. Clark (1987) documents the appalling judicial treatment given to the rape of adult women in late eighteenth-century Britain. Any sexually experienced woman was seen as essentially beyond being raped! But attitudes to the abuse of children were not governed by the same sexual politics:

> The rape of children by men was widely abhorred. In 1786, the *Universal Register* noted, 'The practice of committing the most shocking indecencies on children is quite common.' On the other hand, some popular beliefs such as the myth that intercourse with a virgin would cure venereal disease exacerbated this problem. In 1752, fifty children were admitted to the Lock Hospital infected presumably by adults. Such assaults inflicted terrible emotional and physical injuries on children, and their assailants were popularly detested and severely punished, regardless of the offender's

status . . . In contrast, sexual violence committed by men on adult women tended to be seen as an extension of natural, everyday relations between the sexes, and thus much less culpable. (p. 42)

Compared with a small proportion of jury convictions for rape prosecutions in which adult women were the victims (fewer than one in eight resulting in a guilty verdict), the situation was radically different when it came to child victims:

> In London, out of fifteen men tried in the Old Bailey Sessions between 1770 and 1799 for rape on girls under thirteen, five were found guilty and sentenced to death; four were remanded for trial on the charge of assault with intent to commit rape. Like men convicted of the 'unnatural crime' of attempted sodomy, men guilty of attempted rape were put in the pillory to face the rage of the populace. In one incident . . . [t]he concourse of women who had witnessed the hardened miscreant's shame was immense. They surrounded the pillory, and pelted him with filth and rotten eggs. In yet another case, a man put in the pillory almost died from the abuse. (pp. 48–9)

There is no doubt that broad social and professional issues are intimately bound up with errors in the child protection system. Much of this book is about these. However, as much as anything else, the way in which the notion of child abuse is socially constructed through actions, theory, science and research is important in accounting for errors. To shift the blame on to an unreasonable public is a self-serving act which leaves central professional matters unquestioned and untouched. There is clearly nothing intrinsically 'good' in professional involvement in the protection of children. In this chapter we have seen examples of appalling abuse to children by professionals acting in that capacity. The abusive medicine and surgery of nineteenth-century physicians was not merely the actions of individual aberrant individuals but was made possible by the status of medicine and its 'scientific' basis. While it is relatively easy to relate such professional abuse to broader ideological issues, it is nonsense to imagine that these alone are responsible. The special role of science has to share part of the responsibility, although, of course, there is an ideology in science (Bevan, 1980; Howard, 1985; Kimble, 1984) which also has to be taken into account.

In this chapter, we have seen repeated but varied examples of the failure of professionals in respect of child protection. No matter what fine gloss is put on these, the remarkable feature of the account is that the history of child abuse is a story of professional failure. Error seems almost characteristic of the process. This is not to say that there are not many successes, but these seem to coexist readily with failure. It is important to know why.

CHAPTER 2

GATHERING THREADS

Officers from 18 police forces are to carry out urgent further investigations after identifying 'sinister issues' in 24 cases of bogus social workers entering houses to try to examine children . . . The bogus officials have succeeded in carrying out intimate examinations of 14 children, aged between two and four years. (*The Times*, 15 May 1990, p. 2)

One of the artefacts of child protection activities has been the 'bogus social worker'. In Britain, during the early months of 1990, media attention was directed towards a string of instances of such bogus social workers intent on sexually abusing children. Perhaps a mother, at home with her child, would answer a knock on the door to find strangers there who introduced themselves as social workers. They suggest that her child must be physically examined because of allegations of abuse. Reports came from all over the country and the incidents began to be seen as an epidemic. Grave distress was caused to families by the pretence.

Fear of Child Sex Link Over Bogus Social Workers
The first incident was . . . in Sheffield when two women posing as social workers examined two young children in front of their mother after asking them to undress completely . . . On February 5 one woman returned with a man saying they had warrants to take the children into care. The mother challenged the couple who then left. (*The Times*, 22 March 1990, p. 3)

Bogus social workers are credible only because of the way in which child protection is socially imaged. It is a woefully inadequate explanation of the bogus social worker phenomenon to suggest that the people involved were simply perverts taking advantage of a chance to abuse a child. The social workers were bogus in the sense that they were not officially employed, but in what other ways did they differ? The crucial question is why unannounced visitors to a household could make such requests to examine intimately or to remove a child without being immediately perceived as dangerous paedophiles.

Were bogus social workers an issue in the nineteenth century? Apparently not, despite the earliest recognisable social workers being charitable amateurs. Similarly, was there such a concept as the bogus social worker in the 1940s, 1950s, 1960s or even in the 1970s? While historical documentation on this is not available, one can be confident that bogus social workers were unknown then. This is simply because the characteristics of real and bogus social workers overlap only in terms of modern child protection practices. Without these parallels, bogus social workers would have no veracity.

> Editorial: Bogus Social Workers
> The crime would not be possible if members of the public were not either extremely trustful of social workers, or at worst intimidated by them and by their enormous power to cause the most disruption to family life . . . The social worker has in fact no right without express court authority to gain entry to a family home in order to inspect the condition of the children or remove them to a 'place of safety'. But enough members of the public appear to believe otherwise for impersonation to seem plausible. The bogus social workers sometimes suggest they are checking on allegations of child abuse, and the common reactions of indignant and innocent parents is to produce the child and offer it for inspection to prove the allegation is nonsense, while secretly fearing that an unco-operative attitude will count against them. (*The Times*, 13 May 1990, p. 13)

Bogus social workers do little different from real social workers. The public knows that real social workers turn up on the doorstep, intrude into the parents' authority and care and custody of the child, take children away, have them subjected to medical inspections, cross-examinations and other procedures, do not have to explain why they do what they do, treat guilty and innocent families in identical ways, and sometimes harm children. The public's image of social work, well founded or otherwise, could not be expected to differentiate the real from the bogus precisely because there is no distinction which stands up to examination.

The final denouement of the bogus social worker saga confirms graphically the nature of the problem. Rather than resulting in numerous arrests of paedophiles and paedophiliac rings, the ultimate realisation was that in some cases *real* social workers had been mistaken for bogus ones. The upshot, then, is intriguing. Not only were bogus social workers indistinguishable sometimes from the real thing, but there was no way of knowing in the stress of the situation that a real social worker was not a bogus one! This is a curious state of affairs, but one which needs to be seen as quintessentially the nature of the beast rather than an aberration.

So the characteristics of modern child protection practices gave credibility to such strangers. In comparison, a caller could not arrive at the door and claim with any credibility to be a doctor in general practice wishing to examine a child for sexually transmitted diseases. Part of the disbelief in these circumstances is based on social understandings of the role of general practitioners as well as their activities in relation to families. General practitioners just do not act in the same way that we assume social workers do. While some bogus social workers were identified as such by families, this appears not to have been easy, especially prior to national media coverage of the events. Thus the problem is to explain not so much the behaviour of bogus social workers as that of the real ones, which takes on a bizarre quality in the light of the imposters. In other words, one needs to understand how intrusive and uninvited child protection workers come to take children away from their parents in dawn raids without the approval of those parents.

It is contended that the actions of child protection workers are the result of the way in which abuse is constructed socially. Abuse is seen as a dangerous plague which threatens society through its adverse effect on the child. Part of the engine house of child protection which leads to some devastating errors are a number of ideologically based themes about gender and power in modern society. Child protection activity does not emerge from the minds of individual professionals in the child protection system. No one has woken one morning and decided in isolation that a child ought to be removed from its abusing family. However, it is commonplace that some people with a certain training occupying a certain professional status and fed with certain information may decide to do such things. What they do is as much a product of the ideological support with which their training, reading and profession provides them as anything else.

The science of child abuse

A feature of child protection work is its basis in 'science'. Chapter 1 discussed how the origins of modern concern about the physical abuse of children emerged out of radiography and paediatrics in the 1950s and 1960s. However, science alone does not account for the identification of 'the battered child' as a social problem. For example, according to Kempe and Kempe (1978):

> The battered-child syndrome was first described in 1868 by Ambroise Tardieu, a professor of legal medicine in Paris. He had, of necessity, to rely on autopsy findings. He described 32 children battered or burnt to death. The same year Athol Johnson at the Hospital for Sick Children in London called attention to the frequency of repeated fractures in children. He attributed these to the condition of the bones, since rickets at that time was almost universal among London children. We now know that almost every case he described was, in fact, an abused child. (p. 17)

But such failures do not alter by one jot the importance of the origins of child abuse in the scientific community. It may have taken another hundred years, but the invention of child abuse out of X-ray machinery (the epitome of a science turned into a technology) is the essence of the matter. Immediately following this, the work of Kempe and his co-workers not only provided the factual evidence of the appalling injuries caused to children by their parents, but also presented the solution to the problem. Claims were made, as we saw in Chapter 1, about the ease of prediction of the likely future child batterer. These provided a legacy of science and prediction which structured the entire field of modern child protection. Of course, there would be nothing more inhuman than to fail to act if one knew who would batter children. The scientific ideology of prediction and control may not turn out to be well founded, but it pervades, as we will see, despite repeated failure.

Much modern child protection work is incomprehensible without reference to this ideology. Many of the incidents which are investigated *and* acted upon are, in themselves, essentially trivial. Whatever other functions are served by the removal of babies from their mothers at birth and by child protection registers, they incorporate a belief that future abuse is predictable. Without this element child protection might almost be regarded primarily as a police matter just like any other crime. Prediction leads in two directions. The first is towards empiricist attempts to predict likely abuse. The second is incorporated into professional practice based on a pseudo-empiricism. The system of child abuse registration represents this well – that is, a centralised register of children who are considered to be at *risk* of abuse by their parents. While sometimes it is argued that such registers enable the targeting of resources on 'problem' families, why target a family if it has no greater likelihood of abusing further than any other? Even this function of abuse registers may not be achieved because of the resourcing problems of the agency caused by the volume of child protection work.

Registration as being at risk of child abuse means precisely that. That the predictors of abuse are badly or not at all articulated in the registration process alters nothing. Later we will discuss how registration may be built on the slenderest of evidence and supposition (see especially Chapters 7 and 8). Despite this, previous registration seems to be a strong predictor of future mistaken or even 'catastrophic' intervention by the child protection workers.

This change in orientation towards prediction is no better illustrated than in Tredinnik and Fairbairn's (1980) data (see also Parton, 1981). They consulted UK social services departments to gain information about the extent of statutory removals of babies from their mothers at birth. There were virtually none of these in the late 1960s. By the end of the 1970s there were as many as 42 in one year disclosed to the researchers. In part, this can be seen as evidence of the growth of an interventionist ideology (Parton, 1981). However, it is also evidence of the growing ideology of prediction, since new-born babies cannot be removed at birth on account of having been battered or otherwise abused (except in the case of drug taking by the pregnant mother). This is not to say that the child protection workers did not have good cause to anticipate future abuse. However, despite the plethora of research on child abuse, there does not appear to be any systematic evidence to suggest that recidivism is common in child abuse or that one can predict from minor 'abuse' on one occasion future serious abuse. I am not suggesting that persistent abuse is uncommon or that serious abuse is not perpetrated by parents who had previously committed less serious abuse. The question is one of the extent to which, say, a bruise mark injury due to overchastisement is predictive of future broken limbs or worse. Furthermore, from what we know of sexual abuse it is often a 'one-off' and relatively minor episode (see Chapter 3).

Had the issue been virtually any other than child abuse, it is unlikely that a belief in prediction would have been accepted. For example, had the issue been the prediction of future murderers, it is doubtful whether claims like Kempe's about prediction would have found acceptance. Those who treat children so appallingly surely have to be seen as different from the rest of us! Kempe had 'proven' that they were 'sick'. Of course, it would be marvellous if there were a perfect means of identifying future abusers. But prediction is weak at best, and it has dangers. There are no perfect Identikit pictures of the characteristics of abusers-to-be from which to pick them out. To be sure, they may *as a group* differ in certain respects from non-abusers. However, there is no way that they can be usefully identified on the basis of even the most discriminating characteristics. For example, stepfathers as a group has more than its fair share of abusers. Nevertheless, most abuse is not by stepfathers and the majority of them do not abuse.

Errors inevitably happen when imperfect predictors are used. Using language borrowed from medical diagnosis, a number of outcomes are possible in attempts to predict any event, including abuse:

True positive: Abuse had been predicted and actually happened.
False positive: Abuse had been predicted but did *not* happen.
True negative: Abuse had *not* been predicted and did *not* happen.
False negative: Abuse had *not* been predicted but did happen.

It should be apparent that a certain pattern will prevail if the predictions are going to be valuable. Ideally, all cases should fall into the *true positive* and *true negative* categories. To the extent that false positives occur, then injustice is done to those parents. Conversely, false negatives involve undetected or unpredicted harm to children.

The futility of the prediction approach is readily illustrated by a study by Browne and Saqi (1988) which involved an entire cohort of babies born in an English county. Essentially, a set of measures was developed which correlated with child abuse. These were then incorporated into a screening instrument completed by midwives and health visitors about each of the families. It is unquestionable that some characteristics predicted future abuse. Indeed, a fairly high level of success was achieved; the vast majority of abusing families were predicted. However, the false positive rate was extremely high, thus indicating the disaster which such predictive screening would bring about. For each family correctly predicted as a future abuser there were thirty-six families incorrectly predicted as such.

Most of the predictors used in this research were in many ways ideal – matters which could be readily assessed by relatively untrained personnel. For example, one-parent families were five times more likely to abuse, families with a premature baby with a low birth weight were eight times more likely to abuse, and families with a history of violence were nine times more likely to abuse. But the hidden message of the research has to be of the overwhelming likelihood of errors. It is therefore of some significance that Browne and Saqi do not simply reject prediction out of hand. They prefer to recommend the use of their device as a screening instrument so that more intensive attention can be paid to the families judged most at risk of abuse:

> All families with a newborn child should be screened perinatally using social and demographic characteristics of the child and its family. This will identify a target group for further screening. However, the remaining population cannot be considered immune to family stress and child abuse. Any change in family circumstances leading to increased stress should be assessed and if applicable the family added to the target group. (Browne and Saqi, 1988, p. 80)

In circumstances of unlimited resources this might not be unreasonable, although it is very intrusive (and a price that many would not be willing to pay). However, where choices have to be made between competing demands for resources, to follow such a suggestion, which involves the policing of so many families when only a few families are at risk, is impractical.

A further point warrants mentioning. The criterion of abuse was whether the child became the focus of a child abuse conference during its early infancy. Consequently, it is not clear that the predictors used in the screening instrument and the factors involved in bringing matters to a case conference are independent of each other. For example, if being in a step-family is commonly accepted to be a risk factor in abuse, then an accidental injury to a child is more likely to be mistaken for abuse in such families. A framework is thereby constructed which enables accidental injury to be labelled 'abuse'. As such, Browne and Saqi's criterion is likely to maximise the apparent validity of prediction procedures, not minimise it. There are a number of other studies, such as Altemeier *et al.* (1984), Lealman *et al.* (1983), Gray *et al.* (1977) and Rowan (1979), which show high rates of false positives in research on the prediction of future abuse. Campbell (1991) describes this as indicating 'an imprecision which reflects the complexity of the phenomenon' (p. 261). Avison *et al.* (1986) claim to have developed a 'promising screening instrument' to predict problem parents. However, in order to identify 90 per cent of the mal-adaptive parents, a quarter of all other parents would be further investigated. Similarly, Paulson *et al.* (1977) found that one instrument classified correctly only 65 per cent of the time.

Margolin (1990) captures the issue well when she discusses the prediction of fatal child neglect:

> Only 39% of the neglect fatalities for Iowa had any previous involvement with child protection services. Second, it should be considered that Iowa substantiates almost 3,000 cases of child neglect yearly, of which approximately four involve a fatality. A screening device would have to be extremely precise to locate these needles in a haystack. In the long run, a strategy centered on training and/or deploying more field professionals might save more lives. Perhaps the most efficient strategy would involve expanded prevention services that would provide education and support to all new parents in regard to child safety. (p. 318)

The ethos of prediction may well contribute considerably to the errors of the child protection system. Furthermore, it is a process which clearly risks being self-validating. For example, it may be the case that factor *x* is common in child abuse. Every time abuse is detected by child protection workers the presence of factor *x* reinforces its apparent predictive value. This would constitute 'commonsense' evidence that prediction is possible and that the 'scientific' evidence is valid in terms of everyday actions. It may be no such thing if factor *x* is common when abuse has not occurred.

These may appear to be unusual claims to make about the role of the scientific ethos in child protection in the absence, so far, of any evidence that professionals in the field directly incorporate elements from research and theory into their practice. At a conceptual level, however, the argument has considerable strength. It is not a big step to describe *prediction* as *prejudice*. To prejudge an issue and to predict (especially using imprecise criteria) are virtually indistinguishable. It is not assumed that the influence of the scientific ethos is a simple one of research feeding directly into practice. But we know from the history of the social sciences that research often serves broad ideological needs. In other words, it gives succour to certain views within society (Howitt, 1991a). Furthermore, it has to be said that virtually no modern research on child abuse, with the exception of the occasional survey of the general public, takes place away from the professional setting with the many opportunities for cross-influence that this provides.

Strong protests might be made that there is little evidence that child protection workers make such predictions. Indeed, they do not make statistically based predictions and there is no intention to suggest otherwise. However, it is the practice of making professional judgements in this field which is the key to the use of prediction. There is no assumption that prediction is reduced to anything other than an uncertain formula or 'rule of thumb' in practice. This sort of *formularisation* is to be expected, and it imbues much professional work as it simplifies complex aspects of the task. It is very difficult to deal with statistical judgements in a probabalistic way, so consequently 'rules of thumb' become entrenched. In this context it is worthwhile noting Finkelhor's (1984) survey of the American general public, which asked who were the most likely people to sexually abuse a child. The replies were as shown in Table 2.1.

Now the public's perceptions were wildly inaccurate in most respects. Any survey of sexual abuse would demonstrate that stepfathers are abusers infrequently in absolute terms. What the public appears to have done is to take the notion that stepfathers *as a group* are far more likely to abuse (Lightcap *et al.*, 1982) and turn it, illogically, into the idea that a high proportion of stepfathers are abusers. It is only when the closest family alone is considered that stepfathers can be considered as common in cases of abuse. Even then they make up only a small proportion of abusers.

We will see later how these prejudgements seem to encourage errors in the child protection processes. Errors seem to be most common among families having 'abusive' characteristics, such as stepfathers and unemployment. The prediction ethos, of course, allows not only factors

Table 2.1: American perceptions of the most likely sexual abusers

Stranger	35%
Stepparent	28%
Parent	22%
Friend/acquaintance	13%
Other relative	5%
Older siblings	3%

Source: Finkelhor (1984).

demonstrably related to abuse, albeit imperfectly, to be used, but other characteristics which might have no known foundation at all to be incorporated. These, as we will see, include notions about what sorts of family can be 'worked with' effectively in case-work by child protection workers. Or which mothers whose spouse had sexually abused their children could cope with supporting their children at home to prevent them from being taken into care – to a degree this means mothers who accept only certain views of events which support particular theories of non-colluding mothers.

Child protection practice is essentially theory led. These theories may not be particularly well articulated as such by individuals, but this is irrelevant. The vaguer the conceptualisation of the theory, the fewer bounds there are to its application. In child protection there is probably as close a link between practice and research as in any professional work. The professional literature on child abuse is enormous given the comparative youth of the field, and research is relatively extensive. Furthermore, it is an area in which several powerful theories can fight out their positions. Feminist theory (Dominelli and MacLeod, 1989) and family therapy (Barton and Alexander, 1981; Burnham, 1986; Glick and Hessler, 1974) are obvious examples.

Even social workers who are aware of the problems involved in predicting abuse may get the issue hopelessly muddled: 'There are currently 40,000 children on child protection registers in England. There is no way from the research to tell which child is going to be abused. *To avoid tragedy all children at risk must be registered*' (Higginson, 1989, p. 17, emphasis added). This is an argument that every child should be registered, since we do not know apparently that the children on the register are more likely to be abused than those who are not!

Theory into practice

Many of the concerns about 'child abuse science' would count for little if its doctrines did not spread into professional practice and training. But there is little doubt that they do. Just as older ideas concerning childhood regulated the older, non-interventionist practice, modern doctrines guide a quite different way of working. For instance, Bowlby's (1952; 1973) ideas about the 'crucial' mother-child bond were part of a post-war construction and reconstruction of the nature of childhood:

> As psycho-medics were identifying the important functions of parents, especially mothers, many working-class families were undergoing stressful situations in the social and economic upheavals of the inter-war period. These experiences served to underline the significance of the family for

child health and 'successful' child rearing. But it was the situations created by the war, such as the rise in illegitimacy, the evacuation of children, and the provision of nurseries for children of working mothers, which not only provided so much research material for the whole range of 'caring' services, but also further and dramatically illustrated the family's primacy. (Hendricks, 1990, p. 53)

Scientific support for the ideal of the domestic mother was entirely conducive to not breaking the bond through interventions separating the child from its mother. Bowlby's work, done for the World Health Organisation, was itself a medical science contribution to understanding childhood. It was also convenient knowledge for one view of the nature of the family which feminist theory allowed. But, despite this, it is reasonable to ask: how do we know that there is a link between practice and theory-cum-research in child protection?

Little formal evidence exists demonstrating the extent of the relationship. Obviously it would be a commonsense proposition to suggest that what is learnt may well be put into practice – after all, that is the primary purpose of training. Of course, the argument could be reversed by claiming that 'child abuse science' is used to justify practice rather than to determine it. But this might be a false choice, since influences in both directions are likely. One is strongly reminded here of a similar issue in relation to education. In the 1960s one very fashionable scientific theory in education was Piaget's conceptualisation of the intellectual development of the child (e.g. Piaget, 1952). Whatever the inadequacy of his approach (Siegel and Brainerd, 1978), it remains true that his ideas were part of the training of a great many teachers and were construed as support for many changes in practice within the school and classroom (Schwebel and Raph, 1974).

One therefore does not need a direct one-way relationship between child abuse science and practice in order for the influence to be there. There are a number of ways of demonstrating that the interchange exists and may reinforce aspects of child protection practice and lead to error. So far we have looked only at the match between science and practice in relation to prediction, but there is much else. One could map the use of child abuse science by practitioners writing in the professional journals for practitioners. Another approach is to examine how social workers learn about and process child abuse science. Pertinent research has often not been carried out on all of these questions. For example, one might look at the diffusion of knowledge about child abuse within the professions just as it has been done in other spheres (Rogers, 1983), but there is no such body of information.

So how does child abuse science filter through professional journals into practice, for example? One good illustration is an article by a practising probation officer, Cowburn's 'Assumptions about sex offenders' (1990). In this he assembles a hodgepodge of 'radical views' of sex offenders. For example, he takes Kelly's (1989) definition of what she terms sexual violence:

> Sexual violence includes any physical, visual, verbal or sexual act that is experienced by the woman or girl, at the time or later, as a threat, invasion or assault, that has the effect of hurting her or degrading her and/or takes away her ability to control intimate contact. (Kelly, 1989, p. 41).

Apart from the bald statement 'I would extend this definition to include male victims', Cowburn takes no exception to Kelly's definition, which verges on being deceptive. The use of a word like 'violence' may to an extent describe the typical rape offence known to the police (Howitt and Cumberbatch, 1990), nevertheless it is an inappropriate description of much paedophiliac behaviour. Furthermore, a woman who never comes to see her early abuse as a threat, invasion or assault has, by this definition, not suffered sexual violence! Must a practitioner wait years until a woman finally realises that she has been degraded before intervention is appropriate? Of course not – so why quote a definition which is fundamentally a smokescreen despite its instant polemical appeal? Indeed, one suspects that any child protection worker who employed Kelly's definitions without modification would rapidly cease to function effectively.

Cowburn reproduces other 'radical views', such as those of Campbell on the Cleveland child sexual abuse affair (Campbell, 1988; 1989), which is a revisionist view of the events there which denies that there was any problem other than sexual abuse itself (see Chapter 6). Among the conclusions which Cowburn recommends to his colleagues is the following:

> It could be that a probation officer's first instinct, therefore, in writing about a sex offender would be to minimise the nature and consequences of the offence. I think that this type of response has two effects. It reinforces the offender's distorted and necessarily partial view of his offences, it also colludes with and confirms the dominance of sexist male power in our society . . . This does not mean that we will necessarily be recommending custodial sentences for every sex offender. We need to consider the totality of the behaviour, the effect of prison and alternative options which may offer a better prognosis for change. (p. 8)

Despite minor qualifications, the article essentially does little more than turn the screw of increased punitive sentences. Not to do so is described as collusion with sexist male power!

Is there any direct evidence that such writing affects the thinking of practitioners apart from the fact that these authors are also practitioners? Evidence of this is provided by the experiences of a social worker in training (Sheldon, 1991). She discusses her attempts to minimise the future risks from, and encourage responsible behaviour in, a man convicted of sexual offences against children. While she takes on board a number of views about the nature of offending, it is useful to focus on her treatment of the work of Wyre (1987). Wyre is a modern pioneer in Britain of the treatment of paedophiliac sex offenders and clinical director of the Gracewell Clinic in Birmingham. Sheldon describes Wyre's main assumptions as (a) high levels of denial of offences, and (b) the abuser justifying his abuse by, for example, adherence to distorted beliefs:

> In addition, I took guidance from Wyre (1987) as to how I could best enable honesty on Alan's part. Wyre maintains that sex offenders live in two worlds – the 'normal' world presented to the worker and the 'deviant' world which the offender attempts to disguise . . . I had to give Alan 'permission' to be honest by, according to Wyre, . . . asking questions in a leading way. Thus, instead of asking 'Did you fantasise/masturbate about the victim?' and receiving the expected 'No' (denial) reply, I was to follow Wyre's suggested approach of saying, for example, 'When you fantasised and masturbated . . .', or 'I expect you fantasised', 'It's well known that . . .', and so on. (Sheldon, 1991, p. 16)

In other words, leading questions are both legitimate and essential! However, putting this advice into practice brought its difficulties:

> Alan's first offence, an indecent assault, caused him to immediately ejaculate and he presented it as a spontaneous act. He admitted, however, that subsequent offences were intentional in that he had wanted to repeat the excitement he had experienced by further, and more serious, sexual contact with Caroline. He was resistant to the notion that he had 'actively' thought about and planned subsequent offences . . . It seemed that some progress had been made by prompting Alan to admit a degree of planning between offences, but I was concerned about his vigorous denial of prior arousal and planning. However, I was also concerned not to 'force' Alan to fit exactly into the theoretical framework I had in mind since . . . an over-readiness to accept the views of 'authority figures' (in this case, Wyre) can lead to 'distorted reasoning and perception' . . . This was to be a regular and persistent feature of my work with Alan as I tried to balance a desire to believe him and a determination not to 'fit' him into a theory at any cost with the knowledge I had accrued from the literature. (pp. 21–2)

> Since I had no previous experience of working with sex offenders, I was completely reliant upon the writings of . . . in particular, Wyre, but I was reluctant to presume Alan had to conform completely to these . . . assumptions and theoretical frameworks. There existed a dilemma of balancing my own desire to believe what Alan was telling me with the information I had gathered from these authoritative sources. (p. 30)

These comments, it should be stressed, are no simple, straightforward confirmation of the view that child abuse practice is structured by 'child abuse science'. What they are, however, is an account of the experience of trying to apply 'child abuse science' which partially fails. However, they fully demonstrate the pressure to move from theory to practice despite a somewhat questioning stance. What would have happened had Alan supported the theory and succumbed to the leading questions? What if the social worker had not had a critical attitude to the theory? In the end, the theory was employed and guided practice. That the theory did not ultimately completely win out over experience in this case does not mean that this particular exchange and future exchanges shed the theory. It would be a very small step for this social worker to decide that her failure to match theory with observation was due to her personal lack of skill at this type of interviewing and/or that Alan was indeed avoiding coming to terms with wilful and planned abuse. Eventually the social worker might learn to recognise denial as symptomatic of guilt – after all, here was a man who was clearly guilty but to an extent continued to deny. What would have been her conclusions had Alan repeatedly denied everything? She might well have assumed that Wyre's theory was a very strong one, since denial was characteristic. What if she then met someone who honestly denied some sexual offence he had not committed?

The classic case of theory into practice, however, is the Cleveland child sexual abuse crisis. Here the entire set of events was triggered by the promulgation of the view that a relatively simple 'medical' test would demonstrate that buggery or other forms of anal penetration had occurred. Hanks, Hobbs and Wynne (1988) describe the test as follows:

> Reflex dilation, well described in forensic texts . . . usually occurs within about 30 seconds of separating the buttocks. Recent controversy has helped our understanding of what is now seen as an important sign of traumatic penetration of the anus as occurs in abuse, but also following medical and surgical manipulation . . . The diameter of the symmetrical relaxation of the anal sphincter is variable and should be estimated. This is a dramatic sign which once seen is easily recognized . . . The sign is not always easily reproducible on second and third examinations and there appear to be factors, at present, which may modify the eliciting of this physical sign. The sign in most cases gradually disappears when abuse stops. (p. 153)

Although it does not appear to be the case from this extract (and it is hardly much clearer in the full chapter), Hobbs and Wynne were in fact the paediatricians responsible for promoting the idea that anal dilation was a sign of abuse (Hobbs and Wynne, 1986). There is little doubt that Hobbs and Wynne's theory was put into practice. There is no problem in understanding the spread of information about the diagnostic aid of the anal reflex – their *Lancet* publication of 1986 would have been readily available. That it produced a degree of controversy at the time of publication probably increased the likelihood that it would be seen by attentive members of the medical profession. Furthermore, according to Bell (1988), Dr Higgs, the doctor at the centre of the Cleveland scandal, had attended a seminar at which Wynne spoke and 'the technique was actually introduced at this seminar' (Bell, 1988, p. 50). Dr Higgs is on record as saying of Dr Wynne's views:

> I think I realised for the first time the numbers of children that could be involved in this problem, the importance of the medical examination. The general feeling was that there were not many findings, that the doctors did have a role, really quite a small role to play. I think what was impressive about the Leeds conference is that there were doctors who had been working in this field, who had had a number of years' experience, had children with findings that were actually then able to be related to histories from the child of abuse and also admissions by perpetrators. (Butler-Sloss, 1988, p. 131)

Of course, knowledge of the test in itself does not account for its implementation in practice. But, of course, it is the availability of the knowledge in an accessible form which allows it to be turned into action. Higgs, according to Campbell (1988), had already been involved in child abuse training work as well as therapy with children. So she was perhaps more receptive to the test than others would have been. Such a test could clearly be used only by medical personnel. So the fact that it was a doctor who adopted it, rather than some other involved professional is no surprise.

While it seems sufficiently well established that theory can lead directly into practice, it would be naive to believe that the association between theory and practice is a simple, direct, one-way relationship. Theory, as already suggested, may be sought out to justify practice rather than practice following from theory. An interesting example of this is Pithers' (1990) discussion of the use of fantasy by children, in which some of the problems of ritualistic sexual abuse investigations are highlighted. Pithers, another practitioner, begins with a recollection from his own childhood:

> When I was about five years old I went for a ride with the devil. For some reason we had not gone to our usual friendly, somewhat agnostic, church but to one which I now know to have been of the Calvinist variety. In the high pulpit a lank cadaverous man in a black gown appeared. I was convinced that his waving arms were wings and that he could surely fly. I knew that the devil was the prince of darkness and he was the darkest creature I had ever seen. That night I dreamt the devil came to me, grasped me in his claws, and flew me to hell. The experience came back each night and I became terrified of going to bed. (p. 20)

When Pithers seeks to put this in the context of Freudian psychoanalytic theory, it becomes clearer what the underlying view is. He accepts a theory about the nature of fantasy which is a substantial and convenient modification of anything that Freud said. It provides a simple formula to be used in cases of suspected ritual abuse:

> Both dream and fantasy depend on the day's 'residue'. This concept is to be found in Freud's earliest work on dreams. Events are taken from the day and are symbolically reconstructed to provide visual material for unconscious experience . . . There are no symbols in the dream which do not have their origin in waking life. In the same sense it must be true that children cannot fantasise about events which lie completely outside of their experience. (Pithers, 1990, p. 21)

This is extremely misleading, of course, since it regards as unproblematic phrases such as 'events which lie completely outside of their experience'. After all, Pither's childhood experience with the devil was essentially real, and well explained by his waking knowledge of the devil which he had gleaned from his everyday life. However, in the last analysis he had not seen the devil at all. So to write of children being unable to fantasise about events that are outside of their experience leaves unanswered questions about what sort of experience will be incorporated into fantasy and in what form. Freud's basic task of understanding through psychoanalytic revelations what lay beneath the superficial content of the fantasy is belittled by this modern reformulation. To equate fantasy with experience in the simple way that Pithers does merely encourages the interpretation of fantasy as directly symbolic of real-life experiences, which is far removed from Freud's notions. In Freudian theory, fantasy comes before reality (Freud, 1962; Hall, 1954). The use of theory in this way is unnecessary to establish Pithers' basic concern about improving the work of social workers in relation to satanic ritualistic abuse. Indeed, his use of theory undermines the power of his argument about training, since it provides another good instance of bad science that might be taught to trainees.

The latent theory in the language of abuse

While it might not immediately seem important, there has been a radical change in the use of language to describe aspects of violence and sex perpetrated by adults on children. Knowingly or not, the new language used is freighted with meanings and assumptions which are not merely 'neutral' descriptions. Indeed, the language is so strongly theory laden that it provides the user with an 'understanding' in itself. Language choice is not neutral but a determinant of thought. It is part of the means of changing and maintaining ideas. The choice serves viewpoints (Grillo, 1989; Smith, 1985) and the language is partly responsible for action. These actions can lead to error.

Several key terms in the abuse literature warrant discussion. They are:

1. Abuse.
2. The family.
3. Incest.
4. Incest survivor.

There is little doubt that, for some, the choice of language is no accident. One should not be surprised at this given the extensive and popular literature on the role of language in, for example, cultivating sexism (Spender, 1985; Steedman *et al.*, 1985). Kelly (1988), in a slightly more general context, has commented:

> A vital part of feminist work around sexual violence has . . . been to provide names that describe women's experience. The terms 'battered woman', 'domestic violence', 'sexual harrassment', 'sexual violence' and 'incest survivor' have all been introduced into our language in the past fifteen years. Naming involves making visible what was invisible, defining as unacceptable what was acceptable and insisting that what was naturalized is problematic. (p. 139)

While it is not my intention to take issue with all of these, such a clear statement of the role of language in political and social change needs underscoring. Language, to the extent that it changes notions of the nature of abuse, has to be regarded critically.

Abuse   The use of the word 'abuse' may appear uncontentious. Indeed, it may well be uncontentious to some. However, one has to consider that this word collects certain acts together and labels them in a particular way. Compare the word with others which might be used. For example, would a description such as 'sexual activity between an adult and child' carry quite the same implications? Or would 'illegal adult–child sexual relationship' fit the bill? The answer is no. These alternative phrases do not carry similar implications. 'Child sexual abuse' grants the responsibility solely to the adult: the child is being misused by an adult. Furthermore, the phrase carries with it no implication that there is ever *appropriate* adult–child sex. The alternatives to sexual abuse are either no adult–child sex or child–child sex, as in sexual games like 'doctors and nurses' between similar-aged children. Thus, in the baggage of the phrase 'sexual abuse' is the assumption that it is wrong and improper without any real fuzzy edges to give pause for thought. Furthermore, there is also no assumption of illegality. Many things which are sometimes classified as sexual abuse are most certainly of dubious illegality. For example, an uncle's verbally drawing attention to his niece's developing breasts would be classified as abuse by some definitions, but is unlikely to be illegal.

When applied to physically violent acts that adults perpetrate on children, the notion of physical abuse may also hold assumptions which other language choices would not carry. 'Chastisement', 'overchastisement', 'corporal punishment' and like phrases may be seen as carrying with them built-in justifications. They all suggest that there may be good reason for what is done to the child – it is 'good' for the child and has a rational purpose concerning its social behaviour. In physical abuse, the justification is absent – denied even by the phrase. Once described as physical abuse rather than overchastisement the excuse melts away. But at the same time it is very difficult to define what sorts of physical violence towards a child are not abuse because of the very slippage in the phrase. Thus, although a phrase like 'causing extensive injury' might equate with some people's notions of what is abuse, the use of the term 'abuse' itself abandons precision. Notice, also, that the phrase bears the notion of an action perpetrated by a powerful individual on a powerless person – powerless people cannot abuse. Inevitably the idea is of adult violence against children rather than between children, say in the playground, which might even produce an equal injury. 'Violence' or 'aggression' would be enough to describe this.

The language shift is not arbitrary. It is of rhetorical significance and allows something to be achieved through language which otherwise would have been socially complex. To have to decide whether to hit a child with a cane was 'overzealous' if it led to injury would be to overload and complicate the social decision-making process.

Furthermore, it cannot be ignored that definitions of the different roles in abuse may have profound implications for the disposition of cases. The victim–perpetrator dichotomy may encourage a simple moral decision, since the perpetrator is always completely responsible. Ringwalt and Earp (1988) gave a large sample of US child protection workers cases of father–daughter sexual abuse to evaluate. There was a strong relationship between blaming the father (rather than sharing the blame among the family) and the relatively strong belief that the father should be imprisoned and a modest one that the daughter should be put into foster care. Furthermore, if the mother was seen as partly responsible for the abuse, the recommendation for the father's imprisonment declined. So the language of abuse reflects the course of action which might follow. Not only that, such a finding emphasises the importance of the theories of sexual abuse. While some feminist arguments (MacLeod and Saraga,

1988) pour scorn on the idea in family therapy theory that abuse is a family problem in which the mother often colludes by encouraging or remaining silent about abuse, the implications for increased punitiveness in the feminist approach are made obvious by this study.

The family   The appearance of the word 'family' in this context is odd at first sight. Surely the notion of family is very precisely defined? More importantly, if it is, why raise it as a problem? Surprisingly, the definition of the family has taken a reverse step in the abuse literature. The concept of the family has slid backwards from that of the nuclear family (man, woman and their children) to that of the extended family (husband, wife, children, grandparents, aunts and uncles, cousins, second cousins and the rest). While this is a perfectly acceptable use of the word 'family', one has to ask why the abuse literature bucks the trend of most social scientific writing. In the social sciences literature the family has been regarded as increasingly fragmenting. The nucleus of the extended family, the nuclear family, was seen as becoming increasingly distant physically and emotionally from the extended family. It has suited the needs of many writers to accept such a view, although it has to be said that the notion of the nuclear family substantially mistakes the real situation. For example, Uzoka (1979) has written of the 'myth of the nuclear family', arguing that there is considerable evidence that even the modern family has extensive contact with and support from the extended family. The myth of the nuclear family serves social work well, since it enhances the importance of professionals in comparison to other sources of social support due to the decline of the extended family.

Reversing the definition of 'family' back to that of the extended family was essential in child abuse research, otherwise intrafamilial abuse would have become *numerically* of less significance. To cut short a story that we will return to later, without reference to the extended family, sexual abuse within the family, in particular, would be relatively much rarer. However, taking the extended family into consideration greatly increases the extent of sexual abuse within the family. This is another way of saying that, overwhelmingly, abuse is done by extended family members rather than by those in the immediate nuclear family. Thus, when it is suggested that the family is a dangerous place for children, it is really the extended family which is in the spotlight. The nuclear family, as we will see, is a safer haven.

Incest   This is defined in dictionary terms as 'sexual intercourse between persons regarded as too closely related to marry each other'. Obviously degrees of closeness prohibited from marriage have differed from culture to culture and time to time, but the parents, siblings, grandparents and uncles and aunts of a child cover the most frequently prohibited incestuous relationships. While close blood ties govern our main notion of incest, the legal definitions may vary from this and include non-blood relationships. It is useful to note, for reasons which will soon become clear, that sexual intercourse is defined as 'the insertion of a man's erect penis into a woman's vagina' (*Concise Oxford Dictionary*).

It might be thought that such a description of incest is more or less acceptable as a working definition despite some blurred boundaries. Furthermore, a definition of sexual intercourse may seem superfluous. Increasingly, this appears not to be so. The concept of child sexual abuse would appear to be sufficiently general as to require no return to the more limited concept of incest, with its implications of close blood ties or marital ties and penetrative sex. Sexual abuse requires no such limitations. Sexual abuse may involve just touching or sexual suggestion, and its victim can be any person, especially someone of lower status in power relationships. Consequently, one has to question thoroughly any attempts to redefine a concept such as incest given its previous fairly specific and clear meaning.

Of course, the conception of incest in terms of close blood relationships implies beliefs about the harm done to the offspring by such liaisons. Incest was especially harmful in this perspective because of the risks to the 'genetic stock'. Lindzey (1967), probably in a rearguard defence of this view, claimed that such relationships brought about mutations and bad genes:

> Very simply the formulation I am advancing argues that the biological consequence of inbreeding is a decrease in fitness. This decrement in fitness is present in all animals, but it is particularly pronounced in the case of man for a number of reasons including his slowness in reaching sexual maturity and his limited number of offspring. Given this lowered fitness a human group practicing incest operates at a selective disadvantage in competition with outbreeding human groups and ultimately would be unlikely to survive . . .
>
> The findings most directly relevant to our present interest resulted from a very recent study . . . which . . . compared the children of 18 nuclear incest matings (12 brother–sister and 6 father–daughter) with 18 control matings, rather closely matched with the incest group for age, weight, stature, intelligence, and socioeconomic status. At the end of 6 months they found that of the 18 children of an incestuous union, five had died; two were mentally retarded, were subject to seizures, and had been institutionalized; one had a bilateral cleft palate; and three showed evidence of borderline intelligence (estimated IQ 70). Thus, only 7 of the 18 children were considered free of pathology and ready for adoption. (p. 1054)

Pathology was remarkably absent from the control group, except for one instance of a severe physical defect. Lindzey's case was thereby supported.

The point is not to take issue with Lindzey's views as such, but to highlight the way in which incest is construed as harmful by him. There is not a word of the social or emotional harm done to the children themselves, which is in the sharpest of contrasts with modern writing on the effects of incest (see Chapter 3). Lindzey's views seem based more on a past ideology than on a distinctly 'scientific' approach which originated the idea of adverse biological risks in incest. He even cites an unpublished study by Segner and Collins (1967) which explored myths about incest. Apparently, about a third of these described deformed or infertile offspring as a product of such unions. That such views could be supported by biological science is not at issue. However, it is important to highlight the way in which the notion of incest then incorporated theoretical ideas radically different from recent ones.

The biological argument was a vastly different means of understanding the harm caused by incest. More modern conceptions ignore the consequences for the gene pool in favour of ideas about the social and psychological harm done. Instead of genetic mutation, the abuse of power and vital caring relationships are held responsible. In this regard, no claims are made about 'biological' incest which are at all different from those for other forms of child abuse (though abuse by parents may be seen as the most harmful by some authors). 'Child sexual abuse' would seem to be the most useful portmanteau term.

The use of the term 'incest' has been revived to cover a whole gamut of sexual transgressions perpetrated by adults on children. All the different forms of sexual abuse are lumped together as incest if they are perpetrated by a member of that child's family – or sometimes even if they are not. The following was published in a professional social work journal:

> [F]eminists have found traditional definitions resting on the legal variant with its narrow focus on biological relationships and genital penetration wanting (Nelson, 1982). Feminists have broadened the definitions so that unwanted sexual advances occurring within intimate social relationships which replicate familial ones have come within its ambit. Dominelli (in Dominelli and MacLeod, 1989) defines incest as 'all unwanted sexual advances that occur between individuals who are involved in relationships of trust and in which one individual is subordinate to and possibly dependent upon the other'. This definition highlights the feminist principle that personal relationships involve power relations which make the private realm a political one, thus making sexual politics an integral part of male–female and adult–child interactions . . . [F]eminist definitions suggest there is a continuum of sexual abuse ranging from flashing and being touched up to rape which can be classified as incest if it occurs within a relationship of trust. (Dominelli, 1989, p. 297)

But, of course, the sexually suggestive remark made by an uncle to his niece, once described as incest rather than sexual abuse, may be construed as something different – more serious, more dramatic, and closer to the taboos of blood-relative sexual intercourse. This has the important effect of greatly enlarging the apparent extent and seriousness of sexual abuse within close family ties. Secondly, 'incest' is a word full of heavy significance and emotion. Its emotional overtones are far more extreme than details of the individual acts themselves would sometimes communicate.

Other authors use this device in their writing. For example, Kelly (1988) seemingly feels that the language chosen by women to describe abusive incidents is sufficient to extend the use of the term 'incest' to cover all forms of intrafamilial sexual abuse: 'Incest, as women defined it, involved abuse by either a father figure or a male living in the household. It did not always involve on-going abuse; two women were raped once by their fathers' (p. 89). Although, as it stands, this does not seem objectionable, it becomes a little more difficult to appreciate its value when, for example, the term 'incest' is used to describe sexual abuse by lodgers (apparently not sexual partners of the mother). Furthermore, when we read the following, the risks appear even more complex:

> It transpired that 28 women picked up sexual messages . . . during their childhood, mainly from their fathers or father figures. Other relatives mentioned included uncles, grandfathers, a brother and a cousin. Thirteen women defined their experience as incest: six were assaulted by their biological father; two by step-fathers; two by mother's boyfriends; one by a number of male relatives and lodgers; one was assaulted by a cousin who lived in the same household and was treated like a brother; and one by her grandfather with whom she was living at the time. (p. 89)

It is not clear what had happened to these women. They have apparently 'picked up sexual messages', but these messages appear to have been the 'assault' that they had suffered. Certainly they consist of all of the 22 per cent of Kelly's sample of women who had experienced 'incest', although it is far from certain, due to the confusion generated by Kelly, what proportion of these women would have been seen as experiencing incest using a more conventional definition. One has to look elsewhere in Kelly's writing (Kelly, 1989) in order to find examples of another consequence of such an approach to the definition of incest:

> The woman speaking below graphically illustrates the problems of defining 'incest' when the point of reference is not the experience of the individual who is being abused but a legal or 'commonsense' definition. Her father was a lawyer and made sure he never did anything which would legally be defined as abuse.
>
> > 'It remained quite static . . . it consisted of him coming into my room when I was asleep and sitting on the side of my bed and beginning to

touch me which would wake me up. If I was lying on my back or my
side I would still pretend to be asleep and would roll over on my
stomach so that he couldn't touch my breasts or vagina. He would rub
my back and he obviously was sexually excited (sigh) and would tell
me I was beautiful . . . [He would say the same thing over and over
again.]' (p. 71)

This quotation again confuses the issue and is contradictory. If the father
'made sure he never did anything which would legally be defined as
abuse', why did his daughter roll over to protect her private parts, why
was it obvious that he was sexually excited, and are there not alternative
and more innocent interpretations of the events described in the text?

Blume (1990) offers perhaps the greatest transformation of the meaning
of incest:

> Incest has many subtle faces. Incest can be an uncle showing pornographic
> pictures to a 4-year-old. It can be a father masturbating as he hovers outside
> the bathroom where the child is, or one who barges in without knocking. It
> can be the way a baby sitter handles a child when he bathes her. It can be a
> school bus driver forcing a student to sit with him, fondling her under her
> skirt at traffic lights . . . It can be the way a father stares at his daughter's
> developing body, and the comments he makes. It can be the way an aunt
> caresses her niece when she visits. It can be the forced exposure to the
> sounds or sights of one or both parents' sexual acts. It can occur through
> a father and mother forcing their child to touch or be touched by other
> children while pictures are being taken, or by a father . . . passing [his
> daughter] around to his buddies in the bar. (pp. 8–9)

Incest survivor This conjunction suggests that some do not survive
incest (see Siegel and Ronig (1988) for an example of the use of this
term). While this may well happen sometimes, it is hardly typical of most
intrafamilial sexual abuse. Indeed, I know of no figures which suggest the
extent of death associated with intrafamilial sexual abuse. One suspects
that it is rare, much as it is in physical abuse. Violence to the *extent* that
death could occur is not at all typical of the sexual abuse of children. So
to talk of people who survived what was unlikely to have killed them is
hardly a clear use of the term 'survivor'. What the phrase does is to attach
a meaning to incest which at best only dimly reflects what typically is the
case. Indeed, it distorts the typical patterns when routinely applied.

Perhaps the survival is a question of overcoming *psychological* destruction – or emotional death. But this carries with it similar problems of
meaning. This possibility relies on the assumption that incest is psychologically completely destructive. But this needs putting to proof before
being regarded as typical of sexual abuse within the family – which can
involve non-contact abuse. The situation is made more complicated when

some use the word 'survivor' to refer to severely disturbed hospital patients (e.g. Goodwin *et al.*, 1990). Again, a somewhat distorted view of the psychological impact of abuse is created by the use of 'survivor' here.

Kelly (1988) defends the use of the word 'survivor' by the notion that some women take their own lives as a consequence of the sexual violence they have experienced. Again, this is presumably true but could be applied to all sorts of things which it is typically not – for example, unemployment survivor, divorce survivor, bankruptcy survivor, and, of course, false accusation survivor, since it is not unknown for parents to attempt or succeed in suicide following false allegations. The use of the term 'survivor' is not simply the choice of certain individual and polemical writers. It is noteworthy that the British Psychological Society, in the report on 'Psychologists and child sexual abuse', chose the term without explaining or justifying the choice (British Psychological Society, 1990). The implication is that 'victim' and 'survivor' are more or less synonymous, but that 'survivor' communicates the true situation more precisely.

But this is not everyone's view. In 'a guide for young people who have been sexually abused', Bain and Sanders (1991) present a slogan to their readers: 'Every victim can be a survivor' (p. 22). So to be victimised does not carry the assumption that one necessarily survives. Survival seems in Bain and Sander's view to require help or treatment – a possibility which makes Blume's (1990) reference to 'secret survivors' a curiosity. Quite clearly the word 'survivor' has no fixed meaning and seems to be used in contradictory ways by different writers. One then has to ask what functions its use has other than in purple prose used by commentators ranging from committees of psychologists to radical feminists.

The close interplay between the 'science' of child abuse and practice is important to understanding how some sorts of child abuse errors occur. It is the incorporation of key elements of positivist science into social policy. This mode of thinking, to the extent to which it occurs in the thinking of all professionals involved in dealing with child abuse, is part of the genesis of errors. As with many ideologies, one does not need to be aware of the origins of the belief in prediction in order to be influenced by it. It is part of the training material made available for professionals. Take, for example, the following, which is from Milner and Blyth's (1989) guide for teachers on coping with child sexual abuse. They suggest that the following characteristics, among others, 'all . . . have been found in association with child sexual abuse at some time':

Unkempt appearance.
Dirty appearance.
First to arrive at school.

Last to depart from school.
Refusal to speak in class.
Refusal to undress for PE.
Frequent lateness or absence.
Inability to concentrate.

Such 'symptoms' of abuse seem closer to the elaboration of a stereotype than reflecting the fuller picture of abuse gained from survey work. This is discussed in Chapter 3.

The socially created language of abuse brings its own problems as we have seen. One worrying feature is that its emotive and over-inclusive nature destroys its ability to communicate. What image does 'sexual abuse' create in the minds of teachers, nurses, doctors and other professionals? It could be that the picture chosen from the vast range of options created by the language makes extreme and persistent abuse seem less so, and relatively trivial one-off incidents more serious. In any case, over-inclusive use of language cannot help but affect day-to-day situations no matter what theoretical and political gains it may yield.

During the 1980s, attitudes towards the power of social workers changed, and in different ways according to the social class of the person being interviewed:

> On our first reading 48 per cent of both groups agreed that 'social workers have too much power over people's lives.' Our latest survey suggests both groups are nowadays less inclined to support that proposition, but the wealthiest are *much* less so (34 per cent, as opposed to 43 per cent of the least well off). It appears then that those most likely to have direct or indirect contact with the social services are conspicuously more suspicious of their powers. (Taylor-Gooby, 1990, pp. 16–17)

But the other clear message is that people are more sympathetic to the need for social workers to have interventionist power. Presumably ideas about the extent and seriousness of abuse have been listened to.

CHAPTER 3

PSEUDO-SCIENCE?

> It is often helpful to ask a little boy to stand on the examining table so that he can be face-to-face with the physician. Then the physician can ask the boy to use his own penis to demonstrate what was done to it. Boys often pull on their own penises, hit them from side to side, squeeze them, or pinch them to demonstrate. (Levitt, 1990, p. 233)

That such treatment of a young boy is legitimised in the context of a child abuse assessment is problematic, and the treatment is by no means essential to proving that abuse has occurred. The adult rape victim might just as well be asked to 'mime' her rape, or the woman indecently assaulted to maul herself in front of a video-camera. However, the intrusiveness of this examination is perhaps eclipsed by further procedures recommended by the same eminent US paediatrician:

> To clarify the boy's definition of the sexual acts, the physician can perform a rectal examination that includes the penetration of the boy's anus by the physician's gloved and lubricated examining finger. The physician can ask him what he calls the buttocks or define that as outside and ask him to define whether the touch was at the anal opening or actually inside the anal opening as the finger enters the anus. This allows the boy to compare that sensation with the sensation of abuse. (Levitt, 1990, p. 236)

One wonders whether a boy treated like this could tell the difference! Again, would digital penetration of a vagina 'to compare that sensation with the sensation of abuse' be legitimate practice? Indeed, would it be legitimate practice for parents to penetrate their children digitally in order to decide whether abuse had occurred?

Levitt is well aware of de Jong and Rose's (1989) paper which reviewed the outcomes of 45 randomly selected cases involving criminal charges of vaginal rape and sodomy. The authors selected these since, in their words, such cases were 'more likely to have physical evidence than non-penetration cases' (p. 1022). 'In most of the legally proven cases there was no physical evidence of sexual contact, and the presence of physical evidence did not assure conviction of the perpetrator' (p. 1025). In Texan cases, Bradshaw and Marks (1990) do demonstrate a tendency for medical

51

evidence (and confessions) to be associated with prosecution and conviction rates, but overwhelmingly medical evidence was not available in court. This does not mean that medical investigations for reasons of the child's health or for other reasons are inappropriate (cf. Herbert, 1987).

Of course, it might be that Levitt's advice is not followed by other medics and she stands in splendid isolation. But we can turn, in the very same volume, to Gerber (1990) before we finally suspend disbelief:

> Once a child has agreed to be completely honest, the clinician can assert that while the commitment is probably heartfelt, upon being confronted with certain questions, the boy's spirit will weaken. At that point, it might be wise to tell the client that you are going to ask a series of questions that you don't want him to answer. You can explain that you do not want answers because he will probably be dishonest about them. You can then ask a long series of questions, including the following:
> 1. What did it feel like the first time you put your finger or crayon or pencil inside your ('butt') anus?
> 2. Can you tell me how difficult it was to position yourself near a mirror so you could see what your ('asshole') rectum looked like?
> 3. Can you describe how your ('cum') seminal fluid tastes?
> 4. When did you first become familiar with how your ('butt') buttocks smell(s)? (Gerber, 1990, p. 245)

It is hard to accept such treatment – yet again recommended by an 'authority' in the field. With a few modifications, the abusive telephone caller could use this script to harass and distress adult women and would deserve whatever punishment he received.

Such suggestions are cited here to illustrate the extent to which the imperative of intervention and detection is operative in the child protection rhetoric. If it is generally accepted that there are no bounds to the question of stamping out sexual abuse then the important question 'why not?' needs asking. Indeed, it would seem that, with the notorious child abuse disasters such as those of Cleveland and Rochdale, the public sees the problem as child protection workers stepping beyond the mark. The all-or-nothing quality of some interventions, together with the lack of questioning of what is being done by professionals as against what might have been done by the abuser, gives the appearance of lunacy to these examples of child protection intervention.

This chapter looks more closely at the role of scientific research in creating an *action imperative* which leads to hyper-zealousness and with it the risk of error. Of course, increased vigilance may well help detect more abuse (to argue otherwise would fly in the face of historical trends of the last twenty or so years), but one must always ask: at what price?

That social science is not neutral is an obvious contention, but its implications are sometimes overlooked (Howitt, 1991a). In a social constructionist approach to knowledge, the question has to be: in whose interest was the knowledge created? For whose purposes? It is not acceptable to make generalised and morally loaded suggestions like 'in the interests of children'. There has been no global evaluation which balances out all of the risks. It is clearly a notion based in morality to argue that children should not be subject to harm, and a matter of ideology to decide what is harmful. 'Spare the rod and spoil the child' contains just one view of what is harmful to children. In the absence of a clear understanding of the harm done to children by child protection activities such as intervention, fostering, interviewing and the like, it is impossible to say what should be done about abuse. We are only just beginning to be aware of the direct harm done to children in residential care (Community Care, 1991; Kelleher, 1987) despite great investment of time and resources into examining abuse by parents. Any social constructionist approach to child abuse must question whose interests are served by available knowledge. Just as Freud's denial of the childhood seduction theory of adult hysteria can be seen as serving the needs of patriarchal society as well as the needs of the developing profession of psychoanalysis, similar possibilities cannot be ruled out when directed to modern 'child abuse science'.

The self-serving nature of child abuse science is rarely argued. One exception is the account by Pfohl (1976), whose view is that the paediatric radiologists gained from child abuse an alternative to their then marginal status within the medical profession: 'By linking themselves to the problem of abuse, radiologists became indirectly tied into the crucial clinical task of patient diagnosis. In addition, they became a direct source of input concerning the risk "life or death" consequences of child beating' (p. 318). One can only wonder the extent to which the moral and ideological accompaniment of child abuse does not still have similar pay-offs for disaffected professionals whose roles would otherwise be mundane and lacking in ideological lift (Cherniss, 1980; Eidelwich and Brodsky, 1980).

Two broad areas of 'child abuse science' will be discussed in this chapter:

1. Research on the extent of abuse.
2. Research on the effects of abuse.

Each is a vital element in creating the imperative to action in child protection. Chapter 4 deals with the matter of the detection and prosecution of abuse and extends the debate on the imperative to action.

The extent of abuse

Incest

> Incest is a silent subject. Silent not because it is reported inadequately or inaccurately or because not enough programs have been established to deal with it or even because little is yet written about it – all these are true but are only symptomatic of a larger source of silence surrounding incest. (McIntyre, 1981, p. 462)

Anyone believing that incest was suddenly discovered by feminists and caring professionals during the 1970s (Hechler, 1988) needs to re-examine their knowledge of history. The self-serving history which suggests that incest was unknown to professionals prior to the 'renaissance' of the 1970s is denied by a cursory glance at the criminal statistics. Those on incest reflect a degree of professional involvement by the police, medical doctors, social workers and others which might belie the self-serving notion of past professional ignorance. Examining the data on British incest offences shown in Table 3.1, one finds no great trend for a significant rise in known offences until the late 1980s. Furthermore, it is a crucial feature of the data that incest was common enough and thus known 'within the system' even forty years ago.

Although there is room for endless argument about precisely what the recent upturn in the annual rates means (are they an increase in 'true' incest or an increase in reporting?), other implications are more certain.

Table 3.1: Incest offences in England and Wales, 1950–1989

Year	Incest cases	Year	Incest cases
1950–4	237*	1978	329
1955–9	293*	1979	334
1960–4	294*	1980	312
1965–9	237*	1981	241
1969	275	1982	230
1970	277	1983	243
1971	307	1984	290
1972	323	1985	277
1973	288	1986	444
1974	337	1987	511
1975	349	1988	516
1976	338	1989	471
1977	295		

* Annual averages over five years.
Source: Home Office (1969, 1972, 1975, 1982, 1989).

Incest was most definitely not a major secret forty years ago. While many cases probably went unrevealed to anyone, substantial numbers did come to the attention of the police. They may have been dealt with insensitively and without specialised assistance, but such cases nevertheless happened frequently enough. Furthermore, if the police were aware then it is certain that medics examined victims and that social workers (and perhaps schools) were involved. It is my recollection as a young psychologist in the 1960s that professionals were well aware of incest (Howitt, 1991a).

While these data might grossly underestimate the amount of incestuous intercourse occurring, the question of precision need not bother us unduly here. In the present context the data merely demonstrate the limitations of the argument about past professional ignorance of the crime. Indeed, the relatively small increases in the reporting of incest over forty years is remarkable when compared with, say, rape (Howitt and Cumberbatch, 1990). It is difficult to summarise the trends because of substantial annual fluctuations. The biggest ratio between any two years suggests a doubling of known offences. More typically, the increase is smaller than this (ignoring the recent upswing).

What happened in the 1970s clearly could not be construed as the discovery of incest; it was the transformation of incest into a social issue. That is a very different matter.

It might be tempting to assume that one of the simpler tasks facing a social scientist is to discover the frequency of child sexual abuse. Notwithstanding the problems of embarrassment and reluctance to speak about emotional and taboo matters, the technical problems involved ought to be largely routine. There is nothing unusual nowadays about surveys concerning sexual matters, and society has surely become much more open about these questions. Nevertheless, it is extremely difficult to get a clear picture of the extent and nature of child sexual abuse from research publications. In particular, it is hard to get a precise understanding of who the abusers are.

At first sight this must appear palpable nonsense. Anyone with even a passing knowledge of research on child sexual abuse will be able to point to a number of studies which demonstrate the pervasiveness of the sexual abuse of children:

> Experts in the field of child sexual assault suggest that one in four girls and one in ten boys will experience some form of unwanted sexual activity before age 18 . . . Approximately two-thirds of victims are incestuously abused while someone external to the family molests the remaining one-third of victims. (Regehr, 1990, p. 113)

Even the most casual reading of the literature on child abuse will demonstrate that it is far more widespread and extensive than we are told had ever been imagined in the past. There is no argument that large percentages of both men and women have had sexual experiences during childhood which, more or less, warrant the description 'abuse'. What is difficult to discover is the extent to which this is a problem within the nuclear family rather than in society at large. We have already seen in Chapter 2 that the 'family' has been redefined – or at least it has reverted to its previous definition. It has once more become the extended family in the child abuse literature and not just the nuclear family. There are good reasons for this. Abuse in the context of the *nuclear* family is *relatively* rare. If the prevalence of nuclear family abuse is not particularly great, it stands to reason that relatively few cases of it will be found even in largish surveys. For example, if father–daughter abuse happens to 1 per cent of women, an exceptionally large survey of 2,000 women will include only about twenty cases. This is hardly the most startling of figures. Furthermore, only a proportion of these twenty cases are likely to be legally defined as incestuous intercourse. Even in such a large survey, detailed analyses of people who have experienced nuclear family incest will have very few cases to deal with.

Some of the most vociferous researchers in the field prefer to dwell on the extensiveness of child sexual abuse. But this can be achieved only by including the extended family, wherein lies the power of the data. For all of these reasons, it can be frustrating to unravel the precise nature of abuse within the nuclear family. North American studies are particularly prone to problems.

North American surveys

Finkelhor, Hotaling, Lewis and Smith (1990) were responsible for a national telephone survey of 2,626 American men and women throughout the USA. The questions used to elicit information about sexual abuse were as follows:

When you were a child [elsewhere indicated to be age 18 or under], can you remember having any experience you would now consider sexual abuse:

1. . . . someone trying or succeeding in having any kind of sexual intercourse with you, or anything like that?
2. . . . someone touching you, or grabbing you, or kissing you, or rubbing up against your body in either a public place or private – anything like that?
3. . . . someone exhibiting parts of their body to you, or someone performing some sex act in your presence – or anything like that?
4. . . . involving oral sex or sodomy – or anything like that? (p. 21)

These questions yielded a prevalence rate of sexual abuse of 27 per cent among women and 16 per cent among men. Abuse of 7-year-olds and under accounted for over a fifth of the victims of both sexes. Boys were twice as likely to be abused by strangers, whereas members of the family were nearly three times as likely to abuse girl victims. Nine per cent of men and 13 per cent of women claimed that sexual intercourse was involved, although this may not be accurate. The question actually posed concerned sexual intercourse – or anything like that. What the 'anything like that' might be can only be guessed at. Usually the abuse happened just once.

The relationship of the child to the perpetrator was as shown in Table 3.2. In the case of boys, 31 per cent of the abusers were acquaintances. With girls, this figure was 33 per cent. A relatively low proportion of children experienced abuse from within the nuclear family, although, of course, these may sum to large numbers of individuals. Abuse is much more prevalent in the extended family. But what sort of abuse occurred within the nuclear family? In fact, it is far from clear that this abuse did not largely fall into relatively trivial categories such as verbal sexual harassment. Answers are not provided for this most basic of questions. For all we know, most nuclear family abuse could be sexual intercourse, but it could equally well fall into the category 'or anything like that'.

The opacity of the data is not confined to this one study. Similar comments could be made concerning others, such as Wyatt (1985). She

Table 3.2: Relationship of perpetrator to child in US sexual abuse cases

Boys:	
Parents	0%
Stepparents	0%
Grandparents	0%
Siblings	1%
Uncles/aunts	5%
Cousins	5%
Girls:	
Parents	3%
Stepparents	3%
Grandparents	2%
Siblings	2%
Uncles/aunts	14%
Cousins	5%

Source: Finkelhor, Hotaling, Lewis and Smith (1990).

surveyed a relatively small sample (248) of Afro-American and White American women in Los Angeles. Once again it is impossible to know what sexual acts were perpetrated within the nuclear family, although the abuse studied ranged from the exposure of the offender's sex organs through to intercourse. Wyatt did have a category of 'any other sexual experiences' (e.g. kissing in some instances). As a consequence many forms of non-contact abuse as well as contact abuse became included. However, virtually all abuse by fathers, stepfathers and other relatives was contact abuse. Abuse carried out by members of the nuclear family accounted for 13 per cent of *all* abusive acts in the case of Afro-American women and 9 per cent for White American women.

Russell's (1983) study, although not without its problems, is refreshing among American studies. It is probably the best US study of the incidence and prevalence of sexual abuse of girls. The sample size was substantial (though at 930 adult women not the biggest), but more important was the extensive training of the interviewers for the lengthy interviews. Its major drawbacks were the omission of a sample of males and the fact that it was conducted exclusively in San Francisco.

The definition of child sexual abuse varied somewhat according to the nature of the relationship and the age of the child, and it should be considered carefully. Extrafamilial child sexual abuse (under 14 years of age) was defined as 'one or more unwanted sexual experiences with persons unrelated by blood or marriage, ranging from petting (touching of breasts or genitals or attempts at such touching) to rape'. Extrafamilial child sexual abuse (14 years to 17 years inclusive) was defined as 'completed or attempted forcible rape experiences'. Intrafamilial child sexual abuse (at any age before 17 years) was defined as 'any kind of exploitive sexual contact that occurred between relatives, no matter how distant the relationship'; 'experiences involving sexual contact with a relative that were wanted *and* with a peer were regarded as nonexploitive.' This meant that sex play between peers, for example, would be seen as nonexploitive. A difference of five years or less in age defined whether or not a peer was involved.

Russell clearly takes a definition of abuse which involves physical contact, and disregards non-contact abuse such as sexual suggestions. This is a fairly stringent definition compared to, say, that of Finkelhor. Notice, however, that she defines rather more intrafamilial sexual acts as abuse if they involve older persons than she does extrafamilial ones. This is most important when we examine the rates of intrafamilial abuse compared with extrafamilial abuse. Although Russell presents her data differently, the figures given in Table 3.3 are expressed as percentages of the total sample, since these give the best indications of how frequently abuse occurs in different relationships. By 'very serious' is meant 'completed

Table 3.3: Prevalence of sexual abuse in different US relationships

	VVVVVVery serious	All sexual abuse
Father	0.8%	3%
Non-biological father	0.9%	2%
Brother	0.8%	3%

Source: Russell (1983).

and attempted vaginal, oral, anal intercourse, cunnilingus, analingus, forced and unforced'.

All family relationships (including uncles, in-laws, first cousins, mothers, sisters, etc. as well as closer relationships) were involved in the very serious sexual abuse of 5 per cent of women. The corresponding figure for any form of sexual abuse was 20 per cent of women. In other words, members of the nuclear family are not especially implicated in intra-familial sexual abuse. Such a judgement does not imply that abuse by members of the nuclear family is at acceptably low levels (whatever that would mean), but merely points out an important feature of Russell's data. All told, mothers, fathers, brothers, sisters and stepparents or similar were involved in the abuse of 8 per cent of the women, and for 2.4 per cent of women this sexual abuse was serious. While these figures may appear very substantial, they actually need to be compared with all other forms of abuse. The rest of the family were the abusers of 12 per cent of the women and the very serious abusers of 2.5 per cent of the women. Again these are disturbing figures in terms of the extent of sexual abuse.

Nevertheless, when we turn to the non-familial perpetrators, the figures are radically different. About 50 per cent of the women were abused as children by non-family members, with 26 per cent of offences against the girls being described as very serious ones. In other words, there seems to be little argument that child sexual abuse is extensive, but overwhelmingly outside the nuclear family. Indeed, there is a case for arguing that the nuclear family is far safer than the rest of a child's social world. This is despite there being more 'generous' criteria for intrafamilial abusers in Russell's study than for other perpetrators of abuse.

Wyatt and Peters (1986a; 1986b) discuss methodological problems in research on the prevalence of sexual abuse and the influence of variations in the definition of abuse which may have a bearing on prevalence rates. While important, these do not influence the interpretation that nuclear family abuse is less common than other forms.

British surveys

Baker and Duncan (1985) report British data on the prevalence of child sexual abuse. Their research was conducted in many different parts of the country by a public opinion research company. All the interviewers were female and the sample involved individuals 15 years or over. The definition of abuse given to participants in the research was as follows:

> A child (anyone under 16 years) is sexually abused when another person, who is sexually mature, involves the child in any activity which the other person expects to lead to their sexual arousal. This might involve intercourse, touching, exposure of the sexual organs, showing pornographic material or talking about sexual things in an erotic way. (p. 458)

What this definition includes and excludes is unclear. Just what is a 'sexually mature' person, for example? Would 'erotic' photographs in a daily newspaper qualify the editor as an abuser if he knew that they might 'turn a boy on'? There would be good reason for rejecting the survey on the basis of such major conceptual blocks. However, more detailed questions apparently followed the admission of abuse.

Twelve per cent of females and 8 per cent of males reported abuse according to the definition. Where abuse had occurred it was typically at about 12 years of age for males and 11 years for females. Mostly abuse was a single experience (63 per cent of those abused) or repeated abuse by the same person (23 per cent), with 14 per cent having been abused by more than one individual. Over half of the abuse had not involved physical contact at all. Contact (without intercourse) occurred in about 44 per cent of the cases and intercourse in 5 per cent.

Translated into percentages of people (rather than of those who had been abused), the figures for children who had experienced these different types of abuse were as shown in Table 3.4. These are possibly over-estimates of the numbers who had actually suffered abuse because of the repeated victimisation of some, although refusals to disclose might have had the reverse effect. Turning to incestuous abuse (defined here as sexual intercourse with a *blood* relative – elsewhere parents or grandparents

Table 3.4: Prevalence of different types of sexual abuse in the UK

Abuse without physical contact	7%
Abuse involving contact	6%
Abuse involving intercourse	0.7%

Source: Baker and Duncan (1985).

in the report), the figures are 0.4 per cent overall: 0.2 per cent of boys and 0.7 per cent of girls.

The authors suggest that their data probably underestimate the prevalence of sexual abuse. This is likely to be true (though no one knows for certain), but the point is that there is a considerable 'smog' about the report. It is far from clear, for example, what the extent of *nuclear* family abuse is compared to *extended* family abuse. The authors make the following suggestions:

> We estimate that there are over 4.5 million adults in Great Britain who were sexually abused as children, and that a potential 1,117,000 children will be sexually abused before they are 15 years of age. At least 143,000 of these will be abused within the family. The social and mental health implications are enormous, and the authors suggest that an effective intervention and prevention policy is urgently required. (p. 457)

But, for some, these figures are not bad enough. MacLeod and Saraga (1988) suggest that the 'truth' is worse: 'The methodology failed to take account of the emotional impact on respondents of questions on sexual abuse, so that the results were bound to be an underestimate' (p. 22). Their argument is based as much on the American data producing higher frequencies of abuse as on anything else. But there is no reason why there should be a match between British and American data on abuse – any more than there should be a match in terms of any other sexual offences. They are different countries and cultures.

Nash and West's (1985) study of women on a general practitioner's panel and a further sample of female students unusually did not avoid the matter of 'incestuous' intercourse. They found that as many as 42 per cent of the practitioner's list sample and 54 per cent of the student group had experienced some form of sexual abuse under 16 years of age. Participants in the survey were specifically told that 'adult' meant someone at least five years older than themselves. A list of different types of incident was given, such as 'I was asked to do something sexual by an adult', 'I received an obscene phone call' and 'An adult had full sexual intercourse with me.'

The commonest forms of abuse were 'flashing', 'sexual kisses' and 'adult fondling genitals'. In terms of intercourse and attempted intercourse, Nash and West (1985) are fairly specific about the numbers of fathers, stepfathers, older brothers, uncles and cousins involved. Turned into percentages of the samples combined, the figures are as shown in Table 3.5.

Taking all sexual intercourse and attempts at sexual intercourse into account, almost 8 per cent of the women had been subject to these. It is not possible precisely to break down Nash and West's data any further.

Table 3.5: Relationship of perpetrator to
child in UK sexual abuse cases

Father	1%
Stepfather	0.3%
Older brother	1%
Uncle	0.6%
Cousin	0.3%

Source: Nash and West (1985).

Nevertheless, it can be seen that cases involving sexual intercourse and attempts at this are relatively uncommon within the nuclear family. At most, about a third of cases fall into this category if we include older brothers – excluding them decreases the proportion to about a sixth.

Physical abuse   Few studies directly analogous to the prevalence studies of sexual abuse have been carried out for physical abuse. One exception is Berger *et al*. (1988). This involved US college students and so cannot be assumed to be representative, especially due to the middle-class bias inherent in higher education. Still, it might be assumed that these would give low boundaries to the extent of physical abuse. The findings were notable in many ways. Eighty per cent had been spanked, 35 per cent hit with objects, 20 per cent hit other than spanking, 6 per cent punched, 2 per cent severely beaten, 5 per cent kicked and 3 per cent choked. Twelve per cent had been injured by their parents – 55 per cent of these were bruises, 19 per cent cuts, 7 per cent broken bones, 8 per cent burns, 5 per cent dental injuries and 11 per cent head injuries. Various criteria of estimates of the amount of abuse reached from 50 per cent (using Straus's 1980 definition) to 25 per cent (based on Sapp and Carter, 1978) to 9 per cent (according to Berger's 1981 definition). However, self-labelling as abused was relatively uncommon. Certainly large numbers of the general population would meet social services guidelines of what is abuse.

The dangerous family?

One thing made clear by these surveys is that the *nuclear* family is a relatively safe environment in terms of sexual abuse – a substantially safer haven than is often implied. While it is true that child sexual abuse is largely not perpetrated by strangers, neither is it particularly likely to be carried out by members of the nuclear family. Those known to the children in the extended family and acquaintances are by far the most frequent abusers.

The notion of family dangerousness is also undermined by other evidence on violence against children. Daly and Wilson (1988) note some of the historical evidence concerning the extensiveness of child murders in nineteenth-century Britain. Many of these deaths were ultimately the responsibility of patriarchal Victorian society, which was so cruel to unmarried mothers and therefore made infanticide more likely:

> In the context of the high infant mortality rate, the periodic discovery of a baby's body in the street or river was shrugged off as a grim inevitability. In the early nineteenth century infant life was held cheap, especially bastards. (Rose, 1986, p. 351)

Important as this historical note is, it has little direct bearing on the dangers of the modern family. As Daly and Wilson (1988) point out, the most dangerous time of life is the first year after birth. Figures show similar trends in North America and in Britain. The statistics for England and Wales (Home Office, 1987) have been 'remarkably consistent for the period of the late 1970s to the late 1980s' (Howitt, 1991a):

> The numbers of unlawful killings in the population per million children in the stipulated age group for the year 1987 were as follows: under 1 year, 45 (30 in total); 1–5 years, 10 (26 in total); 5–16 years, 3 (22 in total). Members of the child's family are responsible for about about a *third* of all of these deaths. Although, in this sense, the first year of life is the most dangerous of any time of life in terms of homicide, the rest of childhood is rather safer than adulthood. The child is also more at risk outside the family than inside. (p. 77)

A glance at the British child mortality figures is illuminating. In 1988, for example, there were 2,849 post-neonatal deaths recorded (Office of Population Censuses and Surveys, 1991). Of these, only 22 were entered under the category of child battering and other maltreatment. Accidents and poisonings were a common cause of death. Although the rate of death approaches five per thousand live births in the first year of life, the rate is small after that – substantially less than one in a thousand – from all causes. The data for earlier years (e.g. Office of Population Censuses and Surveys, 1990; 1979) are similar, although the childhood death rate does seem to have declined. Once again, it may well be that child battering is to some extent hidden in other categories of death. However, we have no reliable information on this, and assumptions about the extent of fatal abuse by parents are no more than assumptions.

Similar tendencies to 'overestimate' the extent of physical abuse can be seen in clinical data. So while Kempe (1969) suggested that at least 15 per cent of children under 5 years entering the emergency departments of hospitals were battered, Pless *et al.*'s (1987) intensive research put the figure at 1.2 per cent.

The professionals' experience

Table 3.6: Proportion of US professionals' last sexual abuse cases perpetrated by parents

Mental health workers	69%
Department of social services	75%
Other social services	68%
School	58%

Source: Finkelhor (1984).

One remarkable feature of the research on the extent of abuse is that practitioners often seem to have a radically different experience based on the 'clients' passing through their doors. Finkelhor, Gomes-Swart *et al.* (1984), for example, surveyed the last abuse cases of various American professionals, and found that the percentages of sexual abuse cases perpetrated by the child's parents were as shown in Table 3.6. These figures are dramatically reduced, however, for medical agencies (45 per cent) and the criminal justice system (35 per cent).

Compared to the general population surveys, the differences are quite marked. Truly 'incestuous' relationships dominate in the professionals' experience. Kendall-Tackett and Simon (1987) surveyed 365 adults molested as children who were seeking help from a child sexual abuse treatment programme. The perpetrators of the abuse were as shown in Table 3.7. Again the figures are radically different from the data based on the general population surveys. Another significant feature of Kendall-Tackett and Simon's data was that intercourse was involved in no less than 44 per cent of cases. The authors' explanation of their data's disparity from general survey data included two possibilities:

First, a clinically based population may be more willing to reveal more information about their molestation than victims sampled and assessed from the population at large. Second, persons seeking treatment may have experienced more severe molestations than victims in the population at

Table 3.7: Relationship of perpetrator to child in UK sexual abuse cases where the victim later sought treatment

Biological father	39%
Stepfather	20%
Brother	9%
Uncle or cousin	11%

Source: Kendall-Tackett and Simon (1987).

large, and were therefore more severely affected, causing them to seek treatment. (p. 243)

They also suggest that their use of a telephone survey may have produced more 'revealing' results. All of this is unconvincing. It is difficult to believe that so many victims would have been unwilling to disclose incestuous abuse in surveys, especially as incestuous abuse does not tend to involve the most serious acts. There may, however, be a case for arguing that incestuous abuse is the most psychologically harmful, despite the proposition that all sorts of abuse are damaging.

Similar selectivity can be found in clinical samples of those attending a child abuse referral centre. Reinhart (1987), for example, found that unrelated perpetrators dominated for both males and females (though he included stepfathers and the mother's boyfriend in these). Fathers were involved in the abuse of 25 per cent of boys and 28 per cent of girls. Based on the American Humane Association 1984 figures, Cotter and Kuehnle (in press) suggest that of 100,000 cases of substantial sexual abuse, 56 per cent were abused by a parent.

Whatever else the studies suggest, it would appear that professional experience tends to overemphasise the role of close relatives in sexual abuse. Obviously there are many reasons why such bias or selectivity could occur and, as yet, there is no way of knowing the precise cause. It could be that father–daughter incest does cause far more distress than other forms of sexual abuse, so encouraging more attempts to find professional help, or, equally, professionals may respond differently to incest within the family. Irrespective of what accounts for the over-representation of nuclear family relationships in the professional's case-load, the effect is greatly to reinforce the view that sexual abuse is a matter that largely concerns the nuclear family and so, perhaps, encourage the focusing of attention there.

The effects of abuse

A historical note?

Inevitably, a backward look at the accounts of child abuse's effects puts recent ideas into perspective. Nevertheless, older views concerning child abuse are not just quaint historical artefacts. Rather, they are extremely discomforting, perhaps even alarming. In so many ways they are like an alter-image of current ideas. While the issue of sexual abuse started to attract widespread attention as a social issue in the late 1970s, it is possible to find accounts from even that time which reflect a totally different set of ideas about child abuse. An international conference on love and attraction provides a rich source of such contrasting values. Constantine (1979) came closest to writing the paedophiles' charter:

> A careful review of the literature [from more than 130 sources] on adult–child encounters clearly indicates that immediate negative reactions are minor or completely absent in the majority of cases and significant long-term psychological or social impairment is rare, truly remarkable findings considering that most studies have dealt with criminal or clinical samples. (p. 505)

Constantine argues that the negative consequences of abuse are identified with (a) the use of physical or psychological pressure or coercion, (b) poor intrafamily communication, especially where this leads to a lack of open discussion of sexual matters or strong negative family reaction when the abuse is disclosed, or (c) the child possessing little sexual knowledge or a view that sex is dirty and shameful.

> From a radical perspective, children have the right to express themselves sexually even with members of their own families. Is incest, as some have argued, categorically a harmful experience? . . . Nearly all the published literature derives from studies of clinical and criminal cases and is therefore hopelessly biased, yet the only general conclusion warranted is that not even prolonged incest is necessarily harmful . . . Unpublished studies of incest in non-clinical, non-criminal populations . . . and accumulating anecdotal data indicate that many people have incestuous experiences which they regard positively and which do not appear to have impaired them socially or psychologically. (p. 507)

Even in a research-based discussion of paedophilia, Bernard (1979) writes in a way which seems out of line with modern thinking and was probably ideologically unacceptable to many at the time. Essentially Bernard obtained accounts of abusive experiences in childhood from Dutch adults. Such experiences were then correlated with the number of neurotic symptoms displayed on the 'ABV questionnaire'. A sample of one woman's account, sets the tone fairly well:

> Perhaps you cannot imagine this but when I was 12 I was very much in love with a man of 50 and he with me. I don't know who made the first move now but we stroked each other and experienced sexuality together. It relaxed me wonderfully, one day my parents found out and the police were called in. The examination was terrible; I denied it and denied it again. Then I gave in. My older friend was arrested. My parents, after my forced confession, made out a formal complaint. Nothing then could be of help any more. I have never been able to forget this. It wasn't just. It should have been such a beautiful memory. I am married and have four children. I would not object to their having sexual contacts with adults. I regard it as positive. (p. 501)

Bernard's provisional conclusions, though not objectified in general, were as follows:

1. Some children perceive sexual contacts with adults as positive.
2. Love, affection and security are being sought by the children as well as the sexual aspect.
3. The people with childhood experience of sex with adults did not appear to be traumatised. They were similar in neuroticism to the average Dutch person.
4. Adult sexual orientation was not affected by the type of youthful sexual involvement.
5. The sexual activity was mostly of a masturbatory kind.
6. 'The attitude of society has a negative effect.' (p. 501)

Perhaps as food for thought, he also suggests: 'But it is still too often the case that science is only welcome so long as it leads to conclusions that fall in with the ideology of the community' (p. 499).

The curious notion of 'the participating victim' was created by Ingram (1979) for his account of paedophiliac involvements with boys:

> The children . . . looked on these men as models of sexual prowess, and were happy to receive their sexual initiation at their hands. It was only in later years they came to understand the real meaning of what was going on, and came to expose the men with whom they had had such enjoyable experiences . . . It will come as no surprise . . . that those who reported the incidents to their parents were among the most disturbed or the least disturbed of the children. (p. 514)

But Ingram ventures to raise the rarely asked question of what it was about the abuse and the situations in which the boys found themselves that brought about the damage:

> Where the child was assaulted by a stranger . . . there were violent family scenes, mother crying, or having hysterics . . . father pacing up and down threatening to 'kill the bastard with my own hands' . . . Children were questioned and cross-examined . . . in a way that must have been more disturbing for the child than the actual sexual experience. As one psychiatrist put it of one child, 'If he had not been buggered by the man, he certainly had been by the police and doctor'. (p. 514)

While it is obvious that abuse has to be dealt with, in part, in the family context, there is little formal research. Regehr (1990) describes research on the range of emotions and other reactions experienced by parents of children who had suffered extrafamilial sexual abuse. However, Wolters *et al.* (1985) suggest that 'most parents were obviously perturbed but reacted objectively' (p. 572) in a study based on Dutch police officers' reports concerning sexually 'exploited' children. There might be a cultural difference here due to different attitudes to sex in general.

Ingram's point is that some children's families reacted in a way not conducive to harm, whereas others reacted differently. Although there has been considerable progress in the use of more sensitive means of presenting children's evidence in court – through video techniques, for example (Flin and Boon, 1989) – remarkably there has not developed a strong interest in evaluating the effects of the child protection system in general on the child. But, of course, most of the improvements in handling the children's evidence to the courts concern only a small part of the 'system abuse'. They are primarily designed to serve the needs of enhancing the prosecution of the abuser rather than dealing with the psychological needs of the child.

Modern research

> In 19 years of working clinically with hundreds of adolescents and children, I can recall *not a single case of a client significantly psychologically damaged by sexual experiences.* On the other hand, I can recall several tragic cases of children (and adults) *psychologically devastated by stupid adult reactions to the discovery of sexual relationships.* (Ryder, 1989, p. 333, emphasis added)

This statement is a challenge. Strongly worded, it was hardly made at a time when professionals disregarded or ignored sexual abuse. It quite clearly places the blame for the psychological problems associated with sexual abuse on the way in which society deals with abuse. In other words, ironically the damage is done by the child protection system rather than by the sexual activity itself. Of course, this is not an either/or situation in that abuse and society's response may both be damaging. Taking the implicit challenge on board ought to present few difficulties. Should it not be relatively easy to demonstrate that abuse has effects even when it is not disclosed at the time? Regrettably, despite numerous claims about the effects of abuse, virtually all of the relevant research is primitive and unsatisfactory. Two reasons are the most important:

1. System or societal abuse is not high on the agenda and is virtually unexplored.
2. Notions like 'abuse' and 'victim' inhibit the exploration of the possibility that some children might willingly participate.

Fordyce (1989) commented on Ryder's views:

I found the whole tone . . . scary in that it mirrors the excuses of perpetrators of child sexual abuse by minimising, denying, laying the blame inappropriately on the victims and professionals involved, echoing the words of many an abuser in accepting that some victims do suffer . . . 'but not those with whom I have had contact.' (p. 443)

One should not have to look too far for the evidence with which to dismiss Ryder's claims. But the evidence is just not there. If we were able to show that children who were abused differed in terms of their mental well-being from non-abused children then we would have to examine the influence of the key possible confounding variable – the effects of the child protection system. There is little point in relying on the opinion of therapists, counsellors, social workers, psychologists and the rest, since they have a vested interest in not accepting any blame for damage they or the system they operate may cause. Of course, a simple research design is superficially possible – that is, to compare abused children who enter the child protection system with those who do not. This would begin to unravel the problem and allocate responsibility. But no such research, to my knowledge, has been carried out despite a body of research on the 'effects of abuse'.

A good study of the genre is Lipovsky *et al.* (1989). They compared children sexually abused by their fathers with 'matched' siblings from the same family who had not been. All had been referred by agencies. This study found that the abused siblings were rated by their parents in terms of their behaviour dysfunctions, although they did not differ in terms of self-rated manifest anxiety or self-esteem. They were higher in self-rated depression. The research design was clever because it allowed control over family pathology, which might lead to abuse in the first place. However, it was totally flawed in that abuse and system abuse were confounded.

Or take Mannarino *et al.* (1989), who compared girls within two weeks of disclosure of sexual abuse with well-matched controls from two ordinary schools and a clinical control group. Abused girls were significantly more anxious than the other two groups and differed from the normal controls on a range of symptoms and characteristics. But, again, what would we expect if the system itself did harm? While some of the effects of abuse might be difficult to see as problems of the system (such as delinquency as rated by the parents), one still cannot be sure what caused what. Curiously, however, there did not appear to be any differences due to the type of abuse itself – for example, intercourse versus fondling – which is hard to explain on the basis of the effects of abuse but much easier to explain as a consequence of the effects of the child protection system. In contrast, Conte and Schuerman (1987) found differences between abused and non-abused children based on *parents' and social workers' ratings* which varied in terms of the type of abuse involved. The question, then, is open as to the extent on which this reflects theories held by social workers and parents as to the relative damage caused by different types of abuse.

Clinical samples Countless publications are to be found in the sexual abuse literature which argue that abuse has a major influence on the psychological and emotional health of the victims in *adulthood*. A typical example is Goodwin *et al.* (1990). They discuss a number of 'adult survivors' of sexual abuse who were participants in a three-month support group for victims of incest. Each woman had been hospitalised for psychiatric reasons at least once. Flashbacks, frequent traumatic nightmares and a readiness to be startled were typical. This they say is typical of post-traumatic stress disorder. All but one were abnormal on anxiety and depression measures. All had some sort of problem with their sexual functioning. Forty per cent were anorgasmic; 30 per cent had relations with women because of their sexual difficulties with men; 15 per cent masturbated compulsively; 10 per cent inserted objects into their vagina to a degree which caused pain and bleeding; 10 per cent had abused young boys sexually; 40 per cent had detailed plans to murder their abuser; several described violent actions that had not yet been detected; two described involvement in murders; and two women with caretaking jobs described physical abuse of charges in their care.

The authors go on to describe other outcomes which extend the list of types of effect considerably:

> Fifteen of the 20 women had an eating disorder . . . Five had bulimia and at least one episode of anorexia. Five had bulimia but were of normal weight. One had anorexia without bulimia. Almost all of the bulimia patients described forced fellatio . . . Several were able to control their bulimia by avoiding food that reminded them either of a penis or of semen . . . Arrests related to their impulsive actions, including assault and related charges, drug possession, driving while intoxicated, and prostitution. Sixteen of the 20 had a prior or current diagnosis of alcohol or substance abuse. (p. 29)

This frightening array of psychological and social symptoms nevertheless raises a number of caveats which must be mentioned. All had been subject to extreme abuse of various sorts. For example, 19 had suffered from multiple sexual abusers, 16 from multiple intrafamilial sexual abuse, sexual abuse began in all of them before the age of 8, in 17 of them the incest lasted more than five years, all of them had suffered physical abuse, all of them had witnessed violence, all of them had suffered emotional abuse and 11 of them had parents who abused alcohol.

Furthermore, in addition to a history of abuse, the women were also selected because they had previous psychiatric hospital admissions. Consequently, it is unclear whether it was their selection on the basis of both abuse and mental history which brought about the association between abuse and these appalling symptoms. The difficulty is that by selecting extreme cases in this way the 'typical' effects of abuse may be exaggerated. In other words, that these women showed extreme symptoms is not surprising, since they were selected for psychopathology in the first place. Obviously better research methods are needed than this.

Still in the clinical vein, Shearer *et al.* (1990) found that, among diagnosed borderline personality disordered women psychiatric inpatients, abuse was present in the histories of 40 per cent of them. It was particularly associated with eating disorder and drug abuse disorder. Physical abuse was found in a quarter of the sample and proved to be associated with antisocial personality disorder. But Steiger and Zanko (1990) found that, although eating disorder and psychiatric cases in general showed signs of more sexual abuse in childhood, it did not emerge that symptoms were different for the abused group. Schaefer *et al.* (1988) found that about one-third of their sample of male alcoholics had been physically abused. They reported more severe psychological symptoms but there were no differences in terms of the onset or severity of their alcoholism. The definition of abuse was in terms of being spanked or hurt hard enough to cause bruises, welts, or needing to stay in bed or see a doctor. Gale *et al.* (1988) looked at under-7-year-olds on the records of a community mental health centre and, comparing physical with sexual abuse, depression, anxiety, withdrawal, non-compliance, affective disorder, psychosomatic complaints and suicidal tendencies did not differentiate them. However, inappropriate sexual behaviour was far more common among the sexually abused.

Non-clinical samples   Clinical samples constitute only part of the research. Roth *et al.* (1990) studied victims of sexual assaults. A questionnaire was used in their assessment which measured psychiatric criteria. Those surveyed were either staff or students at an American university. The researchers report a significant difference between victims and non-victims. Victims more commonly exhibited characteristics which could justify their admittance to a psychiatrist's case-load (43 per cent of victims as opposed to 24 per cent of non-victims). However, no evidence at all is provided that they were actually being treated. (Despite this overall comparison, the detailed examination of the cases reported actually only compares groups of victims; there is no comparison with the non-victimised group.)

These data on psychiatric case-load suitability are intriguing. The highest level of symptoms was found among those who had experienced *a single assault by a date*. Multiple childhood victimisation or being the victim of incest with repeated assault yielded fractionally lower scores. The lowest levels of symptoms were for victims of a single assault by a stranger and adult multiple assault victims (virtually all boyfriends or husbands). Intermediate symptom levels were found in those who had experienced a single assault by an acquaintance or a boyfriend or a husband and those who had suffered repeated assaults irrespective of any 'romantic' involvement. These are, of course, rather curious data, since they suggest that nothing is especially extreme about abuse in terms of its psychiatric effects. It is possible that these women were 'over' the problems caused by abuse of a few years before; perhaps they had had help with their problems. However, we are not told that. The data do suggest, though, that childhood problems tend to be overcome, or may not be as severe in the first place as case study data suggest.

Alexander and Lupfer (1987) surveyed 586 female undergraduates at a US state university. The students filled in a questionnaire which asked about a situation 'in which they had been fondled or touched by a family member or older adult in a way which made them feel uncomfortable'. About 25 per cent had – which roughly matches some claims about the incidence of sexual abuse experienced by college students. (No details are given about the types of abuse described in the report, although the authors do appear to know the cases in which penetration occurred.) Nuclear family abuse was most common in those families demonstrating traditional family ideologies, but such ideology made no difference to abuse in the extended family or to that by outsiders compared to the families of women not having experienced abuse.

Certain aspects of the self-concept were more positive in the non-abused women, but these differences were not statistically acceptable as evidence. Furthermore, an analysis taking the women who had been subject to intercourse showed no special effect of this on self-concept, although it has to be said that as few as six cases were involved. Measures of sexual functioning and sexual satisfaction were unaffected by abuse, although abused women had an increased likelihood of having had sexual intercourse (apart from abuse) later on. The type of abuse made no difference to this. Abused children also had a greater risk of being subject to sexual assault later in their lives, but this was unrelated to the type of abuse involved.

Research in Piedmont, North Carolina, looked at the relationship between abuse and psychiatric disorder in a community sample of 1,157 women over 18 years (Winfield *et al.*, 1990). However, it is not clear what proportion were involved in abuse and what proportion were involved in sexual assaults as adults. Sexual assault was defined by a positive response to the question: 'Have you ever been in a situation in which you were pressured into doing more sexually than you wanted to do, that is a situation in which someone pressured you against your will into forced contact with the sexual parts of your body or their body?' (p. 337). They were given the National Institute of Mental Health Diagnostic Interview Schedule, which apparently can identify psychiatric disorders. The prevalence rate was 6 per cent for the entire sample. This was substantially affected by age: roughly 7 per cent for 18–44-year-olds but down to 3 per cent for 45–64-year-olds. A number of psychiatric illnesses were more common in victims, including major depression, alcohol and drug abuse or dependence, panic disorders, obsessive–compulsive disorder and post-traumatic stress disorder. Virtually all of these had their onset after the first attack. However, no attempt seems to have been made to compare a matched sample of non-victims in terms of their onset of psychological problems.

Finkelhor (1984) describes a further analysis of data from a late 1970s study of child sexual victimisation. A scale to measure 'sexual self-esteem' had been developed. Among the things asked on this questionnaire were:

1. 'I find I spend too much time thinking about sex.'
2. 'I really like my body.'
3. 'After sexual experiences, I often feel dissatisfied.'

Childhood victims of child sexual abuse were found to have significantly lower sexual self-esteem – irrespective of their sex. These relationships remained after background factors such as social class, ethnic origin, family size, family values and the like were eliminated. Evidence emerged that those sexually victimised before the age of 13 were more likely to be victims of later sexual violence (forced sex). The figures were 32 per cent of child victims compared with 22 per cent of non-victims. Nevertheless, this was not an effect of sexual abuse but was due to other factors which could be eliminated in the data analysis. Additional evidence showed that girls who were frequently punished by their mother for masturbation or sexual curiosity were the most vulnerable to sexual victimisation in both girlhood and womanhood.

This investigation was extended by examining the relationship between childhood homosexual experiences and their own adult homosexuality (though curiously the equivalent analysis is not presented for heterosexual activity!). Perhaps the analysis reflects a homophobic bias, since, in this context, homosexual activity is presented as if it were a pathological state analogous, say, to 'sexual low self-esteem'. Finkelhor's data suggested that there was a relationship between the childhood experiences of a boy and his adult activities (see Table 3.8).

What are we to make of the apparent effect of childhood experience

Table 3.8: Proportion of sexually abused boys engaging in
homosexual activity in the last year

Childhood experience:	
None	11%
With peer	20%
With older partner	45%

Source: Finkelhor (1984).

with other children, since it appears to increase the incidence of adult
homosexuality substantially? It is a good example of how childhood
sexual experience might influence later life. However, it is far more
typical that all forms of peer sexual activity are left uninvestigated by
researchers. It is then a moot point whether peer sexual experience in
childhood is harmful or merely harmless sexual exploration. Obviously
the answer to this question would have important implications for social
policy as such contacts might have effects similar to those claimed of
abuse. For example, in an intensive study of paedophiles (Cumberbatch
and Howitt, 1991) it was notable that, although a proportion of them had
been sexually abused by adults as children, the overwhelming majority
had been abused by adults and/or had had sexual contact with other
children of a similar age. The startling thing was the close overlap between these early experiences and the content of the adult paedophiliac
activity. It may well be, then, that by concentrating on the effects of abuse
we ignore the importance of childhood sexualisation in general.

The tendency to regard the issue as one of adult abuse of children,
while similar-age sex between children is seen as relatively harmless or as
a radically different problem, has its problems, of course. One difficulty
is to explain why one should be damaging and the other harmless.
Perhaps part of the explanation is the assumption that abuse is cyclical, so
that abused children become abusing adults. Indeed, such an argument
tends to lead to an optimistic attitude in that eliminating abuse from the
present generation of children will reduce abuse of the next generation. It
happens, though, that the evidence on cycles of abuse is quite weak.
Kaufman and Zigler (1987), in their review of studies, suggest that only
30 per cent (plus or minus 5 per cent) of abusive parents had themselves
been abused. This is about six times the rate of abuse in the general
population, they claim. But what of the involvement of peers? In a survey
of US undergraduates, Haugaard and Tilly (1988) found that 42 per cent
at under 13 years had had a sexual experience with another child. The
figure reached very nearly half of the males. Most typically, the sex acts
were kissing and hugging (26 per cent), exhibiting (33 per cent), fondling
(15 per cent) and genital fondling (16 per cent). There were signs that

experiences with adults and children were not so very different in their effects on such feelings as current guilt – except where there was no coercion in this childhood sexuality. Johnson (1988) found that, in a sample of boys who coercively abused other children, about half had been sexually abused themselves. But this does not seem to be typical of all children involved in sexual activity with other children. Only 23 per cent had used physical coercion – verbal coercion was more common.

A later study (Finkelhor *et al.*, 1989) was based on the telephone survey of 2,626 adult Americans mentioned earlier among data on the prevalence of abuse. The survey makes the important distinction between abuse involving sexual intercourse and other forms of abuse. Unfortunately, the questions asked about abuse, as we have already described, asked about 'someone trying or succeeding in having any kind of sexual intercourse with you, *or anything like that?*' (emphasis added).

Finkelhor himself points out the problem: a person might well reply 'yes' to the question on the basis of having been touched on, say, a breast rather than having been subject to intercourse or an attempt at intercourse. Those who have been involved as victims in penetrative abusive intercourse were separated and compared with the rest of the sample. Various measures were taken in the survey. These were as follows:

1. Sexual satisfaction: 'Generally speaking, would you say that your intimate relations with the opposite sex are very satisfactory, or fairly satisfactory, or very unsatisfactory?'
2. Marital status: this is fairly self-explanatory and refers to divorce and the like.
3. Religion: 'Would you say you are a strongly religious person, or only moderately religious, or don't you really practice a religion?'

Factors which might have produced spurious relationships between abuse and these measures were controlled for. Age, race, geographic region, father's education, family structure, number of siblings, happiness of family life, closeness of mother, adequacy of sex education and strictness of parental authority were taken into account. After all of this was done, the following findings emerged:

1. *Men* who were 'victims with intercourse' were more likely to be religious non-practitioners.
2. *Women* who were 'victims with intercourse' were more likely to be dissatisfied with their sexual relationships.
3. *Men and women* who were 'victims with intercourse' were more likely to suffer marital disruption.

The fundamental problem with these data is fitting them to a satisfactory model of the adverse effects of abuse. Finkelhor's analysis is based on the ideological stance that there is something wrong or bad about being a religious non-practitioner, dissatisfied with intimate sexual relationships and divorced. However, none of these necessarily fits easily with the notion of adverse effects of abuse. For example, Finkelhor simply has no data from the men and women in his study that they regarded these things as bad. After all, and one would not wish to press this very far except as an illustration, it might equally well be argued that not practising religion, expressing dissatisfaction with intimate relationships and being willing to divorce are all indicators of psychological strength rather than of having been harmed.

Finkelhor questions the conceptualisations about the effects of abuse which have been put forward by researchers including himself. He points out that the concern is with the long-term effects of abuse on adult functioning. 'The bottom line is always how does this event affect adult adjustment, adult feelings, adult capacities, and adult attitudes':

> This preoccupation is a kind of ethnocentrism on the part of adults. The impact of an event on childhood itself is treated as less important. It is only 'childhood,' a stage which, after all, everyone outgrows. (Finkelhor, 1984, p. 198)

Inherent in Finkelhor's views are ideas which are essentially rejected by the Dutch researcher Sandfort, who questions the use of the term 'sexual abuse':

> Sexual contacts are considered as such *regardless* of the way they came about or the way they have been experienced by the child. Some investigators even included in their concept of 'sexual abuse' events in which no physical contact took place, such as exhibition of the sexual organs, making improper suggestions, showing pornography, talking erotically about sexual matters . . . Does the term 'sexual abuse' not start to lose meaning when it comes to encompass virtually every kind of sexual experience a child can have with an adult? (Sandfort, 1989, p. 5)

It is interesting to note that, when Sandfort (1988) looked at child–adult sexual contact in terms of whether it was *consensual* or *non-consensual* there were considerable differences in outcome. He found that *non-consensual* childhood sex was associated with problems in their current adult sexual relationship and higher levels of psychosomatic health complaints. On the other hand, *consensual* activity was associated with higher adult sexual desire and arousability and fewer anxieties about sexual contacts.

It is established in the literature that certain sorts of 'criminal' behavioural consequences are associated with abuse. So, for example,

Cavaiola and Schiff (1988) showed that fairly substantial rates of physical and sexual abuse, most of which was not previously reported, sexual promiscuity, legal involvement, acting out and running away were more common among abused children than among children who were not but who were drug abusers, and those who were neither abused nor drug-abusers. Dembo and his associates (Dembo *et al.*, 1987; Dembo *et al.*, 1989; Dembo *et al.*, 1991) found similarly that physically and sexually abused youngsters who were interviewed in a secure unit for young offenders showed higher levels of criminality than non-abused youngsters.

However, a follow-up analysis of these same youngsters was carried out a few years later (Dembo and Howitt, 1991). Although physical abuse at this time and a previous history of physical abuse predicted the extent of current problems, things were quite different for sexual abuse. Once background factors were controlled for, it was current sexual abuse, not the history of sexual abuse, which predicted current problems. In other words, the behavioural problems associated with sexual abuse seemed to subside once the abuse stopped, although this did not seem true of physical abuse. Quite clearly, this is a radically different outcome than that implied by most of the research on the effects of abuse, which tends to indicate that the long-term consequences of abuse are important – at least for the clinical samples. These new data seem to fit in well with the survey data, in which it has proven difficult to find the extremes of damage reported in the more selected samples of research based on clinical patients.

> Initially, the behavior of these traumatized children may seem only a bit different from that of other children. Upon continued interaction, however, the therapist is able to discern more clearly through the child's behavior patterns the damage that has resulted from abuse or neglect. (Fatout, 1990, p. 76)

Quite clearly the outcomes of abuse may be varied and to a degree un-predictable. It is not the intention here to quarrel with the research findings as such. It is the way that the conceptualisation of the effects issue has emerged which should be the focus of attention. Although there are severe critics of the methodology of the child abuse research literature (e.g. Plotkin *et al.*, 1981), these are not our concern. The question is the functions served by constructing the discussion about child abuse, based on 'objective' research, in a way which first of all creates a view of the extensiveness of intrafamilial abuse that is a distortion. The nuclear family is not the main arena of sexual abuse and childhood may be physically the safest time of one's life. The dangerousness of the nuclear family is very much a myth which detracts from the more extensive consideration of sexual abuse. Secondly, the research on the effects of abuse considers the matter in a way which prevents the effects of abuse from being separated from the effects of the interventions of the child protection system. The use of clinical samples inevitably brings to the matter extreme and dramatic cases. It is notable that surveys of the general population have tended to find rather insubstantial effects. Indeed, it might be suggested that there is very little consistency in the effects found.

In terms of error this debate is important, since the extensiveness of abuse and its harm are mainstays supporting anti-abuse activity. Certainly, given that most public child abuse errors and those which I investigated involve the immediate nuclear family, the creation of the problem as one of the nuclear family might explain the focus of the system on the child's closest relatives. A comment from West (1991) provides extensive food for thought:

> In reality, incidents of sexual victimisation are so varied and the effects so dependent upon attendant circumstances and individual characteristics that any sweeping generalisation is certain to be fallacious . . . undue emphasis on the worst possible prognoses is not always in the victim's best interest. In cases involving children excessive and over-hasty intervention may satisfy feelings of outrage at the cost of further damage to the victims. There is a great need for recognition of the diversity and complexity of the 'victimisation' and for this to be followed by appropriate and discriminating responses. (p. 69).

CHAPTER 4

ENLARGING THE NET

A young girl, about eight years old, was admitted to my ward. I was told that in the last few days she had been the victim of a criminal sexual assault . . . I examined the child and confirmed the existence of severe lesions on her body. The vulva showed all the symptoms of a violent and extremely acute inflammation. She was literally bathed in a creamy green pus . . . Her labia major, enormously swollen, looked like the segments of an orange and completely masked the vulvar orifice. (Fournier, 1880, p. 108)

What might to many modern eyes appear to be a clear case of child sexual abuse was disbelieved. Using a theory of the detection of lying through its characteristic appearance in a child's language, Fournier, a distinguished nineteenth-century physician:

was struck . . . by the disproportion between cause and effect, clinically speaking, and I could not find an explanation for the singular intensity of the inflammation . . . I questioned the child repeatedly in an effort to get her to divulge new information. And soon she made what was from my point of view an important remark: it suggested that she was reciting a lesson learned by heart rather than telling the truth, a truth which comes from direct experience, a truth dependent only on her own (albeit negligible) intelligence. In fact, she invariably retold this tale in the same words, with the same inflections in her voice, with the same mistakes of grammar, etc.; in short, in the manner of children who repeat flattering civilities or fairy tales. (p. 109)

This 'realisation' was followed by a disclosure interview which finally elicited the 'truth':

I attacked her position by means of friendship, kindness, compliments, etc. A few sweets and a few coins succeeded in winning the little patient's confidence and friendship. I will be brief: a doll with moving eyes was a crucial factor in my triumph. Conquered by this irresistible munificence, the child, after much difficulty and after a long time, finally told me that it was not a *man* who had touched her but her mother, who on three different occasions had rubbed her genitals with a *waxing brush*, forbidding her to tell anyone and threatening her with more of the same if she said anything. (p. 110)

There is every encouragement for researchers to promote the belief that they have special skills which help detect and prosecute cases of abuse. Not only does this enable research to be tied to what would appear to be a challenging social issue, but it is also a source of funding and other forms of kudos for their research. This may do little to promote a questioning stance about child abuse theory and practice. While it is good to know of the real-world applicability of psychological and other findings, simply to assume that assisting in the prosecution of abusers is the main imperative may be more problematic than at first appears. After all, some means of achieving this may not be good things.

One important thread in abuse research concerns the problems of prosecuting offenders – especially as there are often no physical signs to be found. Genital fondling and oral sex, generally, leave no physical damage. Testimony by children may then become essential in prosecutions. Consequently, the question of the truthfulness or reliability of the evidence of children becomes central in cases of abuse. But, of course, views concerning the truthfulness of children's testimony have undergone various stages, ideologically underpinned and linked to changing ideas about childhood (Goodman, 1984). So there is nothing new about the question of the veracity of children's evidence.

Furthermore, there has been a long history of using 'technologies' in order to sort lies out from the truth. The classic example of this, the lie detector test, uses electrical recording apparatus to detect changes in the conductivity of the skin. These variations are claimed to be symptomatic of stress and, more importantly, strongly predictive of lying (Levey, 1988). There is no point in reviewing the evidence on this here, but it has to be stressed that many researchers see the test as invalid (e.g. Gale, 1988), although it is legally admissible evidence in some parts of the world. Truth detection has been recently revived in a superficially different form. This depends no longer upon the detection of emotion but on a theory of key differences between 'truthful' accounts of events and 'constructed' lies. Nevertheless the search for simple indicators of truthfulness is at the root of electrical lie detection, 'Fournier's theory' and these new methods. Accounts of events such as abuse can be seen as involving both content and form:

1. The nature of the events described (what happened).
2. The structural features of the description (the amount of detail given, how well organised the description is, the amount of self-correction of minor errors, and so forth).

So some have argued (e.g. Raskin and Steller, 1989) that the structural features of true accounts are not the same as those of lies. Consequently, if it could be demonstrated what the structural features of truthful accounts are, then properly trained experts could advise courts whether a witness is lying. This is not a futuristic scenario and has been carried out, particularly in continental Europe in connection with child sexual abuse cases.

For example, Trankell (1972) describes what he terms 'statement reality analysis'. He refers to a number of 'criteria of reality', including the following, which we can take as an example for the moment: 'If an account contains details which have a unique character there is increased reason to consider it as an account of an actual observation' (Trankell, 1972, p. 129). As Trankell provides no psychological research evidence to justify this assertion, it might be that he was writing in ignorance of the major psychological studies of naturalistic memory (e.g. Neisser, 1982). Furthermore, he offers what he describes as a 'competence' criterion: 'If a witness has no competence which enables him [sic] to invent the events he describes in his testimony, there is an increased probability that the witness has actually observed these events' (Trankell, 1972, p. 128). He goes on to argue that the competence criterion is frequently used when sexual abuse is being reported by children. However, this is dubious as it takes for granted, for example, that children have poor knowledge of sexual matters. Possession of sexual knowledge does not have to be gained through direct experience and some sexual knowledge is not rare in children (cf. Jervis, 1987). The belief that children are normally 'innocent' of sexual matters is difficult to reconcile with one's passing knowledge of children.

One German forensic psychologist (Undeutsch, 1982), while essentially rejecting the use of laboratory experiments to evaluate the adequacy of his and similar methods, claims success for statement analysis in a large number of sex abuse cases. In his examinations of the statements of children claiming to be victims, he decided that about 90 per cent (out of 1,500) of them were 'truthful' claims. The rest, apparently, did not go to court. It is only the 'truthful' cases which can then be assessed for validity. Undeutsch measures this as the proportion of his 'truthful' cases in which a conviction was secured. By this criterion, Undeutsch claims 95 per cent success in identifying 'truthfulness'.

The question is, of course, what does this prove? It could prove several things. First of all, it might demonstrate that psychologists share similar criteria for assessing evidence with jurors in a court of law. Secondly, it might reflect the fact that most tried cases (including those which do not use such psychological 'expertise') result in a conviction. Thirdly, it might show the power of the statement analysis techniques. But that is the matter in contention, especially since there seem to be no clear scoring procedures involved. The apparent validity of the approach may simply be a further indication that the subjective judgements of psychologist experts and jurors are remarkably similar. Nor should we ignore the possibility that the psychologist actually gave evidence in court about the probity of the witness's evidence. In this case, we could be dealing with a self-validating process, since the psychologist, in effect, is merely convincing others that his or her interpretation is the correct one.

The structural features used in statement validity analysis and similar techniques include the following:

1. Logical structure.
2. Unstructured production.
3. Reproduction of conversation.
4. Spontaneous self-corrections.
5. Raising doubts about one's own testimony.

The psychologist assesses the statement in terms of the presence or absence of these features, essentially forming a judgement about the truth of the account. There are no commonly accepted guidelines about quantifying the various patterns to give some sort of index of the likelihood of truth versus lying. Thus, although it may appear that we are dealing with science, in fact judgement rules in the recommendation to the court. There is no need to point to the catastrophic implications of bad judgements. The likelihood of spuriously high success rates for the technique needs underlining in this context.

Bekerian and Dennett (1990) also believe that there is no satisfactory validity research for these procedures currently available. They turn to basic research, however, for evidence that statement analysis procedures are suspect. For example, they point to basic research which shows that repeated experience of 'autobiographical' events can lead to less accuracy in recall by young children, though the accounts were more complete. Different but similar episodes become confabulated and consequently confused on specific details. Or, in more technical language, we have 'schematic (generalised) accounts'. Thus basic research questions the idea that the unstructured production of memories is typical of honest testimony. Such 'psychologically' based technologies in other contexts have often been conceived as serving oppressive functions, the classic example being intelligence, ability and educational attainment testing. This has been used in ways which justify, for example, racial disadvantage (Howitt, 1991a). Furthermore, it is worthwhile noting that these are not merely intraprofessional judgements, but sometimes a view supported by legal judgements (Burnstein and Pitchford, 1990).

Lying children

A sixteen-year old girl who told a jury her stepfather raped and sexually abused her, denied a barrister's suggestion she was telling a 'tissue of lies' to revenge his strict treatment of her . . . Under cross examination . . . the girl admitted she had told lies in the past – including claiming at school she was a satanist in order to avoid an educational religious outing . . . She also admitted she lost her virginity aged 12 with a boyfriend – and since then had had sex with three other boys . . . The girl agreed she had previously made an allegation of rape against a boyfriend which did not result in criminal proceedings . . . She also agreed she felt hatred for the defendant over his extreme strictness . . . The girl's mother said the defendant told her he had another girlfriend at about the time her daughter told her about the alleged sexual abuse. (*Leicester Mercury*, 22 March 1991, p. 39)

In stark contrast, the research and professional literature on child abuse tends to present a rather different view, which regards children as reliable and honest:

Children, particularly those under age seven, rarely have the capacity to lie, says Gail Goodman, assistant professor of psychology at the University of Denver . . . A study of almost 200 child abuse cases in Boston concluded that roughly 95 percent of the children's accusations were accurate. The study was conducted by Jonathan Horowitz . . . (Silas, 1985, p. 17)

Taken from a professional journal of the American Bar Association aimed at lawyers, this view is intended to influence professional thinking. While it might well be true that children are overwhelmingly honest about abuse allegations, this is only part of the issue. Estranged partners, professionals and others have an additional role to play in the supply of evidence in child abuse cases. Chapter 8 gives some worrying examples of the provision of evidence by professionals. But the 'children never lie' thesis is a doctrine which provides another formula to guide thinking.

The article goes on to reinforce further the truthfulness conception of children's accounts: 'Through repeated questioning, children can often become confused, and, although they are being honest, inconsistencies may suggest lack of truthfulness, said Donald Bross, a sociologist and lawyer . . .' (p. 17). What this seems to be saying to the reader is that, despite the appearances of lying, children are in fact telling the truth. The honest child and the lying child may not differ at all in their testimony. In other words, unless one is prepared to abandon children's testimony entirely, there is little choice other than to believe it. This then leads to a final device which might be expected to lead to exaggerated confidence in one's own judgement, even when others apparently disagree. For the lawyer, failure to convince the jury need not take on any value for altering the subjective view that the children do not lie: 'Juries are often reluctant to convict on the basis of the word of a child' (p. 17).

Irrespective of the intention of the writer, the article carries a string of implications which constitute an account of false accusations which is distinctly constrained. It is misleading in that it locates the problem with children rather than with the system. These misleading impressions would include:

1. The idea that false accusations by children are responsible for errors. This is far from always being the case, and concentration on research into the honesty of children's testimony deflects attention from the problems of the child protection system.
2. The corollary that, where children do not make accusations or deny accusations, the child protection services take no action. This is simply not true. Many of the errors of the system involve overriding or disregarding children's denials of abuse.

In other words, although there is a temptation to dwell on the issue of the worth of children's evidence, since this is pertinent to the prosecution of abusers, other perhaps more significant issues are raised by the study of child protection errors. In particular, the question of when a child will be believed and when it will not emerges in disputed cases of child abuse. This, however, is a question not of the validity of children's accounts but of how these accounts are processed by child protection workers: 'Later he was regularly questioned about ritual dances and sex abuse. It was all rubbish, he said' (*The Times*, 6 April 1991, reporting the experiences of a 15-year-old boy taken from his home in the Orkney satanic abuse case).

There is a tendency for some writers to provide a simple solution to the practitioner's anxieties about whether a particular child is telling the truth. That is to insist that the lying child is a myth:

> *Myth no. 1: Children and women lie.* This is an ancient myth which has particular implications for allegations of sexual abuse made by children and their mothers. There follow several subcategories of this myth: (a) children invent accusations; (b) adult women fantasise about childhood experiences; (c) vindictive mothers for their own purposes cook up stories of abuse to their children. (Driver, 1989, p. 27)

This is clearly a dangerous formulation in terms of its potential for generating errors.

Research on false allegations

Everson and Boat (1989) carried out one of the most thorough studies of false allegations by children, although they incorporated the 'system' bias common in this sort of research. They surveyed experienced officers of the child protection services in North Carolina. Information was requested concerning the number of investigations, the number of substantiated cases and the number of cases which were thought to be false allegations of sexual abuse made by a child or adolescent. The *personal experience* of the respondents during the year prior to the survey was the time-frame of the study. Broken down by the child's age group, percentages judged to be false allegations were as shown in Table 4.1. This table is adapted from the original, which does not give the unclassified category in this form.

The interpretation of Table 4.1 is crucial, of course, since there are a number of possiblities which might paint several different pictures. Everson and Boat offer two. The first is to use the figures found in the false allegations column. As a consequence of this choice, false allegations seem infrequent, in general, but increasing substantially during adolescence. Their second interpretation is based on the same data, but with those in the unclassified category excluded. They assume that the 'majority of substantiated cases of abuse among children approximately 3 years and older involve verbal disclosures by children and adolescents' (p. 231). This omission inflates the false allegation rate somewhat to 3, 7 and 13 per cent for the last three age groups respectively (ignoring the under-3s). There is, of course, an oddity in this. It raises the question of how the initial allegations were made, since it is possible that some of the substantiated allegations were not actually allegations by the child in the first place – they might have been made by parents alone without any substantiation by the child, for example.

There is, naturally, a third way of looking at these data which the authors fail to explore. That is to say that the rate of substantiated cases is the best

Table 4.1: Proportion of substantiated, false and unclassified allegations of sexual abuse in North Carolina

	Substantiated	False allegations	Unclassified
Child			
Under 3	48%	2%	51%
3–6	60%	2%	38%
6–12	55%	4%	40%
12–18	57%	8%	35%

Source: Everson and Boat (1989).

indicator of 'safe' allegations. The unclassified together with the false allegations may actually provide the best estimate of the risk of injustice caused by the child protection system. No detail is given about what sorts of thing the children were claiming in the unclassified category. Furthermore, there is the very important question of quite what action was taken in the unsubstantiated category – were the children placed on a child abuse register, for instance? In how many cases had the children been taken into care or their fathers forced to leave home temporarily? If one takes this approach, the uncategorised category provides a considerable wealth of opportunities for injustice.

There was some evidence that certain sorts of case were most common among allegations judged to be false. Overwhelmingly, they were female 'victims' but, in addition, the alleged perpetrators tended to be of low educational level, and they tended to be non-biological fathers (but partners of the mother nevertheless). The type of abuse alleged was much more likely to be fondling rather than (attempted) intercourse. The main reasons for deciding that the allegations were false were retraction by the child (55 per cent) followed by factors related to the credibility of the child (improbability of the report, 20 per cent; insufficient details, 10 per cent; inconsistencies in report, 10 per cent; and conflicting evidence, 10 per cent).

But it should not be forgotten that the evidence of the apparently low rate of false allegations was largely based on the views of the social workers involved. In other words, the evidence of false allegations can be conceived as part of a *self-validating process* by the child protection system. To a degree, this assumes that the system is neutral in relation to the process. It cannot be known, in this formulation, how adequate the judgements of substantiation are. They may, for all we know, be false substantiations of allegations constructed by the system itself. Importantly, the study provided evidence of the relationship between beliefs about the likelihood of false allegations and actually detecting such cases. Those who had experienced false reports were the most likely to think that the rates of false allegation are high. Such experiences tended to double the estimates. In other words, we might expect that beliefs lead to increases or decreases in 'recognising' false allegations.

Taking a somewhat different starting point, Thoeness and Pearson (1988) interviewed people in key roles in a number of large US domestic relations courts involved with children's custody decisions. Varying opinions were expressed about the veracity of claims that a former partner had abused the children in such circumstances. Not all false allegations made at this stage were necessarily out of maliciousness or spite:

> Family court personnel suggest that there is possibly a certain subset of cases in which abuse clearly took place. One court administrator suggests

that perhaps half of all the allegations heard may be such cases. More problematic are those cases in which all the professionals remain uncertain about what, if anything, actually transpired. These cases often involve very young children with very confusing, vague stories or totally unwilling to talk. These cases may also involve an accusing parent who seems seriously mentally disturbed and an accused parent who is conceivably abusive. These cases may also involve clear evidence of abuse by a variety of possible perpetrators. (p. 23)

The fact that such allegations coincide with custody hearings does not necessarily invalidate them. While there may be personal gains to be had from alleging abuse at this time, some of the abuse itself may be precipitated by factors, such as stress or opportunity, associated with the divorce. Consequently, it is difficult to decide what evidential value such allegations have in terms of the 'children never lie' dictum. Given that Thoenes and Pearson fail to provide even systematic estimates of false allegations in such circumstances, the most we can get from their research is that there is evidence that some professionals are well aware of the possibility of false allegations in the domestic court setting.

Once again, however, the evidence tends to focus on factors outside the professions involved in child protection work. If the problem lies with those alleging abuse then the professionals cannot be faulted. But this seems radically different from the experience of public inquiries and the later case studies on child protection errors. It dodges the question of how the false allegations are dealt with. One can only wonder at the confidence of Spencer and Flin (1990) when they summarise the results of the research as follows:

[T]he most recent scientific evidence shows that a significant proportion of false allegations are in fact made by adults on behalf of children (e.g. in custody disputes), and that false complaints made by children are very rare . . . when children do make a false report it is generally for identifiable reasons, and psychologists and psychiatrists are developing a better understanding of the distinguishing characteristics and symptomology of such cases. (p. 269)

As we have seen, this may be misleading in detail. But it is also misleading in that it ignores many of the stages at which other crucial questions about the use of children's evidence by professionals emerge. While one can appreciate that research has shown that the evidence of children may be of a quality which more or less matches that of adults, none of the evidence to date warrants the 'children rarely/never lie' tag irrespective of the 'hard-nosed' psychological research that has gone into the question of the characteristics of children's testimony (cf. Davies, 1991).

Playing at dolls

Elaine [one of the children in the Cleveland sexual abuse controversy] then moved on to the larger anatomically correct female doll. She undressed the doll but paid little attention to its prominently displayed body parts. Elaine quickly adopted a mother role, treating the doll with great care and stroking its hair and making everything neat and tidy and nice. Perhaps the most revealing part of the play session, if there were revelations at all, came near the end . . . when eventually the seven year old got round to the problem that had truly been troubling her. It had worried her ever since she was taken from her parents and placed in a foster home . . . She had missed a school trip. (Bell, 1988, p. 284)

One of the investigatory procedures employed by child protection workers is to use 'anatomical' dolls in evaluations of child abuse. Boat and Everson (1988) carried out research on their use which yielded some interesting findings. At the time they did their research, over ten commercial companies in the USA were advertising such dolls for sale – several times the number of just a few years earlier. Their findings, in general, point to the inept use made of such dolls. For example, child protection workers in three-fifths of cases used dolls with mouth openings, whereas only one in five doctors did. Virtually all child protection workers used dolls with vaginas compared to less than one in five of the police. While four out of five law enforcement officers used dolls with anuses, only about a quarter of doctors did. Dolls with five fingers were used by three-fifths of physicians but by fewer than one in five of child protection workers. In other words, many of the dolls were incapable of demonstrating what anatomical dolls were designed to indicate. Even an adult could not use a doll lacking enough fingers to demonstrate accurately digital penetration.

What different professional groups considered as 'very convincing' evidence of sexual abuse included 'avoidance of or anxiety about unclothed dolls'. For example, about one in eight social workers, a quarter of mental health workers, a twelfth of doctors and three-tenths of police saw this as evidence. But the professions could not even agree about what were and what were not normal things to do when playing with such dolls. So whereas virtually all workers saw undressing the dolls as normal behaviour, police officers were the least likely to see the touching of the dolls' breasts, genitals and anal area as normal. A quarter, more or less, saw having the dolls kiss each other as *abnormal*. Half of the social workers saw the laying of the dolls on top of each other as normal – only one-fifteenth of law enforcement officers did.

The research was done on professionals who themselves used anatomical dolls in their work. The lack of competence in assessing the accuracy of work with anatomical dolls and the incorrect belief in the diagnostic signs of abuse present in doll play are matters of concern. Edwards and Forman (1989) may have shown (though without statistically significant data) that dolls are useful in enhancing the quality of testimony of witnessed events (albeit in a non-abused sample), but that is a very different matter from reading the 'tea-leaves' of doll-play activities. Furthermore, it is not in conflict with Vizard's (1991) view that 'there is a strong consensus that sexually abused children may show more directly sexualised play with dolls' (p. 120). Probabalistic outcomes of research, however, are clearly dangerous in terms of diagnosticity. So, for example, Jampole and Weber (1987) showed differences between sexually abused and non-abused children in terms of their style of play with anatomical dolls. But this was not a perfect separation and some non-abused children appear to show what some might see as sex play (penetration of the doll's genitals with fingers). Clearly, mistaken assumptions could be made by relying on the doll-play techniques.

The problem lies in the formularisation of doll-play activity in a way that leads to beliefs that abuse may have occurred.

Is child abuse overreported?

Creighton (1985) describes an analysis of the children placed on the child abuse registers serviced by the National Society for the Prevention of Cruelty to Children in Britain. Well over six thousand children were placed on the registers between 1977 and 1982, a period of rapid expansion of concern about child physical abuse in Britain. At first sight, following Creighton's figures, the rise in numbers of registered children is quite alarming. The rates of physically injured children on the register expressed per thousand children in the appropriate population was approximately 0.4 in 1977 and 0.6 in 1982. This is a rise of approximately 50 per cent, of course. Taken at its face value this is quite a staggering figure. However, when we take a look at a breakdown of the percentage of these physically injured children who were fatally or seriously injured, different trends emerge. The percentage falls from about 17 per cent in 1977 to 10 per cent in 1982. In other words, more intensive child protection activity led to a greater increase in the proportion of non-serious cases that were identified by the system.

Despite the trend for the *proportion* registered as having serious injuries to decrease, it could be that greater *numbers* of seriously injured children became registered. But this appears not to have been the case. It is possible to estimate from the figures that there were 0.07 per thousand in the serious category in 1977 and 0.06 per thousand in 1982. It would appear that greater surveillance does not bring more serious cases into the net.

In the USA, the question of the overreporting of child abuse has been an issue among certain commentators. For example, Besharov (1988) claims that the number and percentage of unfounded reports of child abuse have steadily increased since the 1970s, with a commensurate rise in the amount of distressing and coercive state intervention in family life. Part of the argument is that 'non-serious' reports have become very much more common. Such claims are important matters, of course, since they might indicate a clogging up of the child protection system with 'trivial' cases.

Besharov's ideas are roundly criticised by Finkelhor (1990), who argues that the data on which Besharov bases his arguments are essentially flawed. He indicates, contrary to Besharov, that substantiation rates have not changed systematically and that much the same applies to the number of non-serious cases. Of course, any social statistics tend to be problematic and there is always opportunity for the redefinition of what is serious and what is a founded report. Irrespective of such criticisms, one can regard Besharov's basic point as a matter deserving attention irrespective of the statistical adequacy of his argument.

Of course, there are serious questions about what should be classified as abuse and what resources should be given. It should not be forgotten that a case conference attended by, say, five or six workers involved in child protection (social workers, medics, police, etc.) which takes an afternoon has used up the equivalent of half a person for a week. This is an expensive matter for a tiny mark, as in the case of some of my case studies discussed in Chapter 7. A few years ago Geach (1982) reported that a case conference cost as much as £540 ($900), although the figure has doubtless risen since. Once registered, necessarily or otherwise, a child will be subject to a case conference every few months.

In Britain, there is no doubt that there has been a substantial increase in the number of child abuse registrations made. While these might be appropriate if it were shown that registration was being used as a means of targeting resources on children needing help, registration does not necessarily do this. According to Burke (1991), there are a number of factors which give rise to worry about the registration process, including the following:

1. The criteria of abuse have changed. So, for example, non-accidental injury, no matter how slight in extent, is a government-recommended criterion of abuse.

2. Moves towards changing criteria from actual to 'probable' abuse would increase the numbers of registrations made.

As a consequence of such things, Burke's comments are somewhat pessimistic:

> I admit to being fearful of the higher numbers of children named on protection registers. Registers should be an alerting device to justify removal of the child from situations that continue to prove unacceptable, or prompt deregistration if the home situation stabilises. We do not need registration for registration's sake. I am sure no agency would condone such a position but I suspect such a position is current in some departments, due largely to the uncertainty of grey registration and attempts to predict based on past failure, not success. (p. 29)

In the USA, Rycraft (1990) has investigated systematically the consequences of changing the definition of child abuse to include only serious cases. A definition, suggested by the National Association of Public Child Welfare Administrators:

> specifies that only recent acts or the failure to act by a parent or caretaker resulting in the death; serious physical, sexual, or emotional harm; or imminent risk of serious harm to a person under age 18 should fall within the mandate of child protective services. (Rycraft, 1990, p. 15)

The different states of the USA have different definitions of child abuse such that, for example, Rycraft could look to see if the inclusion of the qualifier 'serious' or 'substantial harm' made any difference to the outcomes of the activities of the child protection services. The number of *fatalities* was not affected by variations in the child abuse definition currently employed by the state. Furthermore, case substantiation rates did not alter with the type of definition used. However, the statistical analysis did reveal that the adoption of a definition which involved some measure of seriousness would reduce the reporting rate of child abuse cases. Fatalities, it should be mentioned, are relatively uncommon. The US national figure is one child per 56,000. For every fatality, there are on average 1,800 child abuse reports made. Furthermore, it is not at all clear how many of the children involved as fatalities had previously been the subject of a report to the child protection system.

There are many questions raised by such data – especially that of the degree of protection that society expects to grant to children.

Prejudice and intervention

While the thrust of this book concerns the injustice done to individual families through child abuse practice, it would be naive to disregard the relationship of injustice in the child protection system to broader social injustices such as sexism, racism and the rest. (We can leave the question of sexism to the next chapter and those case studies in Chapters 7 and 8 which suggest that child protection can be regarded as anti-woman.) The question of racism relates, of course, to deep social structures bringing injustice to black people (Howitt and Owusu-Bempah, 1990). There is no reason to assume that agencies involved in child protection work are free of this. On the contrary, the reverse is almost inevitably true. Stubbs (1989) makes the case strongly:

> [S]ocial workers and, particularly, the police, tend to treat black families with a degree of suspicion – as undeserving, deviant, even criminal . . .
> In our own research in the North of England, two incidents involving allegations of sexual abuse against 'Asian' children have a striking similarity to each other. In both cases, the police action was premised on the assumption that 'Asian' families and the community as a whole would 'stick together and protect its own'. Consequently, since the perpetrator was not known in either case, the police harassed and arrested a large number of men within the extended family and in wider friendship networks. In one case, the child was removed from home at great speed and taken some distance to an all-white environment. This action appeared to be premised on an assumption that 'Asian' children are not merely hostages within their own family but within the community as a whole . . . (pp. 102–3)

The survey evidence from America on the relationship between race or ethnicity and sexual abuse is reasonably clear-cut. Russell's (1986) US survey found very similar levels of what she defines as incestuous abuse among the groups of women she studied – white, Afro-American and Latin. The main exception to this was that Asian girls were only about half as likely to suffer incestuous abuse. Wyatt (1985) found that child-hood abuse was more common in white girls than Afro-American ones. No statistically significant differences emerged for 'family' abuse, although stepfather-type involvement and male cousins were slightly more common in the black families. Some of these differences might be explicable on the basis of differences in opportunity due to differences in household composition. Certainly there is no tendency for the Afro-Caribbean population to be more accepting of abuse. Giovanni and Becerra (1979) found that the black American participants in their research rated different forms of abuse as more serious than did their sample of white people.

It is intriguing to find that, once we examine data on race and abuse not taken from surveys, a radically different picture appears. This suggests that in terms of *intervention* in abuse there tends to be an overrepresentation of black families. Powers and Eckenrode (1988) found that black people in New York were more common in cases of physical and sexual abuse and neglect than their proportions in census data would suggest. Substantiation rates tended to show the same pattern, but not strongly. Cupoli and Sewell (1988) looked at the cases of over one thousand sexual assault victims in the emergency room of a hospital. Black people were overrepresented by 50 per cent, although Latin people were underrepresented. (Watkins (1990) reviews several studies of the prevalence of abuse and concludes that Hispanics were less likely than non-Hispanic whites to experience childhood sexual assault, so perhaps this finding about their underrepresentation is not surprising.) White people were in perfect ratio to their occurrence in the general population.

It was shown by Segal and Schwartz (1985) that the race of a child influenced the likelihood that he or she would be discharged back home after a period of time at an American emergency treatment centre. Not only were black children less likely to be returned home, but the majority of the children in the study were black. Some have suggested (Department of Health, 1991; Downey, 1991) that even the British inquiries into abuse in the 1980s (eighteen in number) tended to ignore 'peripheral factors'. Only one – concerned with the death of Tyra Henry (Department of Health, 1991) – raised the issue of race. In this it was suggested that the child's social workers may have been through some 'unconscious' process leading them to believe that a black mother under great stress and in poverty should be able to cope!

Certain writers have found parallels between the experience of racism and abuse:

> Children need to learn in order to survive and to grow. They are taught the ABCs of racism and anti-Semitism. Black and/or Jewish children are taught that they are inferior, guilty of some quality that makes them unworthy and somehow dirty . . . These are exactly the messages that children receive when being sexually abused. (Droisen, 1989, p. 160)

The question perhaps ought to be whether similar messages are sent to black families by white institutions, including child protection systems. The evidence gives cause for concern.

Social class provides another possibility that social injustice is applied to broad groupings of people through social work. Again, things at the survey level are very clear. It is known that social class is associated with sexual abuse in an unexpected way. If anything, Russell's (1986) study suggests that the higher the family's social status, the greater the probability of incestuous abuse. In Britain, La Fontaine (1990) compared cases in a survey of child sexual abuse among a general population sample with those in a child sexual abuse unit in a hospital. Broadly speaking and in percentage figures, upper-middle-class children were twice as likely to have been sexually abused as to enter the child abuse unit. On the other hand, working-class children were about twice as likely to be in the unit as to have been abused. In other words, there is a bias towards the over-representation of working-class children by the system. While this may be to the 'advantage' of some children from those classes, it also seems to explain the overwhelming working-class composition of my sample of families who were complaining of unfair investigations and dispositions of abuse.

Nightingale and Walker (1986) studied the judgements made by workers on a childhood early education programme in the USA. Descriptions of the physical abuse of a child were varied in terms of factors such as social economic status and previous referrals by the child protection service. Families of higher social class with prior referrals for child abuse were judged as being more likely to result in successful interventions than families without such previous referrals or lower-status families, although many other comparisons showed no difference.

It might be argued that so far this account of prejudice and abuse interventions is a little abstract and relies on sweeping generalisations from statistical data. However, not too dissimilar conclusions have emerged in a study of child abuse case conferences observed by Higginson (1990), a manager in a social services department:

> My research into 40 case conferences indicated that when professionals assessed risk there were distortions of the evidence presented. In half the cases, minor risk was exaggerated or serious risk minimised. In the other half of the cases, the right decisions were taken, but often for the wrong reasons. Distortions were evident in all cases, but least marked when evidence was clear and strong . . . Information was ignored or distorted to support stereotypes of whether parents were the type of person likely to abuse children. There was a strong link between abuse and parents exhibiting deviancy against 'community values' (e.g. alcoholism, drug addiction, violence and criminality) . . . Parents thought to 'wilfully' transgress community values became the subject of heightened concern unwarranted by the evidence. Deviant behaviour became confused with abuse. (p. 20)

The problem is to know precisely how such prejudices and others are effected.

In this chapter some of the social processes which might unfairly draw families into the net of child protection have been examined. These have ranged fairly widely across broad areas of concern. The notion of false allegations is worrying because of the relatively constrained view which is applied to it. However, the subtext of the discussion essentially holds that false allegations are made by the general public and that practitioners are distanced from the issue in that sense. Of course, they may have to deal with the falsehoods. But the research concerning evidential procedures (like the anatomical doll-play situation) shows how the net of abuse can potentially be widened further by the inadequacies of knowledge and resources in this aspect of abuse work. The rhetoric which undermines serious questioning of what sorts of abuse should be acted upon risks leaving the net so fine that small fry are enmeshed. Certainly, the distinction between non-abuse and abuse can be very little in the case of non-accidental injuries. Finally, evidence that broad social characteristics of individuals (such as their race or their social class) may contribute to their involvement with child protection services should not be dismissed. While not all of these cases by any means will be errors, they reflect some of the biases which may lead to error processes.

Jervis (1988b) describes her experiences with a London child protection team concerned with sexual abuse. In doing so, she highlights some of the issues discussed in this chapter:

> By and large, [the social worker admitted] the received knowledge . . . is culled from research in the United States. It includes contentious statements such as 'children do not falsely report abuse' and 'a child's story must always be believed' . . . But then at other points [she] says . . . 'if the child retracts the story the worker should continue to express to the child their belief that the abuse happened.' Retraction, the guidelines state, may occur for a number of reasons, none of which appear to be that the abuse did not happen. I mention some of these apparent contradictions . . . to illustrate how confusing the current state of knowledge is on sexual abuse. How it is not easily reducible to coherent guidelines. (pp. 22–3)

CHAPTER 5

ABUSE AND THE NATURE OF SEXUALITY

There is another important reason for the current questioning of the long-held assumption of a preponderance of male sexual abusers of children in the fact that some mental health professionals and researchers are ideologically uncomfortable with the idea. Due to their discomfort, they may be overly eager to accept the possibility that it might not be true. (Russell, 1986, p. 312)

The notion of child abuse, both physical and sexual, carries messages about the nature of sexuality. No simple, single mechanism fully accounts for how this happens. However, throughout the extensive discourse on child abuse, gender plays an important part. Abuse is not an issue which can be seen as involving a dichotomy between parents and children alone. Parenthood needs breaking down into gendered categories – fathers and mothers. Similarly, children need to be seen as sons or daughters. Justification for such dichotomies may have something to do with the nature of abusers themselves, but it is more probably the result of hitching abuse to sexual politics. This is not only an issue of gender and power; it is also about the nature of sex and sexuality, masculinity and femininity. Common modern notions about masculinity and femininity underlie much of the debate.

This gendering of abuse is an old theme present in attempts to control incest and other forms of adult–child sex. For example, incest became an offence under criminal law as opposed to ecclesiastical law in Britain at the turn of the century. Queen Victoria disbelieved that a grandmother could have intercourse with her grandson. Consequently, such relationships were never brought under incest legislation. The gendered nature of abuse is clearly apparent in this familiar example. That it seems a somewhat silly situation rather than an outrage should itself give pause for thought.

The definition of incest in the Sexual Offences Act of 1956, according to Smith and Hogan (1983), is as follows:

It is an offence for a man to have sexual intercourse with a woman whom he knows to be his grand-daughter, daughter, sister or mother . . . It is an offence for a woman of the age of sixteen or over to permit a man whom she knows to be her grandfather, father, brother or son to have sexual intercourse with her by her consent. (p. 419)

This and Victoria's actions contain evidence of the assumption that the sexuality of women is different from that of men. That Victoria was also unable to support legislation against female homosexuality is a further indication of the traditional belief that 'sex crimes', other than prostitution, are the province of males and that female sexuality is a radically different affair.

The clearest modern equivalent to Victoria's reticence over deviant female sexuality has to be feminist writing about child abuse. Even the briefest review of this reveals strongly the view that abuse is endemic in male sexuality itself. Male sexuality, though, is seen not as some purely male eroticism but as the articulation of male power and patriarchy through the penis and otherwise. Male sexuality and male sexual violence overlap so considerably that ultimately they are virtually indistinguishable. Modern views about rape are central to this theorisation. Brownmiller (1975) claims:

Man's discovery that his genitalia could serve as a weapon to generate fear must rank as one of the most important discoveries of prehistoric times, along with the use of fire and the first crude stone axe. From prehistoric times to the present . . . rape has played a critical function. It is nothing more or less than a conscious process of intimidation by which *all men* keep *all women* in a state of fear. (p. 15)

This should not be seen as an overstatement, since it is a precise expression of the view that male sexuality is power and female sexuality as a consequence is powerlessness. Although it is a very big step to say that power in society translates relentlessly into individual sexuality, much of this feminist writing is a vast improvement on previous anodyne conceptions of rape as lust. So the feminist analysis seems to account well enough for the following sort of situation:

He had given me a good talk; he was a good con man and I was looking forward to having sex with him. I was horny and feeling neglected, and I love my sex. He took me outside and down an alley and threw me on the ground. I asked him what he was doing – told him he didn't have to do it there if all he wanted was a screw . . . I told him I wasn't a slut or whore that did it in an alley. It didn't matter . . . He started getting real mad. Then he said he was going to urinate on me . . . He rammed his fist up me twice and he bit my breasts. Then he stood up and piddled all over me and said, 'I feel better.' (Burgess and Holmstrom, 1979, p. 15)

Indeed, it is worth noting that so strong is this feminist notion of power as a virtual synonym for male sexuality that some rush to reject the view that rapists may be different in their sexuality from other men. For example, Chesney (1991), in a somewhat autobiographical account of his reading of research, writes:

> Rapists were compared with child molesters, heavy users of pornography and violent offenders. Never with the ordinary bloke in the street, research lab or psychotherapy clinic. It is very tempting to think of rapists as being somehow fundamentally different from the rest of us men . . . I began to feel that the way these research questions are being asked was in itself a defence against dealing with our own sexual aggression. We had to show that rapists were different or we might be confronted with our own hidden desires to dominate women sexually. But it seems to me that we shall make very slow progress in understanding rape if we cut ourselves off from exploring our own dynamics. (p. 3)

The rhetorical structure of this argument is fairly obvious, as are the devices it employs. Clearly anyone who does not subscribe to Chesney's views is labelled a rape-prone person, or someone who has patently failed to come to terms with the 'dark side' of his masculinity. Failing to toe Chesney's line is tantamount to a disclosure of personal inadequacy. While there is no doubt that a thorough examination of coercive sexuality cannot look only at convicted sex offenders (Howitt and Cumberbatch, 1990), Chesney goes too far by implying that to believe offenders are different is 'a defence against dealing with our own sexual aggression'. In other fields of research, superficially similar arguments have been made about the importance of recognising that racism is not merely associated with extreme bigots such as members of the National Front (cf. Howitt, 1991a). Everyone, professionals included, should be vigilant concerning possible unacceptable aspects to their thoughts and actions. But that is not the same as saying that there is something 'healthy' about individuals who accept this point of view and that those who do not subscribe are 'unhealthy'.

It is in such notions as Chesney's that we can gain further understanding of the way in which child abuse theory leads to damage and error in the child abuse system. There is nothing particularly original in Chesney's argument – perhaps its main contribution is in its patent crudity. Numerous writers have made the connection between 'normal male sexuality' and rape (Brownmiller, 1975; Burgess and Holmstrom, 1979; Burt, 1980; Russell, 1988). What is significant is that a practitioner of psychology such as Chesney reduces the theory into something tantamount to a formula. It is easier to think in terms of simplistic dichotomies and clear-cut generalisations. One should be careful not to assume that it is particularly useful to draw close parallels between rapists of adult women and sexual abusers of children. The point is about what theory does rather than what it says in this instance.

Bayer and Connors (1988) have their own way of expressing a related set of ideas:

> [T]ears, fears, vulnerability, and smallness are not appropriate for males. However, it is not human to deny all vulnerable feelings and needs or to be always powerful. We all feel sad, lonely, scared, needy, and weak at times. Consequently, men often face a dilemma: How can they be male and human at the same time? . . . Most abusers are men who were strongly affected by this socialization and some were victimized as children themselves. Their inability to live up to an impossible definition of maleness – being all powerful and in control at all times – causes them to attempt to gain feelings of control and power by abusing those less powerful. Abusers often express such feelings during therapy sessions by making such statements as 'I had been feeling so insignificant and powerless. But in that moment, when I took her sexually, I felt on top of the world – even though I felt guilty, too, I could be the man of the house.' (pp. 13–14)

Some male therapists dealing with abused children, however, well aware of such views about gender, recognise in them dilemmas for their own work (Frosh, 1987).

Two major issues will be discussed here concerning the social construction of child abuse:

1. Notions about the gender of offenders. More specifically, the belief that female perpetrators of abuse are rare can be seen as nothing other than a statement about the nature of femininity.
2. Beliefs about the effects of child abuse which essentially construct a view of the vulnerability of females which has widespread implications.

The very idea of female abusers

> A single mother indignantly informed the police of the sexual practices of her 9-year-old daughter. In the course of the investigation she explained to the social worker that in her country of origin some mothers regularly verified their daughter's virginity until puberty by introducing their fingers into the child's vagina. She herself had been the object of such verifications, and it was in verifying her daughter's virginity that she had realized what had transpired between her daughter and the neighbour whom she had previously trusted. 'But,' she added angrily, 'if he had to do that kind of thing, he should have done it with me.' (Criville, 1990, p. 125)

While theories may have the function of encouraging thought, sometimes they can serve to limit it. There is not necessarily anything in the theory itself which determines the nature of its influence. Like any other ideas about human nature, religious or otherwise, theories may be adopted for many reasons and put to many purposes. This is as true of feminist theories as any other. Feminist theories have gained wide attention – not simply in the political sphere but in terms of understanding a whole range of issues which more conventionally would have lacked overt 'political' aspects. Furthermore, and closer to the theme of this book, some child protection employees describe themselves as 'feminist social workers' and feel this to be enormously helpful to their professional work (Dominelli and MacLeod, 1989). Irrespective of the benefits which can emerge from such feminist orientations, feminism is no different from any other set of ideas in that it can be used to do something over and above what was originally intended.

The question of female abusers is not a very comfortable issue for feminist theory for a number of reasons. If one considers the research on domestic or family violence which became increasingly common in the 1970s and into the 1980s (Gelles, 1979; Gelles and Cornell, 1985; Pagelow, 1984), there is no question at all that the violence of men against their women partners was readily construed as mirroring their political and economic power. Indeed, it was one means of maintaining dominance. Violence and masculinity were ultimately intertwined in this revelation. The older ideology of male violence as biology's legacy was gone. Male violence was no longer to be understood as analogous to male animals posturing aggression for dominance over each other, as the ethologists of the 1960s had taught us (Howitt *et al.*, 1989), but men beating women for dominance over women. Violence was integral to family life, and extensive. 'The ways in which violence, or its threat, functions as an effective form of control of an individual woman, and, in turn, of women in general are very much the same as we have seen through rape' (Hill, 1982, p. 51).

That the family merely reproduced the broader social dominance of men, that violence within the family established the father's power, and that its extent was hidden for so long, among other things, were probably responsible for the view that gender was also at the root of the abuse of children. After all, it is a small step from saying that male sexuality is based on violence and domination of women to saying that similar processes underlie the abuse of children. But inconveniently such a view does not work particularly well in relation to most child abuse. It is a stark fact that much child abuse is perpetrated by women *not* men. This is certainly true for physical abuse and neglect, arguably the most common forms of abuse. The following examples illustrate this well enough:

1. In Corse *et al.* (1990) 69 per cent of cases involved the mother as the sole abuser and 16 per cent the father as the sole abuser.
2. Rosenthal's (1988) survey of a central register for Colorado between 1977 and 1984 showed that women were the perpetrators of 42 per cent of serious injury, 43 per cent of minor injury, 9 per cent of sexual abuse and 64 per cent of neglect. Overall, 47 per cent of perpetrators were women.
3. Gelles' (1979) survey of US families revealed that 68 per cent of mothers and 58 per cent of fathers had acted violently at least once in the previous year towards children. Virtually all classes of violence showed mothers to be the most frequent perpetrators. In terms of ever having done certain violent acts the distribution was as shown in Table 5.1.

Table 5.1: Proportion of US men and women perpetrating acts of violence towards children

	Women	Men
Threw something	11%	8%
Slapped/spanked	74%	68%
Hit with something	24%	16%

Source: Gelles (1979).

It is interesting to note the outcomes of studies of fatalities in physical child abuse – and neglect – discussed by Alfaro (1988). Nine separate studies were reviewed in a total of six different US states. Men are not always involved in deaths which involve women. The range was from 40 to 88 per cent, with an average of 62 per cent involving men. Quite clearly, although men are the most dangerous in terms of fatalities, one cannot dismiss women as innocents. Also of significance is the fact that those investigations which compared fatalities with non-fatal cases found that men were more responsible for fatalities. In Texas, for example, 65 per cent of fatalities versus 33 per cent of non-fatalities involved men. A New York study showed that 59 per cent of fatal but 25 per cent of non-fatal cases had a father or father substitute living in the home. Women, perhaps, can be described as less physically dangerous but more abusive in general.

Whatever can be said of such data, they hardly show that males characteristically dominate through violence directed at children. Of course, the data can be protested. For example, it might be said that it is typically the case that women are the primary child-rearers, and consequently they have greater opportunity to abuse. It is difficult to see how this 'contact' explanation salvages the 'masculinity equals violence' thesis. First, contact and not the need to dominate would be the primary determinant of child abuse by this explanation. Secondly, it already carries the built-in assumption that male and female violence are differently caused. The matter of neglect, of course, is rather less straightforward. To suggest that women are the main neglecters of children may beg the question why more women are put in the position of caregiver. Of course, desertion by the male partner, the economic underprivilege of women in single parent families and similar explanations may reflect broad social structures, so making the feminist point to this extent.

So an analysis of child physical abuse in terms similar to other forms of domestic violence including that towards adult women would not fare very well. Recently a number of pointers have suggested why it is inadequate. Particularly important is the evidence of the extent of violence within personal relationships, which is not incompatible with the data on women's violence against children. Recent survey evidence has begun to show that women's use of violence against men is common in dating relationships. For example, Riggs *et al.* (1990) surveyed students in New York. Nearly 39 per cent of females and 21 per cent of males reported some form of physical violence against their dating partners (see Table 5.2). There was a tendency for women who behaved aggressively to have aggressive personalities and problems with relationships. Men who were aggressive to their dates had a history of fighting and also had relationship problems.

Even where it has been possible to find evidence of female violence in the family abuse literature, there has been a tendency to interpret it as the consequence of or a response to male abuse (Gelles, 1979, Chapter 8, is a good example). Gelles and Cornell (1985), while acknowledging female violence against their spouses, claim 'when injury is considered, marital violence is primarily a problem of victimized women' (p. 80).

Recently the question of female violence has been raised somewhat

Table 5.2: Proportion of New York male and female students acting violently towards their partner

	Men	Women
Threw something	5.6%	15.0%
Pushed, grabbed or shoved	19.2%	29.6%
Slapped	8.0%	22.4%
Kicked, bit or hit with fist	5.6%	14.9%
Hit or tried to hit with something	4.8%	11.3%
Beat up	2.4%	2.5%
Threatened with a knife or gun	0.0%	0.4%

Source: Riggs *et al.* (1990).

acrimoniously in the psychological research literature. In response to Walker's (1989) paper, which Mills (1990) implies is a one-sided (feminist) view, Mould (1990) argues that the evidence suggests that *unilateral* domestic violence is roughly as common in women as in men. While it is possible, as Walker (1990) argues, that male violence is typically more extreme or dangerous than female violence, in the context of child abuse many of the injuries are relatively trivial, well within the physical abilities of most men and women – and even children. Perhaps partially as a consequence of these realisations, feminist attention in the area of child abuse has tended to concentrate on child sexual abuse. Here, apparently, was an arena in which the battles could be fought over the expression of male dominance without issues being clouded. Child sexual abuse seemed to match the feminist theory well. This was overwhelmingly what men were doing to girls – more or less.

Are there no female perpetrators of sexual abuse? Knowledge of the extent of such cases would seem to be vital in assessing the validity of the feminist view. The lack of such cases would lend support to the theory, their presence reducing its strength. The mere absence of known cases may not, in itself, be conclusive evidence. There are many reasons for this – we may not be too clear what sexual abuse by females consists of, and a number of things might contribute to the underreporting of offences by females. What is clear from the literature is that very little attention has been paid to the matter of female sexual abusers.

One of the few examples of discussions of female offenders is Rowan *et al.* (1990), who describe cases of female offenders among child molesters in America known to the judicial system and social service agencies. It has to be said that these were relatively rare, only one case in about sixty involving a female perpetrator. Working from their nine cases, it is note-worthy that only one case out of the nine involved a child other than the mother's own (in sharp contrast to the survey data, in which abuse by mothers was virtually unknown (cf. Russell, 1983)). In four of the cases, the women were acting alone; the remainder were cases of joint abuse, although not necessarily simultaneously. A fairly typical example of one of the cases is the following:

> Case 3. This 27-year-old woman was charged with performing fellatio on her two-year-old son. She was drinking and 'under the power of a being from another dimension who made me steal and do sexual things.' This woman was a college graduate with a previous sojourn into witchcraft and she had been in a cult for a year. She gave no history of sexual contact as a child and at the time of the evaluation was not psychotic. The diagnosis was borderline personality. (p. 81)

Her case was atypical, though, in that she had not suffered abuse herself – most of the women had. The impression created by this account is of something rather pathological, unlike 'normal' women. This may reflect the reality of the situation, the biases in the identification of women abusers, or any number of things.

Barwick (1991) reports how among some workers there is an increasing belief that women make up a substantial number of child sexual abusers. She quotes one worker: ' "I've had some feminists walk out of a talk when I have suggested that women also sexually abuse children", said one female therapist, who asked not to be named, "or I may never be allowed in another support group" ' (p. 8). A further comment reported by Barwick is worth quoting as it appears to set the current upper estimate of the amount of sexual abuse by females higher than anywhere else:

> 'When I started to work as a therapist in this field four years ago the first child I worked with had been abused by his mother,' said . . . a therapist. 'About 25 per cent of the hundreds of children I have worked with since that time have said a woman sexually assaulted them . . . It is no longer a surprise to me when children mention a woman as the assailant, but what is a surprise is that figure of 2 per cent [from surveys]. If that's true, the whole 2 per cent workload for the country is somehow ending up in my casebook.' (p. 9)

The whole question of what constitutes sexual abuse of children becomes inordinately complex when women as abusers appear on the agenda. Just what are abusive acts by women? Intercourse, genital fondling, oral sexual contact of either sort and digital anal penetration are clearly equivalent to the acts perpetrated by men. But what of much more specifically female possibilities? Take breast feeding, for instance. It clearly has a great many valued attributes for the welfare of the child, being targeted as an important part of positive health programmes. But at the same time, at least superficially, similarities exist with the sexual play which occurs as part of adult male–female intercourse. It is pleasurable and it can lead to orgasm – whether an adult or a baby is doing the sucking. So what of the mother who weans her child very late, for example? Is she a sexual abuser? She certainly is getting pleasure, sometimes to an extent which overlaps with her adult sexuality, so does this constitute abuse? It could be claimed that the longer than 'normal' period of breast feeding serves the mother's needs more than the child's. But also there is evidence that the extent of breast feeding might have an important bearing on the adult personality (Whiting and Child, 1953) which could easily be construed as damage. Should not an interventionist child sexual abuse policy deal with such matters? It would seem an appropriate, albeit rhetorical, question to ask. The following is a perplexing comment in this context:

The boy who says of his mother, 'She would grab my penis, pull and jerk and squeeze my testicles. She was weird,' did not appear to have been experiencing a sexual act on a psychological level, nor indeed did the son whose face was shoved into his mother's genital area or the son who charitably allowed his mother to have sex with him when she was drunk. In each instance, the son interpreted his mother's sexual need of him by a unique set of symbols depending on the context of their relationship and their shared history. (Margolin, 1986, p. 113)

But child sexual abuse theoreticians have contributed a lot to the construction of notions about child sexual abuse by women. Indeed, some of them go through the denial and redefining processes which are analogous to those which have been seen as evidence of Freud's denial of sexual abuse. A particularly good example is Finkelhor and Russell's (1984) discussion. Rather than seeking to expand awareness of the possibility of child sexual abuse by females in order to help protect children from such risks, instead they determinedly minimise the apparent likelihood of women's sexual abuse of children. Perhaps it is worth noting that Russell's work is steeped in the modern tradition of feminist critiques of male sexuality. Finkelhor and Russell (1984), although acknowledging some of the reasons why sexual abuse by women might go underreported, seemingly seek to show that child sexual abuse by women is *rarer* than the surveys suggest. Such an objective, keenly sought, may better be seen as another case of what theory *does* rather than what it explains.

The US National Incidence Study (1981) suggests that 46 per cent of cases of child sexual abuse included a *female* perpetrator. However, a reanalysis by Finkelhor and Russell of the data so as to exclude women who were listed as perpetrators but in reality were only aware of the abuse changed things. The percentage of female direct abusers fell to 13 per cent in the case of female victims and 24 per cent for males. Nevertheless, with nearly a quarter of the abuse of males being perpetrated by females, feminist theory of abuse is still on shaky ground. But, perhaps resourcefully, Finkelhor and Russell go on to suggest that:

the study did not clearly link perpetrators with the type of maltreatment they were guilty of. Thus, if in one family a mother neglected a child while a father sexually abused the child, both mother and father were listed as perpetrators . . . Possibly, some of the women who are included as perpetrators of sexual abuse were really only perpetrators of some other kind of maltreatment . . . [T]he study considered an adult caretaker to be an active perpetrator of sexual abuse if the adult provided 'inadequate or inappropriate supervision . . . of child's voluntary sexual activities' in a situation where a child was involved with a person at least two years older and where negative consequences ensued for the child. So here also, some mothers listed as active perpetrators may very well not be persons who engaged in sexual contact with the child. (p. 173)

One is almost required to believe that it is the males who were doing the abuse whereas the adult females were another sort of victim. While this may be true, there is no good evidence for it reported by Finkelhor and Russell (1984). Furthermore, it relies on a commonsense understanding that women are mere tools of male sexual abusers. Again this is not established and it could well be that the female is carrying out the sexual abuse, dominating the male accomplice in the offence. In other words, theories about gender underlie their interpretation: 'The nonsexist approach focuses on the mother as a victim in the family in which incest occurs, rather than as an offender herself' (McIntyre, 1981, p. 464).

Finkelhor and Russell then move on to consider studies based on self-report when they write of Russell's (1983, 1986) study. We have already discussed this in Chapter 3. But Russell posed only half of the question because she dealt only with female victims. Since Russell's survey did not involve male victims, it might be expected that the prevalence rates for female offending were on the low side. Partially as a consequence, the prevalence rates reported in the Russell study can be assumed to be low, with 4 per cent of females offending against females.

The final thrust of the argument is certainly not lost on Finkelhor and Russell, since the ultimate implication of their comments is acknowledged:

The fact that primarily men commit sexual abuse does have discomforting ideological implications . . . For some people the problem of sexual abuse might be an easier cause to promote if it was not entangled in 'gender politics.' . . . *But reality cannnot be twisted to suit any particular ideological or political need.* The solution to the widespread and destructive problem of child sexual abuse can be found only if we face the truth about it – a truth we believe to be well-documented by the evidence and well-fitted to our current understanding of sex roles and male and female sexuality. (pp. 184–5, emphasis added)

It would not be right to encourage the child protection system to chase the new hare of female abusers. A more modest objective is called for. That is to highlight further the basis of child protection activity in theory. What is intriguing is that to date so few clinicians have reported sexual abuse by females leading to psychological damage. This is much the same as in the case of sexual abuse by males until recently. Whether or not this is a matter of seek and find becomes unimportant compared with the notion that professionals are still not finding what is staring them in the face.

No longer writing with Russell, it is notable that Finkelhor just a few years later seems to abandon virtually all of his earlier arguments. In Finkelhor and Williams, (1988) the dismissive rhetoric is no longer applied to sexual abuse by females. In his study of sexual abuse in child care centres (basically set up to meet the child-minding needs of working mothers) there was extensive evidence which directly undermines feminist and other theorising. Although females were, as is typical, most common among these sex abuse victims, they were also the most frequent sexual abusers of children. At least 59 per cent of the abusers of the boys in the study who were known to have been sexually abused were female. The corresponding figure for girls was 50 per cent female abusers. If nowhere else, in the American child care setting much sexual abuse was determined by aspects of female sexuality, not just male sexuality. Although it should be mentioned that women far outnumbered men in terms of employment in child care settings, and men abused disproportionately to their numbers, it is as important to understand female sexuality in understanding abuse in institutional settings as it is to understand male sexuality. It should not be forgotten either that Kelley (1988) found that 64 per cent of perpetrators in ritualistic abuse cases were female.

It is something of an irony to read in Hobbs and Wynne's (1986) paper on buggery in child abuse, which was seminal in spreading among some doctors the belief that the anal reflex test could be used diagnostically and effectively, that six of their thirty-five cases involved a woman. In two cases, this was with a male partner and in one case with a female partner. Three others have women alone as perpetrators, but each of these is given a query by Hobbs and Wynne. This not only suggests the surprising frequency of women in these cases, but also undermines some arguments such as those of Campbell (1988) about the nature of the protest over the Cleveland child abuse scandal.

Female sexuality as porcelain

While male sexuality has traditionally been conceived as fragile and, for example, vulnerable to sexual deviations, this gospel has been reversed in the child sexual abuse literature. This has promoted the view of femininity as delicate and easily damaged. One could ask what strength there is in a feminine character which is damaged by a suggestive remark (Kelly, 1988; 1989). But, as we have seen, the essence of the way in which child sexual abuse is construed is precisely that – as causing personal damage irrespective of the nature of the abuse. The idea that adult–child sexual relationships may be beneficial is not allowed. Even in what circumstances harm is most likely to occur becomes a non-question to some – harm is if the victim feels harmed. While harm is possibly not the only outcome of adult–child sexual contacts, nevertheless it has other implications still.

Some writers seem to be overly keen to pose the matter of sexual abuse of young people as an issue concerning largely female victims. In other words, being a victim is the natural role of females rather than males. While this may or may not be so, it is hardly supported by the available survey evidence. Take the following passage from La Fontaine (1990):

> In our current stage of knowledge in Britain, it appears that girls are more vulnerable to sexual abuse than boys. The Channel Four survey showed 12 per cent of women were abused as girls but *only* 8 per cent of men reported their abuse as boys. (p. 84, emphasis added)

It seems unduly pedantic to view a difference of four percentage points as meaning much. After all, this is roughly 10 per cent of each sex who were abused as children.

How do girls respond to sexual abuse? Notice that the question is not simply one of the effects of abuse on the victim, but extends wider to issues such as *how they deal with* the abuse. There is a danger in the debate of creating a view of women and women's sexuality which is tantamount to an image of fragility, weakness, powerlessness and vulnerability. The more it is claimed that all forms of sexual abuse are damaging, the greater the expectation of damage. This reinforces the notion of femininity as porcelain and equates femininity with weakness. Intriguingly, some non-feminist researchers and writers present a rather more empowered view of femininity than do some polemical writers. For example, West (1985) in his work on sexual crime presents the results of a survey of women's responses to childhood sexual abuse. It clearly emerges that women's responses as girls tended to be robust and the problem seen as external to themselves. Asked about their long-term responses to their abusive experiences, the women gave the types of reply shown in Table 5.3 with the frequencies indicated.

Table 5.3: Long-term responses of women to childhood sexual abuse

Pity/amusement	71%
Anger	69%
Indifference, problem worked through	58%
Wary of men	53%
Guilt/disgust	49%
Regret	41%
Hatred/resentment towards adult	36%
Confused about sexual norms	32%
Anxiety for other children	24%
Emotional/sexual dysfunction	22%

Source: West (1985).

Although not extensive in its detail, the study grants a degree of understanding and strength in the girls which stands in marked contrast to other views of the sexual abuse of children in which abuse is equated only with damage. (A sample drawn from an American sexual abuse centre seems to have expressed more hostile views about the offence, although this may be a function of it being a selected sample rather than West's more general sample (Berliner and Conte, 1990).)

Compared with this, the views of writers who might be expected to wish to construct a view of girlhood as strength rather than weakness seem one-sided. It is very strange reading the literature to discover what some have seen as significantly harmful. Take, for example, the work of Kelly (1988), writing from a 'feminist perspective'. She extends the list of types of 'sexual abuse' damaging to girls very substantially. Her view that the girl's or woman's subjective experience of events as abusive should determine the definition of abuse is an essential step in her argument. Take the following example, which contains a remarkable slippage in logic. This results in an initial misleading impression which does not stand up to close examination. Kelly argues that 'minor' offences which some would dismiss as trivial can in fact be seriously damaging, flashing being a good example. She claims that even a single 'minor' act 'can have profound long term consequences' (p. 69). This argument she illustrates with a number of instances: 'My sister and I used to take the dog for a walk in the park – I didn't understand it at the time but this guy was exposing himself. I've got very dim memories but I do remember it was terrible' (p. 69).

However, Kelly confounds this example with others which are actually of an aggressive and/or degrading nature. In these cases it is not surprising that the consequences were not trivial, since the acts were not trivial. In one case a man *made* a 12-year-old girl 'feel him up', and in another a 13-year-old lay on the floor while the man ejaculated over her.

Kelly then takes some of the women's comments to highlight what she describes as 'a form of verbal sexual harassment specific to adolescent girls, practised by relatives and strangers, peers and adults'. Apparently the woman who discussed this in Kelly's research remembered 'the acute humiliation and embarrassment she felt at the time': 'It was when my breasts started growing and lots of my male relatives just would make comments about it in front of everyone else – it was really embarrassing. When I blushed they'd laugh and make another comment about that!' (p. 70). How acute humiliation is read into this example is difficult to see given the woman's precise words. Is it any different from comments about shaving or voice breaking made to boys? The attempt to see the individual's experience as the key element of abuse ultimately works as a rhetorical device to advance a theory of femininity as weakness and emotional vulnerability.

A study involving police officers, child protection workers and nurses attending an educational programme on abuse demonstrates the differentiation made between male and female characteristics and how abuse is perceived (Kelley, 1990). Participants in the research were given a written description of the sexual abuse of a child. This was described as 'extensive and involved fondling activity, oral intercourse, and (vaginal or rectal) penetration'. For some participants the child was described as male and for others as female. Assignments of responsibility and appropriate punishments, as if on a jury, were the main measurements taken. Significantly severer punishment was recommended when the victim was female rather than male, despite the situations being as similar as possible. It has already been explained why this might be so. However, it might be asked whether the results were an artefact of different attitudes towards anal and vaginal penetration. Abuse of girls may be seen as more serious because of the greater seriousness of vaginal intercourse, although this explanation clearly has gender-specific overtones which may not be warranted.

A study by Finkelhor and Redfield (1984) essentially dismisses this possibility. They created a large number of verbal descriptions of abuse that varied in terms of many factors, including the child's sex, the perpetrator's sex and the sex act involved. As several different acts were involved, the precise nature of the act did not come into the overall trends. Not surprisingly, intercourse was seen most often as abusive, while attempted intercourse and fondling of sex organs was a little less so, but verbal abuse on a sexual theme reduced the perceptions of abuse a lot. The adult–child relationships which were seen as most abusive were father–daughter, male relative–girl, male stranger–girl and older brother–boy. The least abusive were female neighbour–boy, older sister–girl and female stranger–boy. Furthermore, the male perpetrator–female victim combination was the most abusive, and the female perpetrator–female victim the least. These judgements were made largely irrespective of the nature of the sexual activity involved in the abuse. There are clearly many assumptions in the minds of people when they make their judgements.

None of this is to deny the harm that can be done by abuse or to condone it. My concern here is about assumptions that are built into practice and what beliefs are impressed on to practitioners that might encourage erring on the side of action where doubts may exist. The notion of *resilience* is worth some attention. For example, Farber and Egeland (1987) describe how a *few* of the children brought up in physically abusive families transcended this abuse in their psychological development. Even in such circumstances of continuous abuse, there is nothing inevitable about damage. Clearly the response to abuse is a somewhat more complex one than is sometimes presented, with more options than automatic harm. It then becomes a more open question what types of effect might be the outcome of the one-off incident typical of much abuse.

Almost as a footnote to this, Pierce and Pierce's (1985) finding that boy victims of abuse spend *less* time in therapy than girls should be mentioned. The reason for this may lie in professional attitudes, but we just do not know.

> [T]he social work establishment may unfortunately feel the need to reject out of hand some logical conclusions drawn from the evidence: that all men have some potential to sexually abuse and 'the family' can provide a con-genial setting within which this horror can occur. Already the writing is on the wall and we need to recognise that the losers in any future political cover-up of sexual abuse will be the children. (Kidd and Pringle, 1988, p. 15)

One cannot pretend to be able to quantify the influence of the ideas discussed in this chapter on child protection errors, let alone their in-fluence on practice in general. Wherever possible, evidence which links practice and judgements to the ideas of gender which are inherent in theories of abuse has been mentioned. But, of course, detailed know-ledge of precisely how individual decisions have been affected in specific cases is impossible without very intensive studies of the beliefs and decision-making practices of individuals.

Kitzinger (1990) latches on to a similar theme when she questions the notion of the 'passive' victim, images of which she sees adorning pub-lications on child abuse among other representations. The passivity belies what might happen:

> Victimized children also plead and bargain with their abusers or try to repel them by making themselves 'unattractive' – strapping down developing breasts, cutting off their hair, or hiding inside an armour of bulky jumpers in all weathers. Samantha refused to wash, deliberately making herself physically disgusting: 'I told myself that if I was dirty and smelly no one would want to have sex with me.' (p. 164)

Perhaps more attention should be paid to calls for non-sexist social work (Gardner, 1987).

CHAPTER 6

THEORIES OF ERROR

'You have to look at the history of investigation,' says Dr Zeitlin. 'Twenty years ago we weren't looking for sexual abuse and would only do so if it was obvious. It meant the majority of sexual abuse would be missed. Consequently there was a very high likelihood that if it was suspected, it had occurred. As the medical evidence in these cases was overwhelming, the term 'disclosure interview' was merely a corollary to the diagnosis. But then concern about sex abuse grew. Child abuse had become a major focus of child health, taking the place of many of the infectious diseases which had held medical attention in the early part of the century. And once concern was raised, more sophisticated techniques of detection needed to be devised.' (Jervis, 1991b, pp. 27–8)

It is one thing to claim that the very way in which the public debate about abuse is constructed crucially affects how child abuse is dealt with. On the other hand, it is far from certain that this is sufficient to explain all of the problem cases where things go disastrously wrong and which are publicised on a national and international scale. Nor does it deal with the many private tragedies which occur to families. Quite clearly, there are reasons why families become involved in child protection processes – their addresses are not drawn out of a hat to be investigated at random by child protection services. Naturally the explanation of erroneous involvement with child protection systems has to include some understanding of how cases are brought to the attention of such agencies.

Based on my experience, it would seem that there is a fairly good reason why *initially* child protection services should have become involved with all or virtually all of the families involved in error. There was almost invariably a prima-facie case warranting concern and investigation, although sometimes a very trivial one. No doubt this is a sentiment which the families themselves would share more or less unanimously. The problem lies not so much in the investigation itself (though stressful and potentially wasteful of resources), but in a sequence of events which can lead to injustice. It is these processes which should be the vital aspect of any theory of child protection errors. Of course, this is not to ignore malicious or vexatious accusations by a neighbour, ex-partner, family or other people which naturally lead to investigations for child abuse. But these cannot usually be construed as the cause of child protection errors in themselves. False accusations might lead to time-wasting investigations, but the system's treatment of such reports forms the basis of true child protection errors.

Requirements of a theory of error

Any theory of child abuse errors ought to be able to do the following:

1. Account for broad ideological and political influences.
2. Account for the influence of organisational structures.
3. Account for the beliefs and professional practices of child protection workers.
4. Account for situational factors in presenting 'symptoms' of the situation which contribute to errors.
5. Explain the dynamic and process-linked factors leading to errors.

Doubtless it would be a major task to achieve any of these things satisfactorily and an immense undertaking to present a comprehensive theory dealing with them all. With matters of social injustice, there is a need not to wait until the final morsel of information arrives before acting. As a consequence, all the theories of professional error in child protection are rather piecemeal. Much of this theory comes not from the professional literature or from investigations by researchers in psychology, social policy or social science, but from rather different sources as we shall see.

Bureaucratic theory

Not surprisingly, most of the notable cases brought to the attention of the public concerning errors in child protection are associated with legal or public inquiries of one sort or another. A good example of the bureaucratic approach is the Department of Health and Social Security (1982) document *Child Abuse: A study of inquiry reports 1973–1981*. This is essentially based on a review of twenty reports concerning child abuse cases which in some way had been problematic. It presents a summary of some of the main points recommended by inquiries. For example:

> [W]orkers who might encounter child abuse must have the special knowledge, skills and experience to be able to recognise when it is taking place, or is likely to take place . . .

[A] major characteristic of many cases is the failure to bring together all available information and to use it in a structured objective way, by carrying out full psycho-social and medical assessments. These require continuous re-examination and revision. The need for health monitoring is important, particularly in cases of neglect. (p. 69)

While there is little in such recommendations to object to, it is a rather different matter to assume that the availability of guidelines guarantees that they will be followed. The controversy around the satanic sexual abuse intervention at Rochdale in northern England partly concerned the failure of social workers there to follow the guidelines laid down by a government ministry. Furthermore, one cannot guarantee that the use of bureaucratic principles will not itself enable further abuse of the family. For example, the Butler-Sloss (1988) report promoted the following as a 'matter for further thought and wider discussion':

> With the emphasis we place on the need to avoid the necessity of removing a child from home, Social Services Departments should consider the appropriateness of using their powers . . . designed to prevent the reception of a child into care, to defray for a limited period additional costs incurred by the suspected abuser in leaving home on a temporary basis while initial assessment is completed. (p. 254)

There is potential for varying the emphasis of such a comment in order to carry out its 'letter' but at the same time to leave the 'suspected abuser' to carry the burden. If the 'suspected abuser' is out of the family home then the urgency to deal with the case is reduced. The 'needs' of the child, as bureaucratically defined, have been served irrespective of the harm to the family as a whole:

> Innocent fathers accused of child sex abuse are being forced out of their homes by social workers because of new procedures . . . The new technique is known as 'ousting'. But it clearly goes further than was recommended by the Butler-Sloss inquiry into the Cleveland scandal as an alternative to taking children into care . . . An accountant was forced to live apart from his wife and two children after a child psychiatrist accused him of abusing his three-year-old daughter. The allegation was first made by a playgroup leader who believed the girl showed evidence of abuse in drawings and conversation . . . The father was given an ultimatum: 'I was told that if I didn't move out the child would be taken away and fostered.' (*Sunday Times*, 8 July 1990, p. 4)

The father, who incidentally was eventually cleared by the High Court of the accusation of abuse, was presumably seen as very much the guilty party warranting any privation.

It would be the wildest guess to estimate the extent to which professionals ignore or bend rules, regulations, procedures, guidelines and the like in their professional activities. Such behaviour seems not uncommon as far as can be judged from notable public inquiries concerning child abuse. This applies not only to recent examples such as the Rochdale satanic abuse case but to some earlier ones. We know that it happens sometimes, but why, how frequently and in what circumstances would be speculation. Knowledge of the extent of such things is clearly of great importance if the 'bureaucratic' approach to explaining and preventing errors is to be evaluated. What makes professionals deviate from the requirements of their employers and the government needs to be tackled – but by and large it has not been.

Rather than leave this matter at the level of anecdotes, it is possible to glean at least a little insight from American studies of mandatory reporters. Zellman (1990) describes how, in the USA, many groups of professionals are required by law to report suspected child abuse and neglect to appropriate child protection agencies. This sort of legislation takes away impediments to reporting suspected abuse. These laws may involve statutory immunity from legal action if the report was made in good faith, removing the privileged status of information concerning abuse gathered in doctor–patient and therapist–client relationships, sometimes allowing the anonymity of the reporters, and the imposition of legal penalties in many states for the failure to report. So, in a sense, there is nothing more bureaucratic than such legal requirements to report.

The USA is not alone in the imposition of mandatory reporting. The situation in Britain is different, of course, but it should not be overlooked that the major agencies such as social services, the police and the medical profession are required to share information and have joint meetings. Furthermore, some organisations such as educational authorities may require reporting as a condition of service. Mandatory reporting research is primarily important here because of its bearing on the question of rule following.

Zellman presents data from an American national survey of general and family practitioners, paediatricians, child psychiatrists, clinical psychologists and social workers. The study concerned failures to report suspected cases of abuse. The most common reason for failing to report was the belief that insufficient evidence of the abuse was available. A full 60 per cent justified their inaction in this way. Whether or not one believes this to be a sensible decision by the practitioners, it underlies a failure to adhere to the intent and requirements of the law.

There were a number of other reasons for non-reporting which cannot be justified so easily as preventing the waste of agency time and resources. For example, 8 per cent of these mandated reporters claimed that the child protection services overreacted on reports of suspected abuse, 16 per cent justified their non-reporting by claiming that the available child protection services were of a poor quality, 19 per cent felt that they were better able to provide help for the child themselves, and 24 per cent explained that treatment was already being given so reporting was not necessary. Nineteen per cent claimed that to report the abuse would risk the disruption of therapy. Zellman writes of her data:

> The data strongly suggest that most mandated reporters are aware of and accept their responsibility to report suspected abuse and neglect. Failure to report most often occurs when the would-be reporter is uncertain about whether the incident is reportable or when he or she believes that a report will stymie an important goal of reporting: help for the child and the family. Any efforts to increase compliance with the reporting laws should focus on these uncertainties and concerns. (p. 21)

Whether this is a reasonable state of affairs depends to some extent on one's viewpoint.

One should not carelessly drift into the supposition that non-reporting was simply the act of individual professionals. A further report concerning data from the above study (Zellman and Antler, 1990) makes this more than untenable:

> Interviews with agency administrators and mandated reporters suggest that virtually all agencies have raised the threshold of severity for accepting a protective case . . . In some states, screening techniques and models are clear and widely known . . . In others, [Child Protection Service] officials believe that such approaches violate state law of the agency's mission and therefore do such screening 'informally.' In one agency, for example, the age of the child, type of alleged abuse, and type of injury are assessed in the course of a telephone report. Cases are rated urgent, high priority, or low priority on the basis of these characteristics, but all are slated for eventual investigation. The press of more serious calls often result in failure to ever respond to the lowest-ranked cases, however. (p. 32)

There is no intention to argue that failure to report is the consequence of laziness, incompetence, lack of caring or any other such factors. The point is merely that it happens, often for reasons which at some levels appear laudable:

> [A] report introduces new stresses to an often marginal family. Since mental health providers must violate the patient's privacy in order to report, it can seriously undermine or end a therapeutic relationship. Undesirable consequences may also beset the mandated reporter, who often must confront the family's anger and possibly lose a patient or client. (p. 34)

Ultimately, not only do the professionals in Zellman and Antler's study break rules for reasons they probably consider proper, but the researchers virtually invite us to condone that improper behaviour on the basis of its reasonableness. In other circumstances, good intentions may encourage the breaking of other rules or guidelines because this is felt to be in the best interests of the child. Sometimes, these will be embarrassing, public social work scandals.

Kalichman *et al.* (1990) also carried out a study of adherence to mandatory child abuse reporting laws, although they looked at a rather different set of factors and used a vignette approach which varied systematically the circumstances surrounding the abuse. Licensed clinical, counselling and school psychologists completed one of several different versions of a questionnaire. Scenarios portrayed an instance of child sexual abuse in which the child was described as either male or female, and the father admitted or denied the abuse. The vignette read:

> In an individual session, (Andy/Amy) tells you that (he/she) thinks (his/her) father should not be touching (him/her) in certain places. After telling you that this has happened more than once, (Andy/Amy) becomes quiet and refuses to say anything further . . . In the next family session, you bring up the incident described by (Andy/Amy), asking the father to respond. The father sits quietly for a moment, after which (he gets very tearful and upset. Looking down and in a quiet voice he states that what the child has said is true. He realises that he has a problem and wants to change. He then states that he is willing to work on this issue in therapy/ [or in the alternative version the description ends] he becomes indignant and states that he has no idea what the child is referring to and that he believes it is just another way for the child to get attention. He says he thinks therapy needs to return to the real issue, the child's behavior problems in school). (p. 72)

The most significant finding of this research was that 24 per cent of the mandated reporters claimed that they would not report this example of child abuse. (Also noteworthy is the fact that a close examination suggests denial made no difference to judgements of responsibility.)

Errors out of witch-hunt

Stewart Bell, the Labour Member of Parliament, accounted for the events in the Cleveland sexual abuse scandal by analogy to what happened to the 'witches' of Salem, Massachusetts. In 1692 nineteen citizens were hanged – not because they were witches but because they refused to confess to witchcraft. A sort of mass hysteria broke out among schoolgirls, sometimes involving fits, and one girl even 'saw' spectral yellow birds during a church service. The hunt for the witches who had induced such behaviour was extreme:

> The evidence against the so-called witches was spectacular, and, in the first instance, consisted of the touch test. This involved stripping the accused and searching for devil marks, examining minutely by running pins through

any abnormality that was found. In the case of Bridget Bishop, they discovered 'a witch's tet' between 'ye pudendum and anus' and it did not matter that, after her trial, a second investigation revealed that the 'tet' had withered to dry skin. (Bell, 1988, p. 5)

In Bell's account, there are a number of parallels between the events in Salem and those in Cleveland, where numerous place of safety orders were taken out to allow children to be removed from their families by child protection workers. Just as in Salem, the new 'witch-hunt' was achieved through the courts. Of course, there were differences. The witches of Salem revealed their satanic association around their anuses – a simple and sure test of witchery. It was different in Cleveland. There the work of the devil was revealed by the anuses of the *victims* of alleged child abusers. A simple touching of the anus by a doctor would show a characteristic response which signalled child sexual abuse. That such an anal reflex test was diagnostically invalid parallels the witch's 'tet'. But the response of many of the community to the test led to a massive and extreme situation which ended in a major public crisis for child protection.

The parallels drawn by Bell between the two witch-hunts do strike a chord. However, drawing parallels between such situations scarcely explains why such witch-hunts occur in the first place. Inevitably, because such events are not seen as a developing process, there is a tendency to blame individuals for what happened. Thus the diagnosing doctors and the intervening social workers became the focus of attention. By placing the problem with individuals one comes to neglect why these individuals came to think and act as they did. Incompetence, maliciousness and the like are descriptive traits which further blame the individual concerned. But, of course, the central actors in the Cleveland scandal had learnt their lessons extremely well rather than being failures of the system. They adopted a medical diagnosis approach which reflected both their medical training and the 'scientific' nature of child protection. A second problem with 'personal-blame' models is their failure to explain how the actions of individual doctors could have such far-reaching repercussions. Why did not all the social workers or other personnel simply refuse to accept the doctors' diagnoses? After all, some, including the police, refused to accept them. Bell's explanation is essentially ahistorical, despite the historical parallel. Cleveland could not have happened in 1936 or 1961 or at any other historical period than now. A third problem is that similar errors are made by professionals well away from the influence of the doctors in Cleveland.

Parton's (1981; 1985) account of moral panics supplies much of the historical and ideological backdrop which Bell's account omits. As such, one might consider that there is some support for Bell's views. Unfortunately, of course, the mere notion of a moral panic does not in itself account for this sort of child protection disaster. Further elements have to be introduced. One aspect of the theory of moral panics is the imposition of categories of 'good' and 'bad', which facilitates overresponse to events by stressing the urgency of doing something about the 'bad'. In other words, moral panics are facilitated if right and wrong are simplified into a bifurcated structure.

Errors from ideology

One perspective on child protection errors suggests that what may be construed as error is merely the consequence of applying faulted ideologies. From this viewpoint, there has not been an error as such. This notion underlies Pride's (1987) vitriolic attack on what she terms the 'child abuse industry'. It is important to note that Pride's viewpoint is a fundamentalist Christian one, which contributes greatly to the tone of her comments. More importantly, it encourages her to see the issue as one largely of ideology-cum-morality. In Pride's view, child protection is not all it appears to be. Child protection activity is anything but. Rather it is anti-family and, therefore, anti-child zealotry. Taking this basic notion, she converts it into a set of principles or doctrines which determine child protection activities. Errors, in Pride's account, are the consequences of the profession's anti-family ideology. So the anti-abuse sentiment disguises an anti-child practice. A number of doctrines serve this anti-family ideology. These are 'scientised' principles since they are generally held to have emerged out of scientific investigations. Pride claims that there are five major doctrines in child protection:

1. Underreporting. This assumes that there is a plague of child abuse which is hidden in the sense that it is not reported.
2. Underinvestigation. Given that there are numerous unsubstantiated cases of child abuse, one might be tempted to assume that these provide evidence against the child abuse epidemic. However, the doctrine of underinvestigation defines such cases as ones in which insufficient resources were available to investigate them properly, so abuse goes undetected.
3. Blame-the-parents. Irrespective of their knowledge or consent, anything which happens to the child should be blamed on the parents. An example is a mother who reported an extended family member's abuse of her daughter when the child visited her grandmother. Social workers intended to call a case conference to consider placing the child on the at-risk register.

4. Total depravity. This suggests that all families are depraved and abusive, which leads to assumptions about the legitimacy of all state interventions. Pride cites a 'prominent' textbook for social workers which states: 'Most parents at some time have abused or neglected their child or a child who was entrusted in their care' (p. 44).
5. The immaculate confession. This is simply the belief in the word of the child – so long as it says what you want to hear. Since the belief is in the depravity of the family, child protection only believes children when they accuse their parents of abuse.

In Pride's formulation, all of these are involved in the smokescreen disguising anti-child attitudes. Thus one might consider it no coincidence that the growth of child protection work is contemporaneous with the acceptance of legalised abortion, the growth of pornography, the growth of divorce and the 'abandonment' of the family to career. All of these would fit Pride's formulation of the anti-child ideology. Concern about children, in such an account, is something of a sham, a game of caring which does little that is genuinely child centred. It allows the expression of pro-child sentiments upfront of a hidden but more ominous agenda.

Despite the frequent feverish pitch to Pride's argument, it should not be too easily dismissed as worthless. For one thing, it does latch on to a number of issues. At the same time, it has a tendency to be descriptive rather than explanatory. Some of her themes relate to matters we have discussed, such as claims about the incidence of abuse. What Pride allows us to do, perhaps, is to understand how child protection work seems both child centred and harmful at one and the same time.

Cognitive theory of error

It is an interesting proposition to regard errors in professional practice as arising out of the nature of all human thought itself. In other words, thinking is the problem rather than what is thought about. It should be stressed that this is not a suggestion that some individuals have poor thinking capacity and that this leads to errors. Cognitive explanations of errors are not specific to individuals as such. The clearest exposition of the tenets of cognitive theories of error emerges in Evans (1989a and b). The decision making of 'experts' has a number of features which might be understood as 'error proneness'. These include:

1. 'Pseudodiagnosticity'. This notion, taken from Doherty *et al.* (1979), essentially deals with a logical fallacy in which what may be true in a limited sense is grossly overextended. Thus, the doctors in Cleveland

believed that anal abuse led to a positive outcome on the anal reflex test. This is then reversed to assume that a positive outcome on the anal reflex test was a good sign of anal abuse.

2. Diagnosticity of signs. This is the assumption that, for example, the anal reflex test can be used to diagnose abuse since a positive response is common in abused children. However, the diagnosticity of the sign is really dependent on how common it is in non-abused children. Thus if 50 per cent of abused children prove positive on the test but the same proportion of non-abused children do also, then the test has no diagnostic value at all.

3. Metacognition. This is the broad overview that we all have of our own thought processes. This includes our cognitions about the likelihood that we might be wrong. It has been shown by research that people tend to be systematically overconfident in their own correctness. In other words, we tend to trust our own judgements despite the frequency with which we make errors.

Error as a process

One of the few attempts to discuss child abuse errors from a broadly social scientific and research base is to view error as a process, rather than an event (Howitt, 1990b). Basically the argument is that things go wrong because of a number of error-promoting processes in the system. The starting point is that error processes and normal processes do not differ very much if at all. As such, one needs to be extremely careful not to assume that there is something significantly different about interventions in which things go wrong. Obviously there may be differences, but error could easily be eliminated if these had clearly identifying characteristics.

My work stresses that it is vital not to assume that errors are simply diagnostic errors (Howitt, 1990b). It is tempting to think that the problem is that the means of identifying child abuse are simply not reliable enough predictors, thus allowing false diagnoses. If this were the case then it would follow that improvements to diagnostic criteria would help prevent errors. This view certainly seems to influence attempts to improve the adequacy of children's testimony, for example. But unfortunately, things are not as simple as that from the process perspective. This will become clearer when some case studies have been examined in the next two chapters. I suggest three principles to describe how things sometimes go wrong:

1. Templating.
2. Justificatory theorising.
3. Ratcheting.

It has to be stressed that there is no reason to believe that these occur only in disputed cases. Indeed, it is suggested that their cruciality in normal practice provides the very means of such activities appearing uncontroversial and valid in the eyes of practitioners.

What do these three explanatory processes mean?

Templating This might in some ways be perceived as much the same as stereotyping. However, there is a fundamental difference in that stereotyping involves the attribution of characteristics to individuals because of a broad category of people they fit. To attribute the characteristic 'bad driver' to a person because she fits the category 'woman' is a good example. Templating, on the other hand, involves checking the individual against a 'social template' to see whether or not he or she fits a particular pattern. So, despite the frequently voiced warning that abuse happens in all sectors of society, part of the template of the child abuser is being a stepparent. An instigating event (such as a bruise or scratch detected on a child by a health visitor) leads to the 'suspect' person being compared with the template. All the families involved in my research (Howitt, 1990b), with possibly one exception, were working-class, single-parent, stepparent, unemployed, unmarried, or young, or combinations of all of these things. Many of these are the typical demographic predictors of abusing families. The distinction between templating and stereotyping is important because the former is part of building a picture rather than a crude expression of a prejudice. The latter probably would be very obvious to the worker him or herself and likely to be rejected.

Justificatory theorising This is built on the view that child protection activities are led by theory not simply explained by it. Although it might be argued that templating ultimately depends on empirical evidence gleaned from personal experience or research, many child protection errors are dependent on theoretical understanding which justifies particular decisions or plans for action. A classic example of this is what might be termed 'contrition' theory (Howitt, 1990b). This states that, in order for a family or a family member to be 'treatable' (i.e. 'they can be worked with' in the language of professionals), evidence has to be provided that the implications of what has happened are understood and the responsibility admitted. Without this evidence the individual or family is deemed 'not workable with'. This substantially increases the risk that the family and child will be or remain separated. The most poignant thing about this is that, for the family in which abuse has *not* occurred, a truthful denial is no different in its outcome from denying abuse when in reality it did occur. For reasons best known to themselves, some families prefer to risk losing their children despite believing that, if they lie and admit responsibility falsely, their family is much more likely to remain intact.

Ratcheting   This also refers very clearly to a process. It describes a tendency for the child protection processes to move in a single direction. Unwinding, undoing or going back on a decision seems very infrequent (if not unknown), even in circumstances where these might seem appropriate. This is characteristic of some of the cases which have achieved great public notoriety. More mundane examples of this process at work are reflected in the difference between *taking-into-care* and *coming-out-of-care* decisions. It might be commonsensical to assume that the factors which lead to children being returned to their homes are simply the reverse of those which led the child into care initially. For example, a troublesome child may enter care ostensibly to provide respite for the parents. However, when they feel able to cope this may not signal the child's return home. Criteria may be introduced to govern coming-out-of-care decisions that have little resemblance to the taking-into-care criteria. Ratcheting has a 'never going back' quality which may help protect the professional within the organisation by reducing the chances of taking a 'risky' decision which leads to further problems and criticism.

While this is not a complete theory of errors by any means, the above processes help organise and make sense of many of the cases studied in the research. However, the processes need not be independent of each other as the following case study makes evident.

A case study

Mrs Fletcher at the time of the interview was 29 years, her husband 32 years and her son 5 years. Since the time of the alleged abuse, the couple have had a baby son, just a few months old. The key events began two years previously, shortly after the family had moved into a new home. Two key facts should be mentioned. First, the boy, Stuart, was from a previous relationship of Mrs Fletcher – so Mr Fletcher was his stepfather. Already some key information relevant to templating has emerged – this was a single-parent family into which a step-relationship was introduced. Secondly, the couple were married about five weeks before the precipitating incident took place.

   Stuart (then 3 years) was in bed as it was about 10.30 at night. According to his mother, he got up to go to the toilet. Climbing over a safety gate at the top of the stairs, his foot caught and he fell down the steps. The parents were alerted by his call and picked him up. They found a friction or carpet-burn graze on one side of his knee. However, the next morning he complained of having a 'headache' (he called it 'a tummy ache in his head'). Concerned about the possibility of concussion, Mrs Fletcher examined him further but could only find in addition 'two tiny little bruises on his rib cage'. On telephoning her doctor, it was suggested that she should visit his surgery. Coincidentally, the health visitor arrived (Mrs Fletcher was pregnant) and drove them there.

> So we got there and he examined Stuart . . . [H]e said to Stuart how have you done this? And Stuart said I fell down the stairs last night because I climbed over the safety gate and I was naughty, you know . . . and then the doctor said to him has your mummy hit you? And Stuart said no. And he said has your daddy hit you? And Stuart said no . . . and he said I'm very sorry to say this but I think either you or your husband has abused your son, in other words you've hit him: what have you got to say? And I said well that's just ridiculous. I mean this was my family doctor, who'd known me since I was born myself.

She was asked by her doctor to take Stuart to see a hospital paediatrician, whose views were that 'this is just a waste of time' since the injuries and the story were perfectly consistent and that 'there is no evidence in my opinion that this child has been abused at all'. Mrs Fletcher was told to go home:

> at which point there was a knock at the door and a nurse said could she have a word with the paediatrician . . . So he went out, he was gone for 5 minutes, and he came back in. And he said I'm very sorry Mrs Fletcher, but your doctor has rung the social services and informed them that he thinks that the child is at risk, and a social worker was there at the hospital . . . In the space of two hours, this was, social services have been to a magistrate and they've taken a place of safety order, just on the say-so of my doctor.

Notice that the ratcheting process has begun. The general practitioner and the paediatrician disagree fundamentally as to the interpretation of the child's injury. The process of child protection has started and cannot be stopped, let alone undone, by the evidence of the paediatrician. Not only does the no-abuse opinion from a more senior medic carry little weight now compared to the other opinion claiming abuse offered by the general practitioner. The child's account also seems to be dismissed. According to Mrs Fletcher, the social workers' view was 'we don't think these injuries are explained'.

In the meantime, the police arrived at the hospital to interview her. Mrs Fletcher's parents also got there after being telephoned. Eventually her husband also reached the hospital:

> So he came down to the hospital, and as he came into the corridor he met
> with my mum and dad, and he said what's the matter, he thought something
> dreadful was wrong. And me mum said 'Oh well they're saying that some-
> body, that either you or Susan have abused Stuart, that you've hit him.' So
> he said 'Well that's ridiculous, he fell down the stairs'. At which point two
> police officers came either side of him and arrested him.

The events at the police station were even more disturbing:

> They said your wife doesn't want anything to do with you so you might as
> well tell us the truth, because she knows you've been hitting your son and
> she's just totally disgusted with you, in fact you're probably never going to
> see her again . . . And when I rang the station at half past ten and I was told
> that he'd admitted to it, he hadn't admitted to it at all.

The following example of justificatory theorising is important and
cannot merely be seen as a ploy on the part of the police. It is a theory of
why the husband should have abused the child. Notice how much more it
is than just an empirically established relationship between stepparent-
hood and abuse. The police view is a theory of why a stepfather should
physically abuse his stepchild:

> They also tried a tactic which sounds pretty disgusting but I have to say it,
> . . . this policeman sat by him and tried to be pally with him and gave him a
> cigarette, and he said I can't say as I blame you mate, he said because after
> all he's not yours is he. And me husband said well no he's not mine but,
> you know, I think of him as my son. And he said imagine that, he said,
> somebody's been with your wife before you, he said, how does that make
> you feel? He said I bet you hate that child.

In this instant, the templating process permits the emergence of a
justificatory theory which is then used as part of a persuasive technique.
This is not uncommon. There is no sense in which justificatory theorisation can be seen as an abstraction – it is used by child protection workers
in discussions with families involved in abuse investigations.

While the father was not prosecuted, their story had a long way to go.
Within a few days, Mrs Fletcher miscarried and she attributes this to the
child abuse allegations. She claims no prior or later miscarriages. Within
four weeks of the intervention a court application for an interim care
order failed because of a lack of evidence, but a two-week adjournment
was granted. In the end, no substantial evidence was provided, but
justificatory theorising nevertheless emerged in the case made on behalf
of social services to the court:

> All they said was we've visited Mr and Mrs Fletcher in their home and we
> feel because the father is not the natural father, we believe that he, the son,
> is at risk from the stepfather, because he isn't the natural father, . . . they're

a new family, they've only just been married, they've only just moved into this house, and we feel that the son is at risk and should remain on the at risk register . . . and that they should have this care order.

Evidently 'risk indicators' were being employed to justify what 'diagnostic signs' could not support.

But these parents, by appearing in court, had reached a position often not reached by others. The court refused to give a care order and, in the interviewee's view, 'they [the court] actually gave the social services quite a severe ticking off'. This was construed by the family as evidence of its innocence. Many families do not have the opportunity to put the case before a court. Typically, because cases of abuse have to be reported to the police, the outcome of the police investigation is seen as part of the process of achieving a sense of justice. The decision of the police not to prosecute is seen as validation of innocence. The family was also fortunate in that both partners were together when the precipitating incident occurred. The residue of suspicion that can otherwise be left may be extremely painful.

Achieving a sense of justice is not an easy matter. Stuart was kept on the child protection register by social services. This is hardly a neutral thing – Mrs Fletcher had to cease involvement with a playgroup of which she had been a committee member for several years because of Stuart's name being on the at-risk register.

All of this is part of a ratcheting process whatever the original justification for being concerned about the child. In this case, the only known professional concern about the child was based on six injuries during the period of being on the at-risk register. However, these clearly must have been reconstrued by the social services in a rather novel way, since they had happened at the local social services day nursery and had been recorded as such in its records. In other words, it could be argued that the child was being kept on the register because of injuries which could be attributed to the social services department's negligence.

Eventually, the boy's name was removed from the at-risk register. This Mrs Fletcher saw as being the consequence of the threat of a judicial review of the case. Even this was not the end of the story. All through the period of being on the at-risk register, Mr Fletcher's children from a previous marriage had visited for overnight stays. After the removal from the at-risk register:

> my husband's ex-wife was contacted by the social services where she lives. . .
> she had this note saying would she please telephone this particular social
> worker . . . So she went along and the social worker told her that her ex-
> husband had been accused of child abuse, and that in his opinion he didn't
> think that the children should be allowed to come down here and see their
> father unless it was in the presence of their grandmother, like my husband's
> mother.

There is a surprise coda to this. One of the problems of this case is to explain the initial actions of Mrs Fletcher's general practitioner, who reported his concerns about abuse to the social services department. Why did he act so precipitously? Pressed in the interview about the involvement of the doctor, Mrs Fletcher recounted her visit to this doctor after her miscarriage:

> So I went in and he opened this letter [from the hospital] and he read it – oh, you've lost a baby – oh well, in view of what's happened it's probably best anyway. And I – but the thing is, now, I'm repeating this in confidence – the thing is, about 3 years ago, if – yes – 3 or 4 years ago – my doctor, my particular doctor, was actually taken to court for sexually abusing his own daughter. Right. And he was found guilty, in fact he pleaded guilty. He was fined £1,000, and . . . he still had to go before the – I don't know if it's the GMC [General Medical Council] or the BMA [British Medical Association] or whatever . . . he said he'd been depressed and he'd been taking tranquillisers and he didn't know what he was doing, but he still carried on being a doctor.

While this case study demonstrates the templating, justificatory theorising and ratcheting processes I have discussed elsewhere (Howitt, 1990b), other theories of error have something to say about these events. Some of Pride's theory is redolent of what occurred: for example the ignoring of the child's evidence which did not fit the idea that this was a case of abuse. Furthermore, if Mrs Fletcher was correct to hold the intervention as responsible for her miscarriage, this would be a telling but extreme example of anti-family ideology. Given that no support was provided for a pregnant woman at a time of severe emotional stress, it is difficult to see that such a view is entirely inappropriate. The authorities worked to detect the guilt of the parents not to care for the unborn child, which was obviously at risk given a stressful situation.

Evans' (1989b) cognitive theory perhaps also finds an explanatory role. The injury, the carpet burn, was most certainly insufficient to diagnose abuse. Therefore the original diagnosis was a case of overdiagnosis. The problem with Evans' cognitive theory is that it fails to account for the preparedness of some to overdiagnose but not others. In other words, although mistakes of diagnosis may be typical of human thinking, there needs to be an account of why checking processes are not brought to bear during diagnosis. On the other hand, the tendency in metacognition to believe in the validity of one's judgement was very clearly demonstrated in the thinking of the social workers who at no stage (publicly) backtracked on what they thought, despite their failure in court and their withdrawal in the face of the threat of a judicial review. They simply changed direction and contacted Mr Fletcher's ex-wife. Of course, in some people's language that might be considered a witch-hunt, since no evidence would change the accusation. Stuart Bell's theory might, after all, be merely the superficial description of a far more complex process.

And who is to say that a child abuser accusing others of abuse (as was the doctor in this case) does not provide further confirmation of the anti-child ideology of child protection?

Non-error theory

While there might be some consensus that the processes which led to the public inquiries into child protection interventions were evidence that significant errors had been made in those cases, not all writers agree with this. So instead of the problem being to explain why child protection goes wrong, the issue is that of accounting for the inquiries themselves. This is a presumption that no real problem exists in the child protection system, but that there is a problem with a society which sees the system's activities as problematic. This can be described as a *theory of non-error* – how events can be construed socially as child protection errors whereas in reality the protection of children can best be served by such events. They are non-errors in the sense that those involved were doing 'the best thing' for the children involved.

The main advocate of the point of view which leads to non-error theory is Campbell (1988; 1989), who provides a strongly feminist account of the buggery diagnoses of doctors in Cleveland. This was published after the government inquiry (Butler-Sloss, 1988). Essentially, the argument is that the events in Cleveland cannot be properly construed as a child abuse intervention disaster. Thus:

> Among the 26 children whose cases were thrown out by the courts, there are some who will give some professionals sleepless nights. What are we to make of one of the 12 families whose children were subjected to five medical opinions, three of which concluded that there were signs of sexual abuse (the two dissenting opinions only saw the children four months after the initial diagnosis)? The confidential guardian ad litem's report submitted to the High Court concluded that the situation was a mess, mishandled by everyone, that the children should go home, but that there was every possibility that the children had been abused. What, then, prompted Mr Justice Eastham to throw out the case and tell the children that they had not been abused? (Campbell, 1989, p. 15)

This is a post-public inquiry reaffirmation of the propriety of the diagnoses of the doctors involved. Campbell essentially challenges the notion of error in the Cleveland affair. She writes: 'Seventeen of the children lived with fathers or other relatives who had already been convicted of sexual offences' (p. 14). This view resurfaces in Roberts (1989):

What is known about the final tally is that 75 children are still under supervision – be it fostering, residential care, voluntary supervision by social services (a large proportion) or adoption. Another 20 underwent a period of supervision that has now ended. Among the remaining 28, there have recently been five re-referrals. Those families still battling to prove their innocence claim that 63 children were not abused. (p. 1)

But few of these matters encourage the view that the Cleveland inquiry got it wrong in any significant respect. Nothing in Roberts' comments, for example, can be taken to suggest that buggery was common to all of the children. Still being under supervision may be irrelevant to that issue. For example, that a number of children were under voluntary supervision may have been part of a 'plea bargaining' process between parents and social workers into which the parents entered in order to ensure that their children were returned home as soon as possible. Being under supervision is no sure sign that abuse had in fact occurred. That 63 families still battle to prove their innocence may mean that there were more families who gave up the battle once a satisfactory arrangement had been made.

Of course, it is necessary for non-error theory to explain the reasons why many people acknowledge or believe that a dreadful sequence of mistakes took place in the case of Cleveland. For Campbell, the answer lies essentially in patriarchal society's avoidance of the recognition that buggery is an important part of male sexuality. In some ways, then, the Cleveland affair was a fight between patriarchal and feminist ideologies:

> The hidden agenda of the inquiry was the prevalence of buggery and by implication, a challenge to the received wisdoms about the nature of masculinity. For if buggery was being perpetrated by fathers on their children, then that disturbed the belief that it was typically homosexual. (Campbell, 1988, p. 63)

In the feminist literature, Nava (1988) discusses the media representation of Marietta Higgs, the doctor primarily responsible for the diagnoses of abusive buggery in the Cleveland case, in the following terms:

> A number of quite different associations and prejudices are mobilized by the persona of Marietta Higgs . . . We hear . . . that her German mother and Yugoslav father separated when she was two and that she was brought up by her mother and stepfather in a 'splendid' house in Australia. She is herself a working mother of five children and is unconventional in her domestic arrangements – her husband looks after the home and children . . . She is personally neat, dignified, determined and professionally highly respected by colleagues for her dedication, integrity and clinical expertise. Many of the newspapers refer to this, yet it is almost as though these are coded references which simultaneously suggest that she is *too* conscientious and rather *too* clever – neither very English nor very feminine. (p. 117)

Nava sees the image of Higgs as being constructed by the media to be the symbolic representation of feminism. Thus she becomes a foil against which to work out the more 'consensual' positions on the Cleveland crisis being developed by the media:

> We must be aware of the way the Press has mapped out the field and controlled the parameters of the meanings that have been produced. If we are not, we run the risk of being pushed by the media construction of Marietta Higgs as the representative of feminism and anti-traditionalism into uncritically offering her our approval. (Nava, 1988, p. 119)

Theories which recreate the problem of Cleveland as largely that of patriarchal society seem to have fallen into much the trap that Nava seeks to avoid.

There is clearly no consensus in the 'theories of error' which have been applied to the matter of child abuse. But a consensus is not necessary for them to be of value, since they range over a broad set of approaches which are probably not incompatible. Indeed, the theories, by concentrating on their own limited domain, encourage the view that they are complementary rather than competing. They range from human thought processing to ideology to gender politics with a few more in between. It is likely that few situations can be explained simply by reference to just one of them. Equally, one has to doubt that all of them put together would account fully for any of the range of errors in child protection work.

The psychological approaches to errors of everyday action which were developed to account for lapses (certain speech errors or 'absent-minded' mistakes such as filling the coffee-pot with hot water but neglecting to put the coffee in) would certainly have a place in any account of mistakes in general. It is not so clear that they would help to explain errors in child protection. There do seem to be some parallels to be drawn. For example, much of the behaviour which is involved in the error is exactly the same behaviour as would be part of the successful performance of the task (cf. Norman, 1981; Reason, 1979; Reason and Lucas, 1984). Apart from not putting the coffee in the pot, the rest of the behaviour is error free. But then we should note the crucial difference – child abuse errors are not commonly universally accepted as such. Forgetting to put the milk in the coffee would be an error in anyone's book.

The extent to which it might be possible to develop broader theories of error in child abuse work can only be guessed at. What is more important is the notion that error is a central consideration in good practice and well worth understanding.

CHAPTER 7

BATTERING FAMILIES

The child was born in London . . . the third child of recent immigrants from East Pakistan (now Bangladesh). He did well at first, but at the age of 18 months . . . his parents noticed that his appetite was poor and that he was not growing. Three months later, he fell from a chair and sustained a compression fracture of the left tibial shaft without displacement. He was treated in plaster and apparently healed well. He was seen again, because of continuing failure to thrive, at the age of 30 months. At this time, it was thought that bruises were present on the forehead, on the upper chest and over the back, but because of the child's pigmentation it was not possible to be certain of this. However, he was admitted to hospital, and skeletal radiographs revealed what was regarded as a healing fracture through the left radius and ulna and fractures of the right radius . . . The skull radiographs also showed apparent fracture lines . . . Accordingly, the child was regarded as a case of nonaccidental injury, was kept in hospital, and made the subject of a compulsory care order by the local magistrates. (Paterson, 1981, p. 423)

This child was removed from his parents for over two years. It is easy to justify this, surely? The extent of the injuries says it all. However, apart from the medical evidence there was nothing else to suggest that his parents were responsible. Eventually it was recognised that the child was suffering from rickets – an outcome of a deficiency of vitamin D. This may well appear to be a case where a dreadful error was made for the best possible of reasons. After all, a child having once received skull and general multiple fractures might well be in severe danger of its life. But there was sufficient evidence at the time of the intervention that the symptoms were also those of severe rickets. They simply were not construed as that. The interpretative framework of child injuries no longer excludes abuse by parents.

Some might argue that the remedy in this case would have been the early use of specialists to aid diagnosis. This apparently easy solution has snags. One should not assume that error processes are satisfactorily accounted for as failures to obtain the appropriate specialist skills. Important questions remain about why such opinions were not sought. A

133

complete explanation would involve knowing what processes lead to the failure to seek disconfirmatory evidence of abuse. Indeed, sometimes it has to be asked why certain specialist advice is disregarded in favour of alternative diagnoses – this seems to be rather more than a matter of mere ignorance.

Brittle bones

One physical malady that can be mistaken for physical abuse is *osteogenesis imperfecta* or brittle-bone disease. Paterson (1986) writes that it 'readily mimics non-accidental injury' (p. 254). While it is not common in absolute terms, it is the most frequent of the hereditary bone disorders. Its incidence in Western countries is one person in about 20,000. While fairly rare, nevertheless:

> This is not a new disease; a 4000 year old skull from Upper Nubia in the British Museum shows good evidence that the child had this disorder. One of the leaders of the Danish invasion of England in the Dark Ages was Ivar the Boneless, who was said to have been carried into battle on a shield. (Paterson, 1988b, p. 56)

Its medical description, for what it is worth, ought to be considered with the diagnosis of child abuse in mind. In so doing, it is important not to assume that what appears to be a disease 'mimicking' abuse is sufficient to explain the confusion:

> Brittle bone disease . . . is not a single disease, but a group of at least 10 disorders which all cause abnormal fragility of bone. It is likely that in each of these the underlying abnormality is a defect in the structure of, or cross-linking of, the fibrous protein collagen (essential for the strength of bone) . . . Some children are born with fractures, and may have as many as 400 fractures in childhood. Others have few fractures and live a virtually normal life. (Paterson, 1988b, p. 26)

There is no suggestion that injuries to such children are the consequence of rough handling which would be harmless to normal children. 'The fractures . . . occur with little or no trauma. Changing a diaper or turning over in bed may cause a fracture' (Paterson, 1986, p. 254). To a lay person it might seem reasonable to assume that, since such injuries occur without battering, then bruising should be absent. This ought to enable brittle-bone problems and abuse to be distinguished by the absence or presence of bruising. Once again, things are not that simple. Bruising occurs in brittle-bone cases because of the seepage of blood from the internal site of the fracture. Furthermore, unless the fracture is very recent, bruising may not be present in real abuse cases. The problems are compounded by other features of the disease. For example, Paterson (1988a) has seen 'a number of children with what appeared to be a temporary brittle bone disease' (p. 27). The implication is that these children no longer show features of the disease except for past multiple fractures in x-ray photographs.

Not surprisingly, then, a survey of nearly eight hundred brittle-bone patients (Paterson, 1988a) revealed that well over 10 per cent of them had been investigated as non-accidental injuries. Thirteen cases had reached a case conference stage or even that of care proceedings. There is a hint (Paterson, 1986) that parental behaviour may be responsible for the decision to regard the injuries of these children as abuse rather than disease:

> Caution is needed in interpreting parental attitudes. In one case, it was said that the parents were aggressive in an accident department. The parents were angry because they were sent to see a social worker when they wanted urgent treatment for their daughter's fracture. (p. 255)

Furthermore, some parents may display guilt symptoms simply because of their non-abusive involvement in the injury to their child.

But this omits a lot from the explanation. It is too easy to assume that parents contribute to the misdiagnoses because their manner or posture gives the appearance of guilt. For one thing, it is difficult to justify professional decision making being based on such peripheral factors. If decisions about abuse are made on little more than lay psychological theories about how guilty people behave then this is tantamount to a failure in the training and monitoring of professionals. They are the sort of non-evidential factors which are little more than prejudices and stereotypes.

It is clear from Paterson's discussion of brittle-bone disease that not all cases are treated as if they are non-accidental injury. Any satisfactory account of errors must begin to address the question of how some cases are overlooked as possible battering, whereas others are treated as potential abuse, virtually from the moment the injuries come to the attention of professionals. Simply having brittle-bone disease might enhance the possibility of false accusations, as we have seen, but this is an insufficient explanation of sustained false allegations of abuse.

But not everyone shares Paterson's views. Taitz (1987) claims that there is one form of brittle-bone disease (Type IVa) which lacks any obvious indicators such as the blue colour to the eyes. Type IVa, which Taitz sees as being confusable with abuse, is extremely rare according to Taitz's statistics:

[I]n a city of 500 000 people with 6000 births a year the chance of encountering a child under 1 year old with osteogenesis imperfecta who shows no other features or family findings of the disease would be between 1 in 1000 000 and 1 in 3 000 000. This would produce an incidence of 1 case in every 100 to 300 years. The annual incidence of fractures caused by non-accidental injury would be about 15 cases. (p. 1083)

Almost mischievously, Ackland (1987) asks 'How are these children differentiated from other children who present with a radiological diagnosis of multiple unexplained fractures? Often it is only the radiological evidence of fractures and the absence of reasonable explanation alone that leads to the accusation and conviction of parents of child abuse' (p. 1346). In this comment, there is a serious question about how diseases are identified. But there is reason to think that it is not this special type of brittle-bone syndrome which causes the confusion. For example, Holt (1987) suggests that some medics, for example, when looking for 'blue sclerae' imagine that this is a deep royal blue rather than the eggshell blue which is typical. There is something to be said for this, since Paterson and McAllion's (1987) research on brittle-bone suggested that it was not Type IVa alone which gave 'false allegations', although it was associated with the greatest percentage of case conferences and care proceedings.

Taitz (1988) argues that Paterson's views on Type IVa brittle-bone disease are mistaken and have been rejected in some court cases, although Paterson and McAllion (1988) indicate that all uncertain cases of diagnosis were excluded from their research. Furthermore, in all cases that they considered, prior reason existed to suspect the adequacy of the non-accidental injury. Few would argue with Holt's (1987) comment that 'parents should be able to have their child examined by someone with experience of the condition, so that they do not become victims of the probability trap' (p. 1346). The probability trap is the tendency of courts of law to work on the balance of probabilities. This will always favour the abuse interpretation, since abuse is far more common than brittle-bone disease.

Case studies on physical abuse

Six separate cases will be discussed in this chapter, all of which involved allegations of physical abuse. Only the first two of them actually involved brittle-bone disease. The later ones include somewhat different issues. Particularly, the question of 'who abused?' is critical in some of these cases, although the trivial nature of the abuse is also interwoven with this question. The last of the case studies is somewhat different in that it points to a complex set of events which led to sequential injustice.

Case Study 1: The brittle-boned boy

Brittle-bone disease may be relatively uncommon, but it would not be surprising to find that it occurs more commonly among disputed cases of physical abuse. If there is little awareness of the syndrome among doctors and a generalised belief that physical abuse is epidemic, then the mistaken judgement of abuse must be likely in such cases. Quite expectedly, then, my research into disputed child abuse decisions contained good examples of this. In the following account it is important to recognise that processes are involved in the story which help filter the events into becoming error. The family consisted of Mr and Mrs Peters and two boys from the wife's previous marriage; one at the time of interview was aged 5 and the other 8. The interview was conducted with Mrs Peters alone.

> We'd been married for about a year, and Oliver, on one particular night, I always remember, it was a Tuesday evening, we put the children to bed about half past seven. At the time Oliver was about two and a half. And we checked them every so often in the night, say every two hours, you know. We don't so much now, but we did then. This particular night we found Oliver on the floor, my husband found Oliver on the floor. Picked him up, he was a bit mardy, just put him back to bed. And he found him out on the floor again. We both went up and picked him up, and he was sort of crying, he was hobbling round, he couldn't walk, he couldn't put [on] the pressure, he couldn't put his leg on the floor and walk. We weren't very happy about it, he was crying, he was obviously in some distress. We thought oh we'd better do something . . . We took him to casualty, they X-rayed him, and said he had fractured his femur, and they were going to take him up on the ward for observation . . . Next day we went in to see him, and Dr Rice was doing a ward round at the time, the consultant paediatrician. He said how did it happen. We said well we don't know – all we know is we found him on the floor. We picked him up and he couldn't walk. He says well we'll have to go into this further, he says he's got a spiral fracture of the femur, and a spiral fracture results in a twisting motion. He says I'll question you in my office. So he took us both into his office, said he didn't believe us, more or less stated it was very suspicious . . . And he said well, we're not happy with the account . . . He said the fracture required a twisting motion. And I said well there's no bruises on Oliver, no bruises, no swelling, no external marks at all. Which I thought to myself well if you're going to twist a limb like that, especially being a femur, it would need a considerable amount of force, and there'd be marks, but he says oh no.

The case was brought to the attention of social services and the police arrested the husband, although they released him without charge after twelve hours. The children were placed on the child abuse register.

I mean you can imagine I was in a right state. I thought well what are they going to do with him? I've got one kiddy in care now, because he – well one kiddy in hospital, you know, I didn't know what was going to happen to him. One kid in hospital, and I've got my husband, the break up of my first marriage, I thought they were going to take my other little boy – you know, I just flipped, and I took a load of pills I'm afraid. About 6 or 7 Disipan tablets – panicked, I mean – next thing I knew, the police took Cliff off, the next thing I knew there was a police woman in me bedroom.

Oliver returned home from hospital after about six weeks. There were visits from social workers. Then a second incident occurred a year later:

He was three at the time . . . it was the evening again, Cliff was in the bath with the kids, because he goes in the bath with them, the two boys, and he was sort of lying down in the bath with the two kids at the end and Oliver decided to jump – he jumped from the side of the bath. I was in the bedroom at the time, and he jumped and he must have landed funny. He started to cry. He said mummy my leg, mummy my leg, I can't walk, I can't walk – he couldn't put any pressure on his leg . . . we just took him straight down to casualty again at half past seven at night, and they X-rayed him and said he had a fracture of the tibia, which is the knee . . . They plastered him up and said we'll keep him for 24 hours for observation, we didn't think any more about it. We went the next day to visit him, and this same consultant was there, the paediatrician. He says how did it happen again, we told him, he says well its another spiral fracture I'm afraid, we're not happy again. He says it's not conducive with a jump from the bath . . . They said I'm afraid we're going to have to inform the social services again, which they did. And they came to the hospital, and they interviewed us, had a doctor from the community health council . . . The hospital social worker said they were going to go out for a place of safety order, which meant he was going to be taken into foster care.

The evidence of the two children was apparently disregarded and Oliver was fostered a few miles away. A consultant radiologist was asked to view the X-rays by social services in order to say how the injury might have happened. Although there was a police investigation, no prosecution was brought because of the lack of evidence. The parents contacted Parents Against Injustice (PAIN), a support organisation for parents unfairly involved in abuse cases. They were informed of the brittle-bone disease possibility. However, social services claimed that the doctors had tested for the disease. 'I said well that's a load of rubbish anyway, because there's no test for it. I mean even the X-rays of some patients look normal.'

Eventually the consultant paediatrician changed his mind and admitted that this might be a case of accidental injury. It has to be said, however, that this happened only after an independent brittle-bone specialist had been involved. While he did not actually feature directly in the course of events, it is clear that the possibility of his evidence would have made the consultant paediatrician question more carefully the abuse diagnosis. The return of the child to his home is predicated on this change of position.

It is obvious from this account that the error in the process derives not from any scientific failure, but from the failure to push medical questions far enough. While it is possible that the paediatrician was ignorant of brittle-bone disease, the decision that abuse has occurred is not the result of such unawareness but is due to a combination of factors, some of which are in addition to the points mentioned so far:

1. The stepparent relationship.
2. The youth of the child, which facilitates the neglect of his evidence.
3. The failure of the parents to provide a reason for the second injury. That they did not know how the injury occurred is interpreted in a framework of culpability.
4. The repetition of injury, which allows the erroneous confirmation of the first injury as non-accidental and which leads, as a consequence, to the increased likelihood of separating the child from its parents. Of course, a repetition of an accidental injury has no true diagnostic value.
5. The inexperience of the social worker involved.
6. The suicidal reaction of the mother, which appears to emulate guilt.
7. The parents' denial of culpability – a diagnostic sign of guilt!

Note that none of these reasons can be taken as determining errors outside the broader framework of child abuse theory and practice. The brittle-bone issue is not the principal matter. In the medical and social work professions of thirty years ago generally a different view of the injuries would have been taken. The difficulty of diagnosing brittle-bone disease is not relevant, since little or no attempt had been made to diagnose it or enter it as a possible framework for understanding the events. The events templated well with a view of the nature of child physical abuse which probably justifies little more than the tag of a stereotype.

However, there is another factor which ought to be taken into account. That is the tendency to be overconfident in one's own experience and understanding of the world, as identified by Evans (1989a) and discussed in Chapter 6. While it is the case that Oliver returned to his family within three months, there is evidence that the rumblings in the minds of those responsible for the misdiagnosis continued long after the original events. Approximately three years later the consultant paediatrician responsible for Oliver's case wrote to a brittle-bone specialist in the following terms:

I have now had an opportunity to review this boy's X-rays with my paediatric radiology colleague, Dr Armstrong, and even with the most powerful retrospectroscope we cannot convince ourselves that there are any signs of even mild *osteogenesis imperfecta*. Further information which you offer to support your diagnosis would be of interest. Have you independent paediatric radiological support for this contention?

That this letter, from the consultant community paediatrician, was written in such terms suggests that little attempt had been made to research the literature on brittle-bone disease, otherwise the failure of X-rays to identify the condition would have come as no surprise. Furthermore, to ask for independent radiological support further compounds the impression of a failure to understand that there need be no radiological differences. Finally, this belated enquiry suggests that the original attitude to the case had not changed, but that the paediatrician was keen to salvage his belief in the correctness of his own views.

The reply to the consultant community paediatrician included the following comments:

It doesn't surprise me that the radiographs appear normal. This is the rule rather than the exception in the sort of *osteogenesis imperfecta* that we are dealing with in this context. There is a widely held, but fallacious, view that OI is characterised by classical radiological changes, including diminished bone density and Wormian bones, and, while these can occur, they are actually unusual at the time of the first few fractures . . . In Oliver's case the evidence for OI comes from the history, which is very typical. Other suggestive features are the poor linear growth, the excessive sweating, the past history of blue/grey sclerae and the double-jointedness. There are also suggestive features in the family history, but I have not yet had an opportunity to see Oliver's father, who had fractures . . .

The extent to which Evans' (1989a) arguments about metacognition's tendency to overconfidence are built into cognition rather than imposed on cognition is uncertain. For example, could the overconfidence that the diagnosing consultant paediatrician had in his own judgement reflect, among other things, the wish to portray himself as an expert, the fear that a catastrophic misdiagnosis would undermine his status in his professional circle, a personal arrogance, or what? Certainly professional work imposes its own imperatives of playing the professional role rather than that of a confused, bewildered amateur.

Case Study 2: The brittle-boned baby?

Dan (26) and Leslie (23) are the parents of a baby who was diagnosed as suffering major injuries. Unlike the previous case, the outcome of the following case was the permanent separation of the parents from their baby.

[Leslie:] Well . . . the big problem started April 11th last year. What it was, Graham was born on March the 10th. He seemed to be fine in the hospital, but I did have a difficult birth, you know, forceps, epidural, and with me having a heart problem as well, that didn't help. He was breech right at the end, and he quickly turned himself round just before he came out, and he had the cord round his neck. He was distressed and I was distressed. And because they didn't want me to put strain on my heart by pushing, that's why they gave me forceps. But they just whipped him out, didn't they?; he seemed to be fine in the hospital – I was only in there five days after I'd had him – and then at home he seemed to be fine . . . for a week or so.

After that he just started being violently sick. You know, so I kept taking him to the doctors, and at this stage there was still the health visitor, doctor and the midwife coming in anyway, because his cord, you know on his belly button, was still on. So they were coming for that, and they were coming to check my stitches and everything. And they were looking at him being sick and they couldn't find anything wrong, they just said it was his food that was too strong. Well we watered his food down . . . and nothing changed. So we were taking him to the doctor's like two or three times a week, if not more . . . April 7th I was giving him a bath, because that was the day he had to go and have a heart scan, to make sure his heart was OK . . . and he just passed out and went all limp. So I phoned for the ambulance . . . [The doctor] couldn't find anything wrong with him. So when I took him to [the hospital] for his heart scan, I told the doctor about it there, and he checked him over after he'd given him the scan, and everything was fine, or seemed to be. He couldn't find anything . . . [O]ver the weekend, he was still being violently sick, and so on the Monday . . . [the baby was taken to the hospital]. When we got there, they checked him over . . . [T]here was about four or five doctors in the room and they were asking us all these questions. The thing was, whilst asking these questions, Dan was being silly, giving them silly answers you see, because he was just joking about it. But of course we didn't realise at the time that there was any fractures or anything . . . Dan was giving pathetic answers that he shouldn't have been giving.

The baby was left at the hospital overnight for further investigation.

Then Tuesday morning . . . we phoned up the hospital to see how he was . . . and they said I think you'd better come in . . . And they said . . . what have you been doing to him? And I was shocked – we haven't been doing anything to him. Anyway, they tried to make us say we'd done something when we hadn't . . . [The doctor] said there was a leg fracture and bleeding behind the eyes on the brain . . . Anyway, they were doing more tests later that day, and he came back to us, and he says I've got to phone the police and get in touch with social services . . . [T]he police came at 7 o'clock that night . . . and it wasn't until then that we found out that he had two fractures to the skull, as well.

Social workers told the parents that they considered the injuries to be
non-accidental. As soon as the baby was discharged from hospital, he
went straight into foster care.

The parents believe that the difficult birth was responsible for the
injuries:

> [E]ver since Graham was born, I've been having a discharge problem. Now
> I've been to see a specialist about it, and he said it was an erosion gathering
> all this discharge . . . Now when I went to have it frozen out, he had a good
> look inside and he said it looks as though . . . it was a difficult birth . . . He
> says did you have forceps, I said yes . . . And he said well it looks as though
> when they pulled Graham out with the forceps it looks as though they've
> torn you as well, which is causing the discharge problem.

Furthermore, the parents feel that there are problems about the diagnosis
of abuse:

> [T]hey've come to the conclusion that little Graham was picked up by his
> ankles, swung round, and either let go and hit against something, or just let
> go and he's hit something hard, or he's been swung into something . . . But
> [a brittle-bone specialist] said when we spoke to him that if we'd done that
> he'd have had finger marks on his legs where we'd held him, but he didn't.

> [Dan:] And there'd be extensive bruising . . . around his head, more
> bruising than fractures. Plus we did get . . . several leaflets from the brittle-
> bone society . . . well three of the five symptoms were . . . the eggshell
> colour of the eyes . . . the bluing on the whites of eyes, the enlarged
> fontanelle . . . and the profuse sweating, which he had. He had three of
> those three. Which is part of the reason why we did decide to get [a brittle-
> bone specialist] down. But he never came down you see till later . . . it was
> almost a year later, so most of the signs had disappeared.

The 'evidence' against the couple even included the fact that Dan had
been sarcastic in the hospital when being interviewed by the doctors. The
brittle-bone specialist's evidence did not prevent the permanent removal
of the baby from the family. Furthermore, in this case there was an example
of the sort of 'double bind' situation in which parents can be placed because
of the theory that confession is essential before an abuser becomes safe.
The following comments were made to them by a social worker:

> [Leslie:] Right from the start they've said if you admit to doing it, we can
> help you, you know, we can work with you to start rehabilitating you back.
> But if you don't admit to doing it then there's nothing we can do to help you,
> because we haven't got anything to work on. But why should we admit to
> doing something if we haven't done it in the first place?

Young, unmarried parents are perhaps stereotypical abusers. The 'wise-
cracks' might have reinforced the impression of irresponsibility. That the

injuries were viewed by the local doctors as deliberately caused might have been encouraged by these factors. Unwilling to lie about their involvement, the parents were left unable to demonstrate their 'reform' into 'satisfactory' parents. This baby was not allowed back to the family – although the couple have had another child since this time which they have been allowed to keep following 'parenting skills' training.

Case Study 3: Bikers, rats and runners

But, of course, brittle-bones are not a feature of every mistaken accusation of child abuse. There is a 'moral' aspect involved in the way in which some parents become suspected of abuse based on peripheral and irrelevant factors which should not be involved in such serious judgements. Although this was a feature of the previous case, it becomes even more important in this one.

[W]e've been married for ages . . . And, anyway, we had a message that a friend of ours who gone up to Hull – or they were intending to get to Hull, but they hadn't made it – they'd been picked up by the police . . . We're normal Greabos . . . a Greabo is sort of your scruffy . . . with a motorbike. It's a general description for a certain age range – usually riding British machines . . . Anyway, they've been in Hull on remand. I think two of them were up for causing damages to the police station, having been carted off. Apparently the van broke . . . down on the motorway and they were trying to fix it and the police came along. Of course, you're not supposed to fix it, you're supposed to ring for somebody to tow you. And then they got hauled in . . . Mary, that was his sort of wife, they've been living together God knows how long . . . was getting worried and so we arranged to take her up to see him, because Pete had got the car at this stage . . . Anyway we arranged that another friend of ours . . . [Jo] should have Carla for the day. Jo had a young lad, he'll be about 18 months then . . . Anyway, we left Carla with Jo and picked up Mary and headed up to Hull, and saw Simon. And came back, picked Carla up, dropped Mary off.

And a couple of days later, I took Carla to 'Mother and Baby' [class]. Now it was a new health worker, health visitor. The old one she'd just been promoted and she'd been excellent. She'd had children of her own. She was a rural person herself. She appreciated that you had rabbits in the back yard and that you had vegetables and you occasionally had a chicken in the process of being plucked in the kitchen when the health visitor appeared . . . This [new] one she, oh dear, she was a lot younger than me – nineteen . . . She was very town bred . . . She wasn't very happy about the [pet] rats, she wasn't very happy about the motorbike . . . She thought it might have fallen on Carla as she was crawling round and the rats might get out and attack her . . . [A]nyway she'd got a little tiny bruise on her arm. You could cover it with your thumb . . . I showed it to the health visitor, because I thought, you know perhaps they all do things like this. Looking back, I realise that was a mistake . . . [The health visitor examined the child.] Anyway she said, '[D]o you think you ought to take her to the doctor's just to check there's no damage underneath because their bones are soft at this age?' . . . [S]he said, 'Oh, I'll give you a lift.' Nipped back here to turn the dinner down because I'd got a stew in the oven . . .

I saw Dr Noon who . . . was another young doctor . . . Now he just had a good look at Carla, stripped her off . . . Checked her over everywhere else and said, 'That's a bite . . . we know you've been under a lot of strain, we're not saying you did it but is there something you want to tell us?' And they kept on and on. I said, 'Look, she hasn't been bitten you know. I'm going home.' 'Oh no, you can't go home. You are going to go to the hospital . . .' We went to the hospital, we were waiting for ages . . . Then this very tall, thin, woman paediatrician came in. Hardly looked at me. Picked Carla up . . . She stripped her. She looked very carefully at the bottom end and said, 'Yes, that's definitely a bite; this child can't leave the hospital.' At which point Pete came in . . . So more or less words to the effect like hell we are. Picked Carla up, threw her clothes to me and said we're getting out of here. And we ran . . . that probably in the end was [a] mistake. At no time had anybody sort of asked me where has the child been in the last sort of week. They'd all sort of said, this is a bite. They never said you've done it. But, this is a bite, you cannot keep this child.

Anyway, we went to Jo's, and I phoned my parents from there because I knew if we went home there would be people waiting for us. We fed Carla . . . and we put [her] to sleep next door's . . . babies cot . . . She was fine. Me mum and dad thought I was having them on at first and then they realised it wasn't . . . Anyway, Pete said, 'Well, I'm going to have to go home at some stage to get more clothes for her.' So about eleven he went home. And he came back and said there's two CID [Criminal Investigation Department officers] on the doorstep. They've promised they won't take her away, they haven't got a warrant to take her away. But they must see her and they must see you. So we thought . . . we've got to go home sometime . . . [W]e went home, and they looked, and they sort of checked Carla over, um, you could keep her, what's all the fuss about. You know, bloody hell, it is a tiny bruise, it's one mark, it's not even broken skin. You know, overreaction . . . have a good night's sleep and forget about it.

While there is more to this story, it can be summarised fairly simply. There were further police investigations which led to no action. The social workers were also involved further. A case conference was called, although once again that was effectively the end of the matter as the child was not even placed on the child abuse register. This the mother puts down to her own parents' timely and forceful intervention.

In many respects it could be argued that little harm was done in this case. The parents acted unusually in running away with the child, although this touches on a complex argument about what is appropriate behaviour for parents unjustly accused of child abuse. Given the parents' history of involvement with the police and what they saw as a further injustice, they might perhaps have been more inclined to see the accusation as a major threat. But the crucial thing to explain in this case is the action of the health visitor followed by, to a lesser extent, that of the doctors. The mother had her own theory:

> [R]eflecting on it . . . I was a classic case. Post-natal depression, husband with a slight record of violence, record of marital discord, you know, between us. She's just out of college. I mean it's got everything going for it. And . . . then when it's a slightly off-beat household as well . . . I told the other health visitor that me and Pete weren't getting on well. Again, you see, that was a mistake . . . I felt I had to tell somebody. I broke down in tears and it was all sort of, well what's he been doing. And I told her. I shouldn't have told her, I should have kept it to myself. [He was] going out and staying out and [us] having rows . . . all the usual sort of not a happy home . . . he chucked me out in the yard once and I'd walloped him over the head for it so it was sort of equal on both sides . . . I think probably that thinking about it that it was mostly the health visitor's fault because she wanted to find something. This was her first ever sort of place that she was a health visitor. And I think that she genuinely wanted to find . . . brutality and brawling.

This would correspond precisely with the notion of templating (Howitt, 1990b). The family were not stereotyped as abusive because of their history and social characteristics, but a mark on the child's skin was interpreted in such a way that it was checked against the template of abusing families. The family fitted the template well enough and the mark was seen as a bite, being then the closest fitting description of such a mark. (Indeed, it might have been a bite by another child according to the mother.) The diagnosis of a bite is neither accidental nor necessarily a product of the injury's characteristics. However, biting a baby is a bizarre act carried out by bizarre parents on their babies. Thus a trivial mark can carry a much more significant message than would at first appear possible. That this 'diagnosis' passes down the chain from health visitor to general practitioner to paediatrician is not surprising given the interpretative framework which had been established.

Case Study 4: Who did it?

One interview concerned a woman of about 27 at the time of the major events. She then had a daughter aged about 3 years and a son of about 7 months. After about a year she found out that her husband was having a relationship with a 14-year-old girl whom he eventually married following their divorce on the basis of this adultery. The woman's daughter came from the marriage, but the baby boy was the product of a relationship that the mother had had since. The 'father, as soon as he found out I was expecting, he done a runner'.

> He was a very contented little child. Then Robert got a bit bigger, he was more contented in himself, he was lovable – Lorna adored her little brother. Then this, all this trouble started, on the New Year's Eve night.

That evening she bathed the child 'and he slipped as I picked him up, and he banged his head on the side of the bath. I brought him back down but he's OK, there's no marks or nothing.' Satisfied that the child was not hurt, she left him with a female teenage baby-sitter. The woman's brother was also in the house for part of this time.

On returning during the night the mother firstly found the baby bruised around the face, and eventually discovered bruises on his body. The mother having sought help, the baby was taken to hospital. 'He had severe bruises to his chest, his back, his side, his face. They saw he had a pinch on his ear, and they say he had a mark on the top of his gum, on the top lip. That's where the dummy could have been rammed into his mouth, to keep him quiet most probably, I don't know, I don't know how it happened.'

> I asked Lorna . . . was it the babysitter? She says yes mummy. I said where did she hit him sweetheart? . . . She said she hit him across the face, across the tummy, across his back mummy.

The doctors examining the child initially suspected a fractured skull, although this turned out not to be the case. However, the bruises to his body (rather than face) were diagnosed as being between three and ten days old. The mother claimed to have a witness that the baby had been 'roughly handled' by the babysitter: 'Margaret across the road, she said to me . . . that she saw Rebecca chuck Robert into the pram, and this was 10 past 7 that night.'

While these are the brief circumstances surrounding the case as seen by the mother, an important point to stress is the extensiveness of the suggestions about what needed to be done by the mother in order for the baby to be returned home. The mother spontaneously mentioned several such episodes:

> [Social workers] asked me if I were courting, if I were seeing anybody when this happened. I said no . . . But they said if I had – if circumstances changed in my home now, if I got married again, I would have a possibility of getting Robert back. That's why they said to me if I got married, I would have had a better chance to get Robert back. Which to me is stupid – I'm a single parent, so single parents are in the wrong. They're not allowed

to have their children, once they're in social services care. [Well who suggested that to you? That possibility?] Well there's this girl I know. She's had her children taken away. She's married, and she's got her children back now.

[But did a social worker actually say it to you?] Yes . . . the things that they used to say to me I used to think God, should I admit it just for the sake of saying I want my son back. Should I admit that I'd done it? But why admit to something I haven't done. They told me if I admitted it, I would be able to have Robert home, on the supervision order . . . Oh it would be about a month after Robert and Lorna had been in care.

Referring to the original solicitor who handled the court proceedings about 'care':

Me old solicitor, she thought I had done this. She was on their side instead of being on my side. She says they said to me, the CID said to me, if you admit to doing it, you'll get your son back. And that was coming from the social services as well.

Clearly these repeated suggestions and intimations form an expression of an underlying theory about the nature of 'remission of abuse'. Essentially, it is that denial of abuse is an indicator of continuing risk. Or, to put this in the direct form, confession of abuse is a sign of healing of the abusive personality.

The outcome of the story was that, although the daughter returned home within months, the baby boy did not and remains in care for likely adoption.

Case Study 5: Lightning strikes twice

While the previous example demonstrated intervention because of significant abuse – though wrongly attributed to the mother – the following case involves rather trivial injuries which nevertheless led to intervention because, it might be argued, of other features of the situation:

[Caroline, 27 years:] I've got . . . my boyfriend [Tim, 31 years], stopping here. And my little lad's Ian [aged 3 at the time] . . . [A] year last April, I had my boyfriend's little girls stopping with us. Because his ex-girlfriend gave them up, so we had them living here. And they were under a social worker anyway. And they were all in one bedroom . . . I'd had a babysitter, which was a friend of Tim's. [I]t was an adult that babysat. And I got the children up, you know, it was a Tuesday morning, and to get them all dressed, and I come to change Ian's nappy, because he was still in nappies then, and he'd got a mark on the top of his leg. Well to us it just looked like a few little red spots . . . Anyway, at the time, when I was changing Ian, I'd

got the social workers at my house to come and see the girls, because he'd
got twin girls. And as soon as I mentioned this mark on his leg she was down
straight away, you know 'That's a slap mark' . . . I had to take him to the
doctors and he had to spend two days in hospital through this mark. We
didn't know how he'd done it, none of us, because he [Tim] hadn't been in
the house for 24 hours. Because he went out to work on the Monday, and
then he went straight to his crib match on the Monday night, so I didn't see
him – well I saw him on the Monday night but the kids didn't see him till the
Tuesday morning, you know. [Tim] had to spend a week at me mam's
[mother's] because we didn't know who'd done it. Even the hospital said it
was a slap mark . . . From then onwards, I was under a social worker for
the year . . . We found out from a third party [what had happened that
night]. [The baby sitter] had slapped Ian.

[Tim:] [After] about three months . . . he [the baby sitter] was living in a flat
. . . he moved down to London. And after he went down to London, I
didn't know this at the time . . . I went round to see him [at his old flat] . . .
his mate . . . told me . . . we understand your lad was smacked by Eddie
[the baby sitter] . . . Eddie apparently had told him, and he told me.

[Caroline:] We told the social workers and the social workers got involved
with the CID. But apparently he's in prison now . . . for GBH [grievous
bodily harm].

This story may seem to have attracted substantial and disproportionate
concern, since the child spent twelve months on the at-risk register and
the family received regular social worker visits. The injuries, according to
the mother, were 'little red speckles, on the top of his leg'. The implication is, of course, that even had the baby sitter not been responsible,
the marks were very small indeed. The term on the at-risk register was
extended by six months because of a minor injury:

Ian pinched Tim, so Tim pinched Ian back, but he pinched him a bit too
hard, not realised, and bruised him. Of course he was on the list for another
six months through that pinch mark . . . I told them. But I didn't think that
it would make any difference.

But this was not Tim's first involvement with social services. As he
explained it, before being with Caroline he had a previous long-term
relationship:

We, we weren't married, but . . . we lived together for four years. And we
had the twin girls . . . I'm not sure it was the pressure or what, but me
girlfriend kept leaving all the time and coming back and all the rest of it, and
this one incident she'd left, I was out at work, she went, she left a note
saying the kiddies had had their dinner and they're in bed playing with their
toys, and left the kids on their own. And they were on their own for four
hours. From then on, you see, they were under a supervision order which
stood for three years.

Tim, the 'stepfather', unemployed, was not, therefore, unknown to social workers, prior to the precipitating incident. Marks on a child in these circumstances are readily explained by the sort of theory which suggests that Tim's characteristics are typical of abusing partners. In a sense, he fitted the category of 'bad' parent well and concerns about his parenting were likely to follow, as well as enhancement of the extent of the original marks which caused concern.

In many ways, this family suffered substantially less than others might have done. But, of course, the family feels itself to be under surveillance and, consequently, at risk of worse. Childhood injuries are relatively common in play and the fear that such injuries would be interpreted as abuse is not surprising. After all, what they see as a minor injury inflicted by a baby sitter resulted in frequent social work attention. The case contains several of the elements which appear from other cases to lead to a greater likelihood of error – previous contact with social services, a 'stepfather' who matches the stereotype of the abusive parent, and an unexplained injury. Furthermore, the child, who linguistically was not very advanced at the time, was not able to provide any evidence about what had happened to him.

Case Study 6: Giving up under pressure

This final case study concerns a mother who had two of her children put into care by substantially different processes. It is an example of how the self-instigated involvement of child protection services leads to a major misfortune. In this case, the mother, Sandra, suffered considerable physical and sexual abuse from her partner. While this was clearly a problem with which she needed help, none was forthcoming. The interview was rather complicated, with at least four members of the immediate family commenting. However, virtually all of the following account is based on what Sandra said herself. The account starts with a list of her children:

> There's Russell [born 1979] . . . he's with his real father, then there's Natalie [born 1981] . . . that's the one who they blackmailed me with giving up for adoption so I could keep Jilly [born 1983], then there's Nathan [born 1985] . . . I'm married now but [the relationship with Bernie] that was just common law . . . [T]he first two I've had problems with . . . started when I had Russell . . . when I was living up [in a deprived area of the city] . . . I kept getting ever so many people coming round knocking on my door . . . [Health visitors] having to strip him off and checking him over . . . I was getting them every week . . . three times a week [the health visitor was getting anonymous phone calls saying he was being ill-treated]. Bernie's mother she was possessive over Russell all the while . . .

I lived with [Bernie] for five years. Me and Bernie, we was having problems. He was beating me up and all this . . . [he] tried strangling me, broke my leg and I took it out on Russell . . . I smacked his [leg] and he ended up with a bruise . . . this was before the second child was born. [Bernie] even knocked me around when I was carrying . . . he was beating me up no end of times . . . week after week if I didn't do up the place I'd get beat up for it . . . he broke me leg (he kicked me with his [steel-toed] boots on) because I wouldn't go up to his mum's . . . broke me nose, blacked me eyes . . . [the social workers] knew all that – he was cautioned [by the police] . . . I also ended up in the [hospital] for twenty days 'cause I was having five epileptic fits a day through it all – I'm an epileptic . . . he's used screwdrivers on me – sexually I mean. [He was also abusing drugs, and tried to get her to be in pornographic photos – that is why he broke her nose.] After all that had happened, his mum's getting possessive over Russell . . . [health visitors] were coming round . . . saying [that] they wanted him checked . . . I was supposed to have put fag burns on him . . . stubbing fags out on him . . . [I]n the end they decided that it was a spot on his back . . .

Anyway Russell was put into a foster home for three months – 'cause I'd smacked him . . . he was playing me up . . . [H]e had impetigo and the doctor said don't let him keep touching it because it will spread . . . [But] he kept touching it and it was getting bigger and bigger so I walloped him across his leg and it come out in a hand print . . . a bruise . . . I called the social services out and explained . . . [The police] kept querying to see if Bernie had done it – I said no he hasn't but . . . I don't think that they believed it . . . [Social services] put him into a foster home [for three months] . . . we got him back . . . They asked us if we'd agree to a supervision order and we says yea . . .

[In] '81 [Natalie] was born I had to take Natalie up the clinic to get her weighed and sort out her milk because she was allergic to normal babies' milk . . . had her weighed. [The] health visitor says 'What's this mark on her face?' . . . I says well it's a scratch. A doctor called me in and he was on about the mark on her face. I said 'Well it's because she ain't got her scratch mittens on.' 'No it's not,' he says, 'we're going to have to call the . . . baby abuse doctor in or whatever they call them.' . . . [T]hen he was on about a purple bruise on her ear. Well all I could see was like a vein you know like the blue veins . . . So he stripped her off in this room and he had this chart down – drawn this baby . . . diagram and . . . [it] had all pinch marks up her legs . . . Did I have a dog in the house? Did the dog do it? . . . the dog wasn't even allowed in the room when the baby's on the floor . . . I was there for about three hours and [the social worker] walked in.

The baby was taken to the hospital for further examination. It was decided that an interim care order would be sought. Consequently, the baby was taken to a foster home. The injuries were a half-inch scratch and marks on her leg which were diagnosed as pinch marks, but the family feel that they were marks due to an allergy.

The social services got it into court. They said there's no way that you're having her back . . . Anyway I left Bernie . . . after he beat me up in front of [a male and female friend] . . . Bernie was messing about . . . and he was nudging me and all this . . . in the end he started thumping me and pulling me about. [He] stripped me knickers off in front of me friends, started beating me up . . . [The friends] just left. I was sitting on the settee crying . . . Bernie left me alone after that. Russell was . . . down [at] his grandma's for a week . . . I made an excuse and I said I had stomach ache . . . so when he'd gone to sleep I got dressed – well practically – I had a skirt and a top on, didn't get me shoes, legged it out the house, left the front door open, got a taxi . . . [and went to my sister's]. [H]e wouldn't let me have Russell . . . to bring him up to my sister's [the child was at his paternal grandparents].

The couple, at this point, separated permanently. A court awarded custody of Russell to his father. Initially there was overnight access with Russell, but eventually this was reduced to just daytime:

[W]e used to have [Russell] at my sister's you see, he was four years old . . . he was still in nappies, he wouldn't use the toilet or anything . . . But I says to him, right, you're coming out of these nappies, I mean at four he should have been out of a nappy, shouldn't he? . . . And he was poohing, he was weeing on the floor, even in the toilet, he done it in the corner, he wouldn't do it on the toilet. But we got him out of that . . . and he was dry at night and everything. And [the social worker] decided to stop it for just one day [because the staying access 'wasn't going smoothly']. [Bernie] used to teach Russell to tell mummy I hate her . . . He said I hate you, I want to see you cry. I says what you saying all this for, he said well daddy's told me to.

But there were other difficulties:

I went to pick [Russell] up, and [Bernie] kept sending Russell out. He says oh go shop, go and see your little friend before you go up your mum's and that, and he done it five times and I thought what's going off here. He put a video on, a porno, and it was a really hard one. And I stood behind the settee, I says well come on Bernie, I've got to go. I says Len'll be waiting, he'll be wondering where I am. [Len was her new partner, now her husband.] And he says oh do you really love Len, and all this, and I says well course I do . . . he'd got his penis out and that and he was asking me if I'd do oral sex with him and all this. And trying to rub me up. And anyway when Russell come in for the fifth time, I grabbed Russell, got his coat, and I went down the cop shop. And all they could ask was was Russell being touched up.

Access stopped shortly after this, largely because the mother relied on an informal arrangement with Russell's father which was not adhered to. Of course, Natalie was still being fostered. Sandra herself was pregnant, by her husband Len. Sandra describes how she feels that she was 'black-mailed' by her social worker to agree to Natalie's adoption by another family.

[S]he said if [Sandra] didn't sign the papers for Natalie to get adopted, [she] would oppose us keeping Jilly [the to-be-born baby]. She . . . said if the papers weren't signed for Natalie, she'd say that we weren't responsible enough . . . to have a kid, because we was keeping Natalie from a stable home. So we weren't responsible enough.

This was in a private conversation. Although the maternal grandparents were willing to adopt the child, Sandra agreed to the adoption because of the threat to her keeping the baby she was carrying at the time. And essentially that is where the story ends. Sandra married six months after Jilly was born and they have another child. Social work involvement with the family effectively ended following a period during which newly born Jilly was subject to a supervisory order.

One can imagine some of the problems for the child protection workers in this case. Already on record was a sequence of anonymous complaints about Sandra's parenting behaviour. The family are adamant that they believe the complainant to be the maternal grandparents. Of course, explaining why this should be the case is not easy and so they have to characterise these grandparents as 'possessive'. Nevertheless, these things do happen and sometimes the unresponsiveness of child protection workers to relatives' anxieties is a source of criticism (there was one case of this in my sample). One should not forget, however, that there were many other things happening at the same time, including the violence in the household which may have provoked some of the (anonymous) complaints.

With this background, when Sandra self-reported the abuse of Russell, albeit apparently relatively minor, quite clearly a theory about the family as at high risk of abusing the child was empirically justified. Sandra's self-report, although perhaps a cry for help, may also be understood as an inability to cope in the context of a violent relationship. However, rather than working on the situation, the response of the social workers seems rather draconian in the light of the abusive 'slap mark'. The child was removed from its parents for a period of three months at a time when he was little more than a toddler, with the risks of possible damage that this entailed. Furthermore, to the mother, who saw this incident as her only act of abuse at a time of severe emotional pressure, this response by child protection workers seemed unreasonable and unfair.

The next stage is, of course, a period in which surveillance by professionals was likely to be at a peak because of the history of prior intervention. It is not surprising that in these circumstances marks which the mother sees as either non-existent or merely blotches caused by an allergy might be interpreted otherwise by nurses and doctors, given their understanding of the past history of the family. Indeed, although Sandra was adamant that she had not harmed the baby, one cannot be totally sure, for example, that the father had not. That Sandra denied it may mean either that he had not or that she was unaware that he had. That this second child was taken away for its own protection is again not very surprising given what had happened to her brother. This is not to say that it was right, but it was perhaps regarded as appropriate action in these complex circumstances. It should be added that Sandra was presented with explanations of the baby's injuries which have more than a hint of bizarre, almost sadistic behaviour. For example, the scratch was explained as a 'stab from a safety pin' and she was accused of bathing the baby in what she describes as 'boiling hot water', meaning too hot. Such explanations would no doubt create a feeling that it was imperative to do something to protect the child despite the rather trivial nature of the injuries which Sandra describes.

Much of the rest of the story is relatively easy to understand given that the father had no accusations of abuse whereas the mother self-confessed to one incident and was believed to have perpetrated others. The father, with the support of his parents, might be the obvious person for Russell to live with rather than Sandra. His behaviour towards Sandra apart, there may well have been few countersigns to him having custody. Again, from some perspectives, the pressure put on Sandra to agree to have her first daughter adopted might seem quite reasonable, although the nature of this pressure seems rather distasteful and inappropriate. Since this time, though, Sandra has been married and no problems have ensued with her children by Len, her new partner. This seems to put considerable credence on the view that her difficulties were the result of the pressures of considerable and brutal domestic violence perpetrated by her earlier partner. She might be criticised for not getting out sooner, but the price she paid in terms of losing her first two children seems a high one.

The complexity of error processes is readily apparent in the examples described in this chapter. In an area where medical diagnosis might be expected to make allegations of abuse clear cut, no such simplification seems to happen. Although the errors in physical abuse spread well beyond the brittle-bone problem, even that relatively straightforward area shows how varied the matter of false allegations can be, and how errors are built into the system. The range of opinions of experts on this syndrome seems to allow one almost to choose one's position on the abuse-accidental injury continuum. But that facilitates the error proneness of such decisions. Certainty about the frequency and diagnosticity of brittle-bone disease would leave little room for error. That one can pick from extremes leaves the matter subjective.

A further consideration has to be the extent to which errors need not simpy be made in terms of diagnosis of non-accidental injury. The injury may be accepted as non-accidental and the problem lies in the identity of the perpetrator. Sometimes the errors may stem from the lack of support for a parent in need of help, and from overreaction to relatively minor injuries.

The extent to which the errors we have discussed are medical in nature is extremely debatable. They often seem to be the result of factors which are the province of the doctor's surgery. Sometimes the diagnosis is at fault, but more often extramedical factors are responsible for the errors. Nevertheless, child abuse science is far from objective. One cannot ignore cases like that of a child seen as a 'failure to thrive case' (essentially having relatively poor and weak development), typically held to be due to the inadequacy of parenting. That this child was suffering an undiagnosed terminal illness speaks volumes. Human misery may be common in all aspects of child protection work – and piled on by some interventions.

CHAPTER 8

SEXUAL ABUSE

There is something very curious about the professional area of child sexual abuse which impels agencies to respond irrationally even when management guidelines exist. (Dale *et al.* [the NSPCC Child Protection Team, Rochdale], 1986, p. 24)

In March 1991, a 47-day hearing before a High Court judge ended. Ten children were allowed back home. They had been taken from their parents on the basis of teachers' and social workers' belief that they had been involved in ritual abuse of a satanic nature. Three other children had been returned to their parents following an earlier hearing. A further four children from another family were not allowed to return home at this time. The case had been subject to a court injunction which initially banned all reporting in the media, although the restrictions were eased later. Only the general nature of the case and the way in which the children had been taken from their parents could be discussed even with this loosening of restrictions. Up to this point, 'The injunctions ha[d] removed from the families their right to seek advice from their elected representatives, advice centres, churches, friends and neighbours' (PAIN, 1990).

Teachers of one 6-year-old Rochdale boy had become increasingly concerned about his 'complex and difficult' attitude. The boy was having temper tantrums and appeared to his teacher to be very disturbed:

One day he arrived at school 'looking as if he had been out all night. He talked of ghosts the general way, as a child might,' said the judge. '. . . He described seeing a mummy and daddy ghost and a baby ghost that died. The teacher said the child showed 'abnormal emotion' when talking about the baby ghost, as if a young relative had died . . .' The . . . boy was posed numerous questions [by social workers], many of a leading nature, said the judge. 'He talked of going to a house with an adult ghost and other children including his sister and two brothers. He described flying and being given special drinks. He also talked of people touching him and of playing tag games with the ghost.' (*Daily Telegraph*, 8 March 1991, p. 3)

At this point a place of safety order was sought and this family's children were taken away from the care of their parents. Notably, medical

155

examinations revealed no signs of sexual abuse in either this boy or his sister. In a combined police and social services exercise, the children of three other families were removed from their homes in a 7.30 a.m. raid. An anonymous telephone call enmeshed the children of another family in the proceedings. 'The judge added: "Another boy said he had eaten a cat. But his mother said this was probably a reference to pasta creatures in soup they were eating."'

Procedural errors on the part of the social workers included failing to video the interviews properly, failing to take contemporaneous notes and generally failing to follow established guidelines issued following the Cleveland report on child sexual abuse (Butler-Sloss, 1988). The organisation Parents Against Injustice listed nine major complaints concerning failures to observe good practice and instances of bad practice. These included:

1. For a long period of time, the children were denied access to their families.
2. An absence of home and social assessments.
3. The views of the parents were not sought.
4. Information about complaints procedures was not provided.
5. The children were taken from their beds at 'dawn'.
6. The authority failed to follow its own child abuse guidelines (PAIN, 1990).

At this stage the authorities rejected suggestions that they were failing in regard to such procedure and practice guidelines. However, the same council accepted the judge's findings immediately the hearing was over. Its Director of Social Services resigned the following day. No action was proposed against the social workers directly involved. But from our point of view, this is not the end of the case. The rhetoric that organisations use to ensure the least disruption to professional activity is an important consideration. It reflects a reluctance to change which might encourage entrenchment in child protection workers. There were several attempts at this retrenchment. In an instant media response, the British Association of Social Workers rejected some of the judge's suggestions: 'the general secretary, said the demands for children to be seen only at the end of the day and for a psychologist to be consulted first were unworkable and likely to put children at further risk' (*The Times*, 8 March 1991).

Essentially this says that the imperative of instant action to remove the child from a crisis needs to hold sway. Waiting until lunchtime or in-corporating a checking process into proceedings are claimed to increase materially the dangers for the children. The statement also fails to accommodate the fact that wardship of the children had been obtained by social workers up to one week before the dawn raids, which does not rest easily with the claim that these dramatic actions were taken to protect children. It is, however, true that surprise may help protect evidence of a crime from destruction.

An interview with the Director of the National Society for the Prevention of Cruelty to Children was even more remarkable (*Daily Telegraph*, 9 March 1991). In early 1990 the Society had campaigned to promote awareness of satanic ritual abuse. However, a number of defensive language strategies seem to underlie the views of the Director of the Society a few months later. For example, he engages in a degree of victim blaming:

> The social workers, [he] concurs, did not recognise the distinction between fact and the boy's fantasy and went galloping down the wrong path. 'But we still have a boy left in front of a television set half the night, watching appalling material that clearly affects his mind,' he says . . . 'That is a form of abuse.'

He then redefines his terms substantially: 'We are now saying that there is ritual abuse, and that is for sex, not Satan.'

The report goes on to report the Director's fears that 'people will conclude that child abuse in general is an invention of social workers, that parents are the real victims, and that the public will then lower its guard to give parents, rather than the child, the benefit of the doubt'. However, it is unclear why this should happen rather than that they conclude that child protection workers need to obey the rules, need better training and need support from other professionals. The comments preserve the rhetorical dichotomy which places child protection professionals and children on one side, parents on the other. This is a mistaken dichotomy in its assumption that good resides with children and the system, bad with parents. It becomes hopelessly flawed when the system itself proves to be harmful to children, parents can be innocent and there is little that can be defended in what the system has done.

The question has to be asked: why the belief in satanism? The answer is at least superficially easy to find. There had gradually built up a belief that satanic abuse as a distinct entity was actually practised and that it was associated with the most bizarre and inexplicable behaviours. Psychologically, it was extremely harmful:

> Since she first told police that her eldest son, Charlie, was involved with and had been sexually abused by, a satanic ring, her house in Humberside has been under a siege. [They] have returned home to find bizarre signs smeared in excrement and blood on doors and mirrors or bunches of keys and clumps of pubic hair half-hidden under pieces of furniture . . . At the age of eight, [Charlie's best friend's] father had introduced him to a group

of men who performed rituals involving sexual and sadistic acts. He talked about watching pornographic videos and being made to take part in them . . . He said he had been drugged and that, on occasions animals were sacrificed . . . Charlie is not the first such child to be disbelieved. [T]he trustworthiness of victims' evidence is confused by the fact that they may have been drugged and shown videos. (*Sunday Times*, 1 April 1990, p. C12)

The professional journals provided images of satanic abuse which are no less extreme. So, for example, the following description reinforces the impression created above:

Ritualistic abuse refers to repetitive and systematic sexual, physical, and psychological abuse of chidren by adults as part of cult or satanic worship. Reports of ritualistic abuse are often characterized by forced ingestion of human excrement, semen or blood; ceremonial killing of animals; threats of harm from supernatural powers; ingestion of drugs or 'magic potions'; and use of satanic songs, chants, or symbols . . . Reliable estimates of the extent of this problem are not yet available. Many professionals are unaware of the nature of ritualistic abuse and fail to recognize its indicators. (Kelley, 1989, p. 503)

There were also, at about this time, worries being expressed about the *possibility* of satanic abuse. An informative example which reveals the basis of the concerns was to be found in this newspaper report:

Fears that Satanic child abusers *may* be at work in the county have been voiced by organisers of a . . . conference. There is *no evidence* so far that children are being ritually abused . . . but organizers have warned ritual abuse is a growing national problem. (*Leicester Mercury*, 1 September 1990, p. 5, emphasis added)

In other words, satanic abuse was being promoted as in urgent need of vigilance. But it is unlikely that because of the publicity given to satanic abuse professionals simply sought and found such cases. That would scarcely be credible. Satanic abuse investigations have been disastrous in that they have generated controversy and raised the embarrassing spectre of false allegations. Well-documented cases are hard to find. While it is likely that the publicity raised awareness of the issue to new heights, it is what satanic abuse appears to explain which leads to difficulties. Characteristically, satanic abuse is represented as involving bizarre acts, drugging, profound psychological damage and extremes of violence.

In child protection work there are cases which possess similar bizarre, fuzzy, violent and weird characteristics. These might be readily explained by satanic abuse, especially if an inarticulate child could be perceived as muddled or vague because of the effects of drugs. While the notion of satanic abuse might be reduced to questions of fact (does it happen or not?), such a conceptualisation is weak as an explanation of why things go wrong in child protection. It is the belief that satanic abuse happens and not the knowledge that it *does* happen which is responsible for events being construed in this particular sort of way. Such a belief was being heavily promoted just prior to the infamous satanic abuse cases. The social work professional journals carried articles encouraging awareness of such abuse. For example, Wood (1990) cites the case of a 4-year-old, Thomas, who 'described seeing a guinea pig having its genitals cut off. He was told to defecate on a bible while in church. He spoke graphically of being hurt by people with swords and snakes' (p. 18). Lunn (1991) describes the Ritual Abuse Information Network and Support Group which had then been in existence for about a year. One member was in contact with police, social workers, nurses and others 'about the nature of ritual abuse and the evidence for its existence' (p. 18).

Like other 'persistent' theories, satanic abuse carries with it explanations for its apparent failures. In particular, the lack of strong evidence of the existence of ritual abuse is freely admitted by Wood:

> Chanting and mind-altering drugs are used to manipulate the child into confused or hypnotic states in which he or she becomes open to indoctrination and exploitation. In these conditions of emotional and perceptual openness, children may be abused by people dressed as authority figures, cartoon characters, ghosts and witches. *This is an effective way to render a child's account of abuse unintelligible to any adult who may hear it.* Examples might be 'Mickey Mouse did this to me'; 'a policeman in his uniform did it.' (p. 19, emphasis added)

The concept of satanic abuse thus makes intelligible the unintelligible! It is also a theory which carries with it significant imperatives to action – it is judged to be especially harmful to children. As such, satanic abuse is just one of the theories which lead to errors. Few may be so well publicised, but they too risk harming parents and children. (It should perhaps be noted that satanism in itself does not explain abuse, since what might be seen normatively as extreme abuse in those faith-healing sects which refuse medical treatment for seriously ill children may be supported by anti-Satan beliefs (Hughes, 1990).)

The following case studies illustrate various aspects of child protection work involving disputed cases of alleged sexual abuse. It should be stressed that the issue of diagnosis is not always crucial in these cases despite the impression which might have been created by the public inquiries concerning child sexual abuse (such as in Cleveland and Rochdale). Indeed, sometimes the precipitating 'act' is not in dispute (as in Case Study 9).

Case studies on sexual abuse

Case Study 7: Making 'sense' of bad children

This is a complicated case which starts off as a fairly straightforward matter of family discipline problems but suddenly becomes transformed retrospectively into a sexual abuse case. The two parents as well as members of the extended family were present at the interview, and the youngest child was also there from time to time. The account is largely supplied by the mother, Mrs Teasdale:

> I was having problems with me son, James, he was playing truant from school, he was thieving . . . off us, he was thieving off members of the family, his sisters. So I went to the . . . social services for help with James . . . So I had social workers come for James and . . . we still had problems . . . We tried everything. She got a volunteer to take him out once a week and then he wanted to see his natural father because Matt's James's stepfather. Now he's [the] real father to my two daughters but stepfather to James . . . At first I didn't want him to because he never seen him when he was a baby. He happened to stop James on the streets when he were nine . . . and said, 'I'm your dad, here's 50p' and 'I'm going to take you on holiday for a fortnight' . . . James was . . . upset. He wet [his] bed for three nights which he never has done and . . . after that, it were just problems all the time. You know, he got [the] attitude if Matt said anything to him, or his sisters 'You can't say that to me, you know, I don't belong.'

But the older children began to arrive back home late from school:

> Rachel started senior school, age eleven. Up to then, she was the best one I had in here. She was very quiet, kept herself to herself, never brought me any trouble. And when she started seniors . . . she were there a few months and she started going round with older girls of sixteen . . . So then we found she was going to a flat . . . there was young boys aged from 14 to 17. It was a young couple what had [the] flat . . . [S]he kept going to this flat and we found out they were playing games, sex gams, like, or one time they played Strip Jack Poker and Rachel [had] got nothing on.

Some family arguments occurred which also involved social workers in various ways. To cut a long story short, problems with discipline for the children got too much for the parents:

> And I was in a right state, crying and everything, and [the social worker] kept saying, the best thing is to give you a break, because it's either them going away or you'll be going away . . . So of course I agreed in the end to put them into voluntary care, just to have a break. And I signed and it said on it voluntary care – I think it were 48 hours notice if I wanted the children back . . . [W]hen they went into care, Rachel didn't bat an eyelid. Just

packed her clothes – she wanted to go. But James seemed to be upset, because I'd threatened him that many times and never did it, but the day I actually – I surprised myself actually, you know . . . Rachel got moved then to foster parents. James remained at Beauvale [Children's Home] . . . [T]hen there was an incident there where James and these other boys went on to [the] girls' dormitory, James supposedly got in bed with this 14-year-old girl, raped her while she was asleep, and this girl was a virgin, which, you know, we don't believe . . . We spoke to one of the boys, that we managed to get to talk to, and one of the girls who was in the room, and they don't back the girl's story up at all. They believe . . . that she did that to get herself out of a jam, because the boys shouldn't have been where they was, in the room, with the girls . . . Rachel had told us before this incident that he was going with this Annette Brown, and they'd been in the bathroom together, doing whatever they do . . . [A]ll he got from that were a caution [from the police].

After a few months, the parents decided that it was time to have Rachel back home again permanently:

[The social worker] said there's a question mark against that. You can't have them home . . . we feel that there's a strong possibility that Rachel could have been sexually abused either in the home or out of the home – which he denies saying at this moment in time . . . it was in front of both of us . . . They hadn't actually said it, they hadn't actually come out and said Mr Teasdale or Mrs Teasdale, we think you're abusing your children.

About this time an incident concerning the youngest child of the family occurred which has a significant bearing on the sexual abuse hypothesis:

[Tara] wrote a story . . . at school. The social workers went behind our back and took it to a psychologist . . . who interpreted it the way he interpreted it. And what he said, in the first paragraph, was that these symbols was not forced to mean anything; in the last paragraph, he says that 'I hope this child gets the help she clearly needs' . . . It were '[The] Disappearing World of Polly Flint'. Now that were a TV series, and also there's a book. And me and Tara has watched that together, when she's come home from school. And of course Tara's a person what, if she hears or sees anything, she keeps it up here [in her head]. And she wrote this story, and it were more or less as what was in the book . . . like Polly Flint went into a secret world. There were a snowman in this story, there were little people, and they were pulling her through another world . . . And in this story there's a walking stick . . . In the series and in the book, a walking stick . . . [The psychologist] said that walking stick was a penis, hanging down on her face.

The full details of the psychologist's interpretations can be found elsewhere (Howitt, 1990a). The essential facts are that the psychologist, taking the story on its own (he claims to have been ignorant of any other details), without seeing any members of the family and apparently oblivious of the details of Helen Cresswell's Polly Flint story (Cresswell, 1982), interpreted the story as that of a very disturbed child:

> [T]he walking stick appears as a persistent source of anxiety, if not terror, throughout the story. It is menacing and intrudes into the girl's happiest moments . . . There is a sense in which something which belongs, or is projected, outside the family, comes back through into the family again, ie cannot be escaped within the family circle. Clearly this *might* be a phallic symbol. That it appears in front of her face and terrifies her might lead one to wonder whether a penis has been presented to her in this way, and an association between this and oral sex may not be excluded.

Or writing about the mother in the child's story:

> *Mother*. Most significantly, she was seen as reluctant to contact the police. I thought it interesting that the girl wished her mother to contact the police, and equally important that she appeared not to want to. Her mother was also described as going out and returning with the man. There was a sense here of mother being involved with the man and perhaps colluding with him. Tara then went so far as to say that it could be a man or a woman that was bothering her. This might also represent, however, a collusion between a threatening male figure and her mother. When she laid a trap for the man nothing happened, though it is clear that she thought only her mother and father know and are involved with this fear.

The colluding mother is one of the 'dominant images' of families involved in child sexual abuse (cf. McIntyre, 1981). It is a remarkable overinterpretation of the child's story – just as it would have been of Helen Cresswell's original story. What the psychologist's comments indicate is a backwards look at events, in this case a story, with a theory of child sexual abuse in mind.

This theory is most clearly expressed in a letter received by the parents from the Director of Social Services in the locality:

> [W]hile they were in voluntary care, James and Rachel became the focus for widespread concerns. These concerns were centred on their erratic school attendance and disruptive behaviour, their history of stealing and their inability to accept that any controls should be placed on their behaviour. In addition, both children's inappropriate sexual activity was felt to be a strong indicator that either or both of them might have been the victim of sexual abuse.

Notice the choice of the phrase 'sexual abuse'. This seems to imply that the person involved was an adult not another child or other children. This is endemic in the abuse literature. That other children can harmfully sexualise a child is not part of this rhetoric. The theory of sexual abuse therefore places the blame with the parents (or some other adult, but this has not been intimated) rather than on anything which happened to the children in care or in the wider community. Certainly, the main social worker involved in this case was able to draw together a wide range of different 'inappropriate sexual activities':

> Of particular concern was the nature of [James's] relationship with his sister Rachel. Rachel is now aged 12 and complained to the social worker . . . that James had tried to kiss her, had asked her about her sexual development and together with a friend had made sexual advances towards her and tried to put his hand in her pants . . . Rachel was present . . . when James and a group of teenagers broke into an empty cottage and indulged in sexual play activities . . . [At the children's home] James and a friend Bobby S. put their beds together to make a double bed and slept together. A used condom was found underneath the following day . . . Perhaps the most serious incident in which James has been involved was . . . [when] James entered the girls' dormitory with two friends. There were 3 girls in the room including Annette Brown aged 14 . . . Annette was very distraught. She alleged that she was asleep and that when she woke up she had discovered that James Teasdale had had sexual intercourse with her . . . James has admitted to having sexual intercourse with Annette but has alleged that she agreed to it . . .
>
> It was rumoured among the children at school that [Rachel] had had full sexual intercourse with an older boy . . . An older girl at [the children's home] who had been sexually abused reported that in conversation Rachel had told her it had happened to her lots of times . . . [Rachel's] foster parents reported that her regular visits home were upsetting her and had noticed an immediate deterioration in her behaviour after a return home and also that she would suck her thumb and curl herself up in a foetal position. On one occasion when she had returned home from a visit to an aunt's house she appeared rather agitated and went upstairs. Mrs Taylor, hearing a banging noise, went upstairs to investigate and found Rachel spreadeagled on the bed bouncing up and down and spraying deodorant into her vagina because it was sore. They also reported to me that she had shown a marked interest in the Childline advertisements on television [Childline is a child abuse 'hotline'] and also had been totally absorbed in a programme reporting on a rape case.

All the above are contained in an affidavit to the court. It also appears to be a substantial reinterpretation in the light of the hypothesis of child sexual abuse. For example, concerning the rumour that Rachel had had sexual intercourse wih an older boy, the special needs teacher at school wrote in an affidavit:

> [T]here was a rumour circulating around the school that Rachel had had sexual intercourse with a fifth year boy. As a result of my investigation into this matter, I interviewed a third year girl who admitted to me that she had started the rumour as a joke.

Rachel's foster mother wrote the following in her affidavit, which also places a somewhat different stress on the interests of Rachel in the media:

The only time Rachel showed any interest in the television was when the advert for Childline was on and Rachel told me that she was going to ring them. This statement was made in the past tense as if it was something she had considered doing previously . . . Rachel also showed a great deal of interest in a *Juliet Bravo* episode where a young girl had been sexually abused by a man. She asked me if I felt sorry for him. She also read out to us an article in the local paper about an incest case concerning a brother and sister and asked us what it meant. When we told her she said 'You can't get them for that' but we corrected her and assured her that it was illegal and that was why the case had been reported in the paper.

Again this is a somewhat different interpretation from that of the social worker, who seemed to have neglected the matter of brother–sister incest, perhaps because it did not meet the requirements of the sexual abuse hypothesis. Even the alleged homosexual incident with which James was involved is considerably in doubt. According to the parents, the person discovering it said, 'They were just messing about, blowing the Durex up like.'

The behaviour of the children certainly fits the stereotype of children abused sexually by adults. And once the template has been checked out, the pressure to fit these children into the sexual abuse framework becomes very apparent. The recall of events, we know from any amount of psychological research, is very much a reconstruction which fits theories (Bartlett, 1932; Bull and Clifford, 1979; Hall and Loftus, 1983; Loftus, 1980). This seems to have happened in this case – the notion that the children were sexualised by other children is essentially dismissed by the use of the phrase 'child abuse' with its implication of an adult's mistreatment of children.

This case also reveals a straightforward stereotyping process emerging. In a handwritten note by one of the social workers, it can be read that James's 'aggressive attitude leads people to believe that the offence at [the children's home] was rape'. The thinking behind this is unclear, but it appears to imply that rape is an activity of 'aggressive' people – of which James is an example.

Case Study 8: What sort of a mother would do that?

This is an unusual case of a sexual abuse allegation in that it involves a woman. Furthermore, the woman is a Kenyan Asian who had married a Frenchman and used his surname as her second name. She married in Britain in 1973 and within a year they were separated. But then she remet a childhood friend and conceived her son, her only child, by him. She is in contact with the father but she lives alone – although she previously lived with her son who was born in 1977:

Now it's . . . September, 1985. I was shocked because a policeman and a social worker walked through this door and told me that I have sexually abused my child. I couldn't bear to live – I thought I wasn't, it was some kind of – somebody was making a joke, which was a very big shock to me. I never dream of things, being of Indian culture, and a person who lives by her principles, I think it was the greatest [shock] I ever had. I was taken into the police station, asked questions, threatened to be hit . . . by the police people, men and women, that if I don't tell the truth . . . I was released in the evening saying that there were no charges. But the social services did not return my child to me . . . they didn't tell me absolutely nothing [about what I was being accused of].

I know for a fact it's revenge . . . I wasn't very happy with the school and the headmaster because my son was bullied. And one day he came with his front tooth broken and it was bleeding . . . I went to school and [the headmaster] went mad, he said – he banned me from going there, he sent the police here, and he issued an injunction that he will not allow me to go . . . near the school and things, because I have made complaints and he didn't like that . . . he thinks, him being a white person, a graduate and a headmaster, I am being rude to him by making complaints . . . I complained about his inefficiency to look after my son. Like I said, I'm very outspoken and open person, so I told him on his face and he didn't like that a bit. He said to me . . . 'You being a Paki, what do you know about what?' . . . And I said 'I have seen people like you sweeping the streets in India.' . . .

[I]t happened the third day . . . after this row . . . And also there are two women, they have . . . [a play scheme centre] . . . and I had complaints against a woman who was running it, whose name is Mary Granger . . . and I went with complaints because I don't like my son to mix with rough people who were rough and speak bad language . . . the social worker I had . . . prior to my son was taken into care ([the] headmaster sent the social worker round) . . . said the child should not be taught, he should be allowed to go out and play and that's how they learn. I said 'No, my parents didn't let me go out to play, and I learnt things' . . . And she said I'm a very fussy mother. Let the child go out to play. I said 'What he'll learn when he go out? He'll learn to swear . . . When mothers are smoking and yapping, talking about various things, the children are playing on the streets, and there are cars coming', I said . . . But it's the social worker who asked me to send my son there and I was forced into this, by the social worker, and those are her friends . . . [whom] I had complaints against. I wrote them a letter, they took my son to a trip and my son was sick, and [the play scheme worker] pulled my son like this you see and he was sick all over his coat. And they all laughed in the bus . . . He felt very humiliated when he came home, he said why did I send him to that bloody play [school] . . . Well they told the social worker that . . . I'm causing disturbance and trouble, because I wrote a letter to her saying that if the person who has done this to my son had no right to assault my son and I will prosecute that person. So she said to me, oh well, merely a Paki . . . she'll teach me a lesson for life . . . which she did by calling the social worker and she actually made a story that I . . . sexually abused my son and things like that . . . [A]t a [case] conference early this year . . . [I was told] it was them people at the play [school] who . . . went to social services and said things about me and my son . . .

I went to collect my son, as usual, half past three, and the headmaster threw me out, and the policemen threw me out and I came home bleeding on the road . . . I was hauled by policewomen and men and I was humiliated and insulted in front of other children, and the children were laughing . . . They said my son wasn't there: so I said why is my son not there, I asked – I said I want to see the headmaster, why is my son not there, I said. [I] placed my son in your responsibility, and why is he not there I said? So didn't know nothing . . . He might be at home. That's what they told me. Very very sweetly. So I think white women are wicked witches, they are pretenders. I hate white women from that day onwards . . . I didn't know where my son was, and I didn't know whether they'd took my son into care. After that I phoned the police, I went to the kiosk that evening, and I phoned police and to ask whether they could find me my son . . . And then after – and the police came, many, five, six police come and said to me they will [search] in the area . . .

And then after about seven o'clock I think a social worker or a senior social worker, I don't remember the name, and the police, she come with the policeman – a policeman or a woman, I don't remember now. And she had a paper with her, and she asked [me] to . . . accept it. And when I took a look at it, it was my son was taken into care, some magistrate's order . . . She said I have sexually abused my son . . . [T]hey said I was sleeping with my son, 7-year-old child . . . And [they] said my son pulled his trousers down and showed them what my mum was doing, that's what they said. It's very embarrassing, very disgusting things women can say . . . They said because I have no husband I was using my son as a husband. I was living a life through him. I was using my son and sleeping with him . . . And I don't think my son would ever do that. I don't think my son ever knew the meaning of what this woman was saying.

This story is very disconcerting. In some ways it is very difficult to comprehend the implications of what was being said. To accept the story is to accept racism and violence in school and in the police. Quite clearly the mother was a battler on behalf of her son. One gets the impression from these and other things that she said that she was quite willing to be offensive to people during her battles over her son. Furthermore, she had ideas about bringing up children which were firmly out of line with those of the dominant white society. She wanted her son to come home to be educated further, not to play on the streets. This was the cause of her earlier clash with the headmaster and social workers. Whether a difference in cultures totally explains this case is unclear. That an overprotective mother is a bad mother makes sense only on the basis of theories of how children learn and become functional adults. That all work and no play is taboo in child development theory may have something to do with the problems.

Another relevant factor was my own discomfort about what I was hearing. This stemmed from my own latent racism, which I might well share with many of the white people involved in this case – in fact, the mother describes overt rather than latent racism. I write this as an academic who has researched, written about and practised in anti-racism training. But I viewed the mother as a slightly bizarre person. She did not even conform properly to our cultural stereotypes – a divorced Indian woman living in a single person household and having a French surname! Added to this was a difficulty in communication and in her relating of events that as a white person I found difficult to believe could happen – such as the headteacher's racist comments or the police violence. But that could well be my problem.

I do not know any substantial details about how the 'disclosure of abuse' happened or of what it consisted. But whatever it was, there is the question of explaining how the allegation of abuse came to be believed. After all, we have already seen that the notion of female abusers is only recently beginning to be accepted. There might be a link. Why would a woman abuse her child? Perhaps because that woman is 'abnormal'. Quite clearly Mrs Trenet was a very unusual personality in the eyes of the school and the social workers, prior to the allegation. Furthermore, she was very protective of her son, and it might be an explanation of such overprotection that she was sexually abusing the boy – indeed, that is virtually the gist of what was said to her. In other words, the female abuser is a somewhat bizarre person prone to keeping her child too close to the home. This formulation is basically sexist, since it implies that female sexual abusers are reproducing a dependent female role which leads to the abuse. That these may all be based on prejudice rather than fact does not invalidate the view.

Case Study 9: The punishment fitting the 'crime'

In this case, that the events alleged to be sexual abuse happened was not disputed. However, the consequences of the act are seen by the family as being not commensurate to what happened. The household consists of Mr Watson, a 27-year-old car mechanic, and Mrs Watson, aged 34 years. This is Mrs Watson's second marriage. There are five children – Bernadette (17), Alan (14) and Jenny (10) by Mrs Watson's first marriage, and Susan (6) and Laura (5), Mr and Mrs Watson's natural children.

> [Mrs Watson:] [My first husband] committed suicide . . . We'd just come out the army, he'd been out the army a year. And he used to knock me

about a bit and I'd left him and I'd gone to a battered wives' home. I took the three children with me, and I went back to fetch some furniture, because I'd got a house . . . and found him dead. And I'd been left him about two months anyway, so there was sort of no love lost, not on my part, you know. The kids were upset but . . . they soon got over it really.

The couple were married in 1982 but lived together during the previous year:

[Mr Watson:] What happened was . . . a year ago . . . my wife went into hospital. Somehow or another, my wife's youngest daughter, Jenny, climbed into bed with me and I ejaculated over her back. She then went to school three days later, told her teacher, I was arrested and charged with indecent assault. I was placed on bail to live at my parents, not to see the kids – I could see my wife, but I couldn't come to the house . . . my barrister . . . come up with this idea of me pleading guilty because I didn't want Jenny to go into the witness box. And doing some sort of deal with the judge . . . the way it was put over to me was, if I pleaded guilty I'd get a suspended sentence and that it'd be finished completely. But that wasn't the case. I pleaded guilty, I received a nine-month suspended sentence for two years, and fined £100. And since then we've had trouble with social services . . .

[I]t happened during my sleep. That's been the biggest problem . . . explaining how Jenny got into the bed.

[Mrs Watson:] She can't explain it, and Derek can't explain it. And social services, you know, they wouldn't believe he does quite a few strange things in his sleep, he's had to go and see a psychiatrist . . . he's took mirrors down in his sleep, he's tried unbolting wardrobes – because he used to be a removal man before. And a couple of weeks before this happened, my grandma died and I was quite upset, Derek was upset, and then when, you know, when he gets upset or worked up, things like that, I mean he's been fighting in his sleep and all different things . . . he's, you know, done it to me before now, but I mean, I wouldn't talk about, you don't go broad-casting it and that. And he says [to the social workers] well I've done it to me wife and that, he says well you've done it to your daughter . . . [He] says 'Well if you're saying I have, and Jenny's saying I have, I must have done.' And that's where they . . . said he'd admitted it, on that basis.

Mrs Watson specifically claims that her husband had ejaculated on her during his sleep 'many a time'. The problem for her was essentially the lack of any explanation of why Jenny got into bed. There is no doubt that the events had taken place in the parental bed. Perhaps had things ended with the suspended sentence then there would have been little complaint. But there were complications. Mr Watson was not allowed home at first and Jenny had been taken to a place of safety:

[Mrs Watson:] [N]ow you see what happened was, they wanted her to come home. But the way I was feeling . . . I'd just had an operation, and it was such a shock: I'd discharged myself [from hospital]. I weren't supposed to do anything. I was in such a turmoil that I didn't know what I wanted. And they said about stopping here and I says well to be honest, I said I don't think I could have her, I could cope with her. And they says well are you saying that you are putting her in care voluntarily, and I says well if that's what you have to do, yes. Because I don't think I could have done, you know, everything was all that mixed up. And so she went into care.

By the time of the interview, things had changed in a fairly familiar way:

She's not in voluntary care, no, she's been made a ward of court and she's been placed in the care and control of social services. And we go, in fact, we go to court tomorrow, because we had a letter come about a fortnight ago to say that social services have viewed the situation and they think that they ought to put her up for adoption, which we – it come as a bombshell. And the other children are on a supervision order . . . and the social worker, she phoned me up on the day after we got this letter saying could she come and see me. And she came last week to see me, and she says I've got an apology to make, we should never have said that we want to put her up for adoption, we only want to move her to a long-term foster home.

The husband is back home on the understanding that he attends a course run by the probation service for sex offenders: 'for the simple reason if I don't do what social services want me [to] . . . the probability is they'll come and take the children away unless I co-operate with social services'.

Whether or not one believes the husband's explanation of the events, and of course there are good reasons to do so, the offence appears at worst a one-off incident – which is very typical of sexual abuse. But this one act has led to the victim being in care. While it is true that the mother requested the voluntary care initially, it has to be asked what alternatives were available to her, what support she could have expected if Jenny had returned home. Although we might wonder why the child went to her parents' bed, there seems to be little or no evidence that she was encouraged by her stepfather to do so. While, of course, the parents might be withholding such evidence, the relatively light sentence the stepfather received tends to support the view that there is less to this case than meets the eye.

One is left with the impression that abuse has taken on an all-or-nothing quality, such that there are no shades of seriousness. The mother was clearly supportive of her husband, so she might have appeared to be a typical colluding mother, unsuitable to provide the necessary support for the daughter's return home. Whether or not one sees the case as badly handled depends very much on the general perspective taken on abuse. One can see the actions taken by social workers as appropriate or inappropriate in the light of one's stance on abuse and one's tolerance of the notion that there are different degrees of abuse.

Case Study 10: Kids never lie?

We have already seen that there is a general thesis in child sexual abuse cases that children do not lie about sexual abuse (Jervis, 1988b) – or, to be a little more sophisticated, that they rarely do so. The following case is a complicated one of a false sexual abuse allegation. Even if the sexual abuse described here happened, the consequences were largely borne by the nuclear family, including the brother of the child claiming to have been abused. The interview began with an introduction to the family.

> [Mother:] Jason's the boss actually . . . he's 13. And we have a daughter called Samantha, she's 16 now. My husband and myself. And we have two guinea pigs. And we were a very, very happy and close family . . . we used to go everywhere together . . . we actually had old people stop us in the street and say what a happy family we were . . .

> [Father:] Jackie's parents lived in Australia . . . There hadn't been a great deal of love lost between Jackie's parents and us, but they're getting on, they're in the 80s. And every couple of years they'd come over . . . and stay with us . . . They caused a great deal of stress in the family, mainly because they're at the age now where having been without children themselves for such a long time they're not interested in young children. So for the first few years when they came back they totally ignored our two children . . . The last two times they came back, they paid a lot of attention to Jason, and totally ignored Samantha, and we had to tell them to stop it . . . but just before Christmas '87 when Childline started . . . we were preparing for her parents to come back again . . . Now we had a three bedroomed house, and whenever they came back the children shared a bedroom . . . Samantha was just 14, starting to develop physically. And it meant sharing with her brother yet again . . . So apparently she started dropping one or two hints to kids at school, she's not very happy about her grandfather coming. That built up at school over a period of time, and somebody reported it to the teacher. She was called into the class, and interviewed. They sent immediately for the abuse section of social services, who immediately whipped her round to the police station, and she was at the police station three hours being interrogated before we even knew anything of any problem at all. Now when the police took the statement from her, the actual accusation allegedly made was that her grandfather had kissed her improperly when she was six years old. He put his tongue in her mouth. She subsequently wrote in her diary that that was untrue – that was a statement made by the policewoman, and not by herself. Now we were called in, we had to kick [the grandparents] out into the street, at 83 years old . . . having done our homework, gone to the library and read up about all this sort of thing, and we read that where the children tell lies or tell untruths, if there is a family problem as a result they become guilty . . . So we asked at the case conference that she be referred to a psychiatrist because we expected her to feel guilty whether she was lying or telling the truth, and we didn't

know which it was at the time. And the case conference said yes, and they failed to refer her . . .

[A]fter she was taken into care . . . we found her diaries . . . which we handed in to our doctor, and when our doctor read them he said she was emotionally disturbed. And the thing that came out from her diaries is that having been caught in this lie about her grandfather, there is in fact a clear development in her diaries that she starts feeling very guilty, very evil, and she's trying to prove to herself how bad a person she is. She had this struggle between an evil and a good in her and in the family. And as the diary develops, she starts imagining events in her younger life that proved how bad she was . . . But as she progresses in the diary, it goes from having kissed her improperly when she was 6, to full-scale rape, with practical descriptions. And the development is from single rape up until the end of the diary, when the diary finishes . . . she actually claims this 83-year-old grandfather has raped her 900 times . . . with the hate towards her grandfather, and the hate towards herself, it's quite [a] strong pronouncement . . .

But the events leading to Samantha being taken into care are rather different from these events.

Then she had a series of accidents – a bit weird – the first one she was playing with Jason in the garden, and we had a rose bush . . . the ball had caught . . . there you see, so she was trying to get it free, and . . . she'd got tangled up in the bush . . . Wriggling to get it free caused scratches on her back again. At school, when she stripped off for PE the scratches were noticed and comments were made . . . did your dad do that? And it was a nod and a wink and nothing really said. Somebody reported, a social worker came out . . . He came out to investigate. Samantha told him what happened, we told him what happened, and he went away satisfied . . . However, he went back to the school and reported what the explanation was, and they refused to believe it in the first place. And they claimed that they were not scratch marks on her back, but welt marks . . .

The social worker then took Samantha to the doctor, who confirmed that the marks were not welts but were due to rolling around in a bush.

[A] couple of weeks later, Samantha came home from school with a big graze on her arm. And we said how have you done that . . . she said oh I fell off a wall, you know, daft, kids do, you know . . . We were called in to the school by her year head . . . and she'd gone round all the teachers and got a written report about Samantha. And she read these reports out to us, complaining about her behaviour. We laughed. I mean when you sit there and they say that your daughter smirks in class . . . spelled smirk wrong, you can't take the teacher seriously, can you, I mean it doesn't make any sense . . .

While the parents, in retrospect, believe that Samantha was behaving rather differently at school from at home, they feel that they were not alerted sufficiently for such a meeting. The school had involved a psychiatrist at one stage, but after meeting with the whole family no problem was diagnosed. Social workers were again called out a week or two later when Samantha had a bruise on her cheek caused by bumping into the computer table when she was crawling on the floor with her brother. Again no action was taken by the social worker, who was satisfied having spoken to the girl.

> We wrote a complaint to the school, because some of these complaints came from the school. And we got a letter from the headmaster saying . . . come in and see me . . . we were due to see him on the Friday . . . On the Thursday Samantha apparently told her friends at school . . . that she was afraid to come home. They called in the social services again. [This was a different social worker, but one who had been involved with the grandfather 'incident'.] She went out, and got two place of safety orders, one for him, one for her, and whipped them into care . . . The basis of that Samantha claimed that she was in danger at home. . . . [W]e've had three different versions of exactly what happened at the school according to social services and we don't know which one to believe. The first had been that she'd told friends at school that she was afraid to come home. The second version was, which was put out by the school, that the mother of one of the other children had rung the social services and sent them to the school. And the third version, which was told by the year head, was that the school received a telephone call saying that Samantha was ready to reveal all. So we got three completely different versions as to what exactly happened . . . Samantha claimed that she said nothing to anybody . . . The social workers claim that she has . . .

The boy was taken away on a place of safety order along with his sister. It was claimed in court that 'they took Jason solely to keep Samantha happy'. He had not been interviewed at that stage by social workers, nor have any allegations been made concerning him. Jason, who was present throughout our interview, claimed that the social workers told him that his parents did not care that he was taken away from them. One cannot tell whether or not this is a child's misinterpretation of what was intended, but that was the impression created in his mind by professionals. The boy stayed in a place of safety for a relatively short period:

> [W]e persuaded Jason to write to the Queen . . . he give it to us, we sent it off. And we got a letter back from the Queen's secretary on the Thursday . . . It says that she can't obviously get involved with the case, having received the letter from Jason she was passing it, had ordered the secretary to pass it on to the Minister of State for Social Services . . . On the Monday he was given back to us. And everybody says it's nothing to do with your letter.

The story of Samantha, though, continued over a long period of time. She was sent to an assessment unit. There were a number of other exchanges between the family and social services. These are complicated in many ways and are concerned largely with the issue of access.

The parents' view of the possible causes of this catalogue of involvement is as follows:

> Now whether or not it was . . . Childline, and this massive 'let us seek out abuse syndrome' and everybody seems to be having schools invite social workers, that has created the situation, where they're looking for it, without the experience to say [it] could be anything else. I mean if you look . . . [at] all these [child abuse] guidelines from all these social workers around the country . . . you read these guidelines, and there is nothing in there that tells a social worker ever to look for any other causes. If there's bruises, it's abuse. There is nothing in there, nothing in the guidelines, that says to the social worker, step back a bit and let's see if we can find any other reason . . . It is not 'is there any other possibilities'. And by cutting out that section . . . they're looking like that, they're blind-folded, aren't they? They're blinkered. And this is what you're getting both in schools and in social workers . . . these new NSPCC guidelines . . . They're asking teachers . . . if they notice this, that and the other, then they should call social services because it's abuse . . . I think there are five items – erratic behaviour is one of them.

In their interview the parents describe Samantha's actions as seeking attention from peers through telling them fabricated stories of abuse. They explain that she was not well integrated with most of her peers and needed a means of involving herself with them. This is more than redolent of some of the views of professional child abuse counsellors about the social dynamics involved in false allegations of child abuse:

> In contrast to most victims of sexual abuse who want to hide their sexual experiences, a new group of children making false allegations are children seeking attention and acceptance. They seek the attention and pity of others by being identified as victims. If they have friends who are sexually abused, they also want to 'belong.' While school education programs on sexual abuse may offer the motivation for child victims to disclose their secret, it also may offer the desperately needy child the opportunity to feel special and included by making a false allegation. Assessment of these children can be complicated because they may create their own detailed stories from listening to educational programs at school, television programs, or sexual abuse stories from their sexually abused friends. (Cotter and Kuehnle, in press, p. 16)

Case Study 11: Getting help against an abuser

It is the impression given in the feminist discussions of child sexual abuse that child protection work essentially serves the needs of females in response to the activities of men, male social dominance and power being partly effected by sexual violence of one sort or another. As such, one might be tempted to believe that child protection work is associated with social justice. By dealing with sexual abuse it might be expected that some of the worst excesses of patriarchal society are brought under control. The following case study shows how erroneous this view can be. A further belief is that mothers are sometimes accomplices in the sexual abuse of children. In the following case the mother is responsible for the disclosure, but the consequences for her are arguably worse than for the abuser.

> [June:] Well I met Ray in 1966, and we were married in February '67. [W]e'd been together for a while before that you know. And after Ben's birth we decided we were going to get married. And we got married in February '67. And then Liz came along in '69 . . . [In 1976 Ray] went to live with someone else. And after the breakup I went into a relationship with Keith, and that led to the birth of Peter in '76. And I married Keith in the October of that year, again after the birth of Peter. And Penny, she was born in December '77 . . . I would be exactly five months pregnant with Penny when this incident occurred . . . I'd woken up rather early . . . [a]nd this particular morning, there was no lights on at all, he was in Liz's bedroom and I went in to kind of find out what was going on and I found him on the bed, he was doing things at her, he'd got his penis out – he was masturbating on her bottom, things like that, rubbing it against her bottom and masturbating in front of her. My immediate reaction was, you know, I was very upset, and I went downstairs. He kind of rushed out of the room pulling his pants up, rushed downstairs . . . I asked him what had been going on, and he told me that – eventually, after a time – that this had been going on for some months, and it had happened two or three times a week over these months.

She reported the incident to social services. Basically, the outcome was that Liz stayed virtually permanently with her natural father. But this is partly a consequence of Mrs Ford's position:

> There had been a welfare report . . . saying well yes June's got a very nice house . . . but she's got Ben that she finds difficult to handle, she's got Peter, and then she's going to have this other child whenever it is – she's going to have three children, be a one-parent family . . . [Ben] basically . . . wasn't going to school, and there'd been petty theft from me and that kind of thing . . . when this happened there was a great deal of support from him. I leaned on him very heavily and subsequently after that it may have accounted for some of the things . . .

[A]t the time, after the birth, the Probation Office, social workers, marriage guidance, the whole thing were trying to get the family back together . . . and Keith, back into the family, because they felt that he should be back . . . I couldn't stand the man . . . [B]efore the birth of Penny I was on Valium, Mogadon, the whole lot. I'd been stockpiling them for a great deal of time. I mean they was just dished out to me by the doctor . . . I was really quite woolly . . . [Keith] was asking me to do things that I just couldn't comply with. And there was things that I discovered about him, his social worker told me were quite normal sexual acts and he said what happens between two consenting adults and all that kind of thing . . . They were making decisions that I should continue with that marriage when all it was doing to me was getting me high on tranquillisers . . . he started at being physically violent, hitting me, as well, because I wouldn't give in to his sexual demands. And he was doing things like if I wouldn't – if I wouldn't have sex with him, then he would be masturbating on the sheets, you know, lying at the side of you and rubbing himself off on the sheets . . . Or else he would be doing it on my bottom, and then I would get up, and he'd be rubbing himself off on me, you know, so that when he ejaculated, it would come all over you.

Eventually, Keith just left, leaving a note saying, 'I realise you really have had enough', and we had a mutual giving up. He knew there was no way I would accept him again.' Then it became clear that her son Ben had taken up theft again, when he was about 13 years of age:

He'd come in with a pair of trainers – so and so's mum . . . gave them to me . . . And then he come in with an electric train set . . . oh so and so swapped it for something. And once I was out in the garden and I found this thing from a mail order catalogue, and it said Mrs Halfpenny, 1 Harvest Road, which is just around the corner . . . and it seemed to click in my brain . . . Ben had a previous offence . . . He'd stolen this tar spraying machine . . . the purpose of Ben's stealing was quite childish, he wanted to make a go-kart with the wheels. And of course wherever you trailed that thing it had left tar, all over the pavement. So when the police were checking it out . . . it was obvious – there's a little entry at the back of our house down there, they're old terraced houses, and he pushed it in there. So I mean that it was obvious that the police found it. And he'd been put on probation for that . . . I said [to his probation officer] well I think that he's running mail order at this empty house on Harvest Road, and within a couple of weeks of me telling that probation officer, Ben was found to be entering Harvest Road, and apparently all the mail that had been coming to that empty house he'd been taking it . . .

To cut into the story, the mother took a new husband, an American airforce man, several of the family went to America, and then they finally returned to Britain following difficult financial circumstances when this marriage did not work out. In the meantime, Ben was in a special unit for children:

Ben was not going to school again . . . he was going out late at night, and still, . . . we were having petty thefts and things like that. And he was picked up one night with some things that he shouldn't have had, and social services decided with the probation, that Ben wasn't doing too good, and they put him into this place called The Elms – which is run by George Franks . . . They had a programme of regression where they were given baby bottles to drink milk and stuff out of, which I thought was quite damning . . . and really bad for the kids. They had the opinion that any problems the children had stemmed from the parents. That the parent was wholly and totally to blame for anything that happened . . . I was asked to work with the psychiatrist and he said that I was to react to Ben not as if he was a person, as if he was an adult, as if he was a little child. I was not to make him feel that anything he'd ever done was wrong. And if he steals something from you then you're just to ignore it, and not to say anything about it . . . George Franks was taking quite a lot on himself and he was dismissed from The Elms eventually, and there was going to be a court case about his behaviour with the children there. His abuse of the children . . . and when I contacted The Elms I was told that Ben had gone to live with this George Franks . . . I don't know where he is now.

The next stage of the story unfolds:

Keith [the abusing husband] was still having access to Penny and Peter, and in that year he was going to Scotland, and he was going to take the children as a holiday . . . And they went off to Scotland, and apparently Penny wasn't too happy, and she seemed to be distressed on this holiday, and Keith called me up and said could he bring the children back early from this vacation, and he did. And when she came home, Penny was incontinent. She was soiling herself as well as wetting herself. And I couldn't understand this either, but I had a little think about it and I thought it was probably the fact that she'd gone from the infants into the junior school, and this had been stressing her . . . [W]e had involvement with the Family Service Unit, basically because Peter wasn't too good at going to school, and this incontinence went on . . . And the Family Services Unit worker . . . said wasn't I concerned it had gone on so long? . . . why don't you take her to the doctor and see what his views are? [I asked Peter] has Penny said anything to you . . . is anything upsetting her? And then he told me that she had told him that her father . . . had been touching her, sexually abusing her, and it had started on holiday. Then I took her to the doctors, and on the Monday – he investigated it and confirmed that in his opinion there had been some sexual abuse . . .

Though Keith's access visits with Penny ceased, complicity by the paternal grandmother allowed contact with him when the children visited her: 'Penny hadn't even told me, that her dad was there and she was very frightened.'

In November [1986] I had a lot of problems with the children, they'd been abused, it was an awful estate, and I'd become involved with [voluntary] social work . . . Peter and one of the neighbour's boys had had a fight, and a woman came down, she'd got eight children . . . and her kids had been for us – everytime we used to walk up the street they used to be effing and blinding, calling us slime and all that kind of thing . . . spitting at you and throwing mud at you and that. And she'd come down, and she'd got all her children there, and she was effing and blinding at me . . . they'd tried to set fire to us, Peter's had his head cut open, Penny's had an arm cut open . . . And [my] children, their behaviour got worse, and they would be having fights and things like that . . . I had a cane, like a bean cane, and I would say if you don't behave yourself and you don't stop fighting, you're going to get a smack with this. And they knew I wouldn't hit them with it – or they thought I wouldn't. And this week there'd been particularly a lot of pressure, and the kids had really been bad, and the particular night when it happened . . . they'd been fighting and Penny had scratched Peter's face, and he'd hit her, and they'd really been throwing tomato soup at one another in the kitchen, it was all over the place. I told them to stop and they wouldn't, and they got yoghurt out the fridge and they were throwing that at one another . . . I said that's it, I've had enough, you can go to your bedroom and you're going to be smacked . . . I took them to their bedroom and they both got a smack. They got three each . . . [with the cane] . . . and that was on their bare bottoms too.

The events were brought to social services' attention by the children's school. The children were put on the at-risk register, where their names remained for two years. There has been some social services involvement aimed at giving some support to the mother.

One of the consequences of the workload in the child protection system is that the allocation of resources to individual cases is problematic. It may well be that in some circumstances families can be given help to cope with their various needs. Unfortunately, the family in this case was precipitated into events in a previous era of child protection theory. Rather than supporting the wife in a decision that she had taken for herself, essentially, before the involvement of child protection workers, action was taken which in her eyes did nothing to help the situation. Keeping the family intact was the theory which was applied in this case. However, the family that was to be kept intact was one consisting of the abusing father and the mother, since the abused child had been settled with her natural father. That this was not what the mother wanted is, of course, irrelevant in such a theory-driven system: what was good for her is what the social workers believed was good for her! While the events which followed cannot be attributed directly to child protection services – after all, they do not encourage children to steal – they actually contributed to the problem by breaking up the siblings rather than removing the abuser. To create further emotional distress is unlikely to enhance a woman's self-image or to enable her to gain disciplinary control over the children.

While the mother's serial monogamy with a sequence of evidently unsuitable partners cannot be considered the responsibility of child protection services, in the end an awful lot of resources were spent on this family for it to remain a problem. All of the children in the family witnessed events and problems which were not of their making and they were set to reject their parents as a consequence.

A range of case studies have been presented which display different characteristics of error processes. The degree of sympathy that one has in each case probably varies somewhat. In some cases the parent seemingly contributes significantly to his or her fate. Sometimes it is very difficult not to blame the parent in part for his or her own predicament. But that, to a certain extent, is the problem. Why do we want to blame that individual – because it is the easiest thing to do? After all, a mother who finds a partner who commits abuse has to have something wrong with her, doesn't she? When we find that her sons turn into troublesome thieves, who can we blame but her? Worse still, when a man who accepts that he ejaculated on the back of his young stepdaughter while his wife was in hospital bleats about the actions of child protection workers trying to sort out a difficult situation, what should we think?

These may be reasonable viewpoints – but only may be and only in some cases. It is not good enough to take such a viewpoint, since it avoids coming to terms with many issues. Such victim-blaming strategies are not rare among professionals and need challenging. While some of these parents by some standards are not ideal, it does not follow that no difficulties are created by the child protection intervention involved. However, to take each case dispassionately is a tall order and very taxing. Incredulity is an easy response to some of these complex and fundamentally disturbing cases. It is safer to place the blame with the family; it produces a simpler theory and is less psychologically stressing. Such responses were more typical of my own experience of the sexual abuse cases than of physical abuse or neglect; and they tended to be associated with admissions that something had happened. The idea of the abuser as in some way diseased is hard to shake even in research. However, it may well be the case that abuse, justifiably dealt with, can nevertheless be associated with a degree of mismanagement by child protection workers.

The following comments of one interviewee may illustrate some of the antipathic feelings which can be generated:

> Well, 15 or 16 years ago, my wife committed adultery and I caught her and gave her a damn good hiding . . . didn't I? Well, instead of me going out and finding another woman and chucking her out, I was thinking of the kids, you know, and I stuck it for the kiddies' sakes . . . we'd got four . . . [A]bout two or three years after that . . . me mum and dad died, both

within three months of each other, and I was left on my own. I've got no
brothers and no sisters. Nobody to turn to, and I don't know whether
something cracked inside of me but I started drinking heavy . . . I was going
out every day and having seven or eight pints, and probably going out again
at night . . . I was borrowing money to go out to drink and I was on the dole
as well . . . I got as I wouldn't work. I turned to my daughters, you know,
just fondling them. No sexual intercourse . . . Not incest or anything . . .
just pushed my hand up their jumper . . . and sometimes down their
knickers . . . My second eldest says I did try it [sexual intercourse] on with
her once but I were drunk, she said I was absolutely drunk. [I]t had been
going off and on over . . . [ten] years. [It involved] the three daughters, but
my eldest and my youngest they tried to feel me, didn't they?

This account contains a great many self-serving excuses and is fairly
typical of the accounts given by paedophiles to justify their own behaviour.
The sexual touching carried on into the adulthood of this man's daughters.
While some might suggest that his behaviour warranted a prison sentence
and the removal of his children from home, this did not happen, perhaps
because the offences were reported only after a long delay. Instead
he received a police caution and, probably because of the age of the
daughters (some adult by this time), little else happened. The couple by
now had only their son with them at home.

In many ways, however, their grievance arose while they were still
living with their eldest daughter. Her husband was about to leave prison
following imprisonment for incest and rape. Social workers felt that the
son would be in moral danger when their son-in-law returned home. They
gave the couple a short period in which to find new accommodation. This
they could not do and the boy was taken into care. They claim to have
been assured that their son could return to them once they had found new
accommodation, but then the problem of the lack of symmetry in in-
and-out of care decisions arose and the boy was not returned even after
this accommodation had been found. According to the father, 'they
reckon it's just because of me'.

The cases reported in detail in this chapter illustrate the professional
theories which can be brought to bear in dealing with child abuse cases.
That these may well be specific to a particular historical period perhaps
reveals a great deal about the functions that the theories serve. The
'keeping the family together' theory, imposed in case study 11 against the
wishes of the mother, made the setting for a long-term 'problem family'.
The 'abusing mother' theory in case study 8 was based on expressed
conceptions of the proper social development of children, and also
perhaps on judgements about the bizarre nature of female abusers. The
theory that children do not lie about abuse accounts for the family in case
study 10, where the child's statement that she was afraid to return home

provided a setting for action in line with the child's wishes. Finally, it is easier to deal with a case of claimed inadvertent abuse by treating it as abuse, and this is facilitated by initial denials of guilt which are seen as symptomatic of the sex abuser.

CHAPTER 9

THE PRESENT AND THE FUTURE

Anne-Marie is 11, a survivor of sexual assault who broke the silence imposed on her by her abuser and saved herself. In February, she gave evidence in court. Her uncle was convicted and imprisoned for six months . . . She and her mother have received no follow-up support from a social worker, and a request for rehousing had been refused. John, the uncle, is now out of prison and lives a few streets away. (Roberts, 1989, p. 10)

Unquestionably, child protection work is stressful. The police, teachers, doctors and nurses, health visitors, social workers and others are not affected simply by the damage done to children – the horrific injuries, the taboo of incest and the distraught families. They are also vulnerable because of the high profile that child abuse work has. There is no guarantee that a mistake will result solely in their censure by local supervisors or disciplinary bodies. The risk is, of course, that any inadequacies in their work, including those created by their work environment, will be made very public indeed.

Not surprisingly, professionals develop means of warding off some of these pressures and risks. Organisations develop 'coping' strategies to deal with stressful aspects of their functioning. The medical profession, for example, may deal with the harrowing nature of its work by developing strategies to distance itself from its patients. In this way, patients' suffering and death take less of an emotional toll (Menzies, 1970).

Harris (1987) offers a related concept which he terms 'defensive social work'. This covers those mechanisms and procedures which serve to protect social workers from crises in their work and workplaces. Since there is every reason to see the responsibility for child protection errors spread widely across the professions involved, care must be taken not to present the issue as exclusively a social work problem. Consequently, while one might speak of defensive social work, similar defences are likely to be found in other professions. However, social work, with its special legal responsibilities, may well find itself dealing with the problems created by these other professions. We have seen some examples of this in our case studies as well as national scandals involving child abuse.

One novel feature of Harris's concept is his insistence that it applies not just to individual workers but also to social services organisations and at all levels. A nationally publicised incident involving a social worker may have drastic repercussions for the social work department and its senior management. So, in a sense, the avoidance of crises is a crucial aspect of the institution's work. In bureaucratic organisations with complex line-management systems, responsibility is spread widely, almost by definition. Consequently, defensiveness is likely to be endemic throughout the organisation.

Harris suggests that there are three main defensive strategies: *positive* defensive social work; *negative* defensive social work; and *suppressing* information.

Positive defences   These strategies are largely the formalised rules (or bureaucratic procedures) employed in order to pre-empt possible crises. One consequence of such formalised rules is the possibility that excessively large numbers of children might be placed on a child abuse register through the adherence to strict and unbending definitions of what constitutes abuse. One can think of the definitions commonly employed concerning non-accidental injury, which exclude claims by parents that chastisement unintentionally went too far or inadvertently caused a bruise. Furthermore, defining the sort of injury which constitutes a cause for concern as any tissue damage (such as a superficial scratch) widens the child abuse net to embrace numerous cases. This, in itself, can be seen as a defensive strategy, since it ensures at least minimal action by the authority. If, as is often the case, another rule stipulates that children meeting such a criterion must be placed on the child protection register, then some possible criticisms of inaction are short-circuited.

One outcome of this process is that the potential for parental disquiet is heightened. Harris warns that, by introducing stringent rules of procedure, organisations may, paradoxically, make themselves more vulnerable to blame or censure. In the event of errors coming under scrutiny, their procedures are likely to be criticised. The misjudgement of the individual social worker cannot be held primarily responsible if the guidelines under which he or she operates are inadequate. It is common that demands are made for the resignation of higher managers in cases where social work inquiries have found deficiencies in the organisation.

Negative defences   These are essentially not taking actions which might involve risks:

> Consider a child which has been taken into care and is currently in a residential home, or boarded out with foster parents. The situation of the child's family has improved and the question arises of whether the child

should be reunited with its family, perhaps on a trial basis, whilst still under the Care Order. If the child is returned to its parents in this way, the welfare of the child will still be the responsibility of the local authority, just as much as when it is in the residential home or is being fostered . . . To return the child to its parents may seem justified on the grounds of being most likely to benefit it emotionally and psychologically. But it may be presumed that children in care stand more risk of being abused if they are returned to their parents, than if they remain in a residential or foster home (if not, it would be safer to reunite all such children with their families!). By not returning a child to its parents the risk of the local authority and its social workers being held responsible for the possible abuse of the child by its parents is removed. (Harris, 1987, pp. 65–6)

Suppressing information   Here Harris suggests that because the files and other records produced by social workers are at risk of being exposed to scrutiny – either within or outside the organisation – social workers are possibly 'more likely . . . to act defensively by producing records that will help to cover them against charges of having been negligent in their duties, rather than ones that are in the best interests of their clients' (p. 66). According to Harris, this may extend as far as to involve the destruction of records.

Harris sees the solution to the negative aspects of these defensive strategies in educating the public into lower expectations about the power of social workers 'to predict, and to control, the actions of their clients' (p. 69). However, neither he nor anyone else, it would appear, has shown that the public has unrealistic beliefs about the scope for success in social work intervention. What seems to produce public outcry are cases which fly in the face of reason and in which suitable procedures have not been followed. That seems to be a totally different matter from having idealistic notions about social work's potential. Addison (1982) gives other examples of 'defences against the public' used by duty social workers which have a bearing on direct face-to-face child protection work:

> Another feature was the use of 'magic tags', which effectively decided the disposal of a case. 'Possible child abuse?' ensured immediate attention, while a case with 'interesting family dynamics' stood a good chance of speedy progress to allocation, because of enthusiasm for family therapy in the department at the time. Cases which could not attract these kinds of label were less likely to receive priority, even where problems were great . . . (p. 613)

This concept of defensive social work raises a number of concerns. Paramount is the difficulty of establishing which things are done with the intent of personal or organisational defence. They may well be justified for other reasons to which none of us are privy – for example, many of the procedures instituted following the major inquiry reports may be seen as 'good practice' – though 'good practice', of course, may frequently be indistinguishable from what Harris deems 'defence'. But, significantly, Harris presents a description of social work which, when applied to errors, shows them in a totally different light. In Harris's formulation an almost cynical process puts the needs of the organisation and its workers before those of the child and its family. In that sense, these are rational processes which seem to explain certain aspects of error, such as the 'fixed' quality of decisions found in some cases. Nevertheless, there is much more to be tackled in an account of error.

One teacher of social workers described one variant of this notion of defensiveness in a somewhat more direct form:

> There is a tendency . . . to develop a trench warfare mentality, whereby parents are 'the other side' and solicitors representing parents are to be treated with great caution. The mushroom principle comes well to the fore – they must be kept in the dark and fed with . . . (Robinson, 1989)

Who gets involved in 'error'

One of the disturbing features of my research was that those involved were not an approximate cross-section of the general population. My sample of complainants seemed closer to the stereotypes of single parents, working class, unemployed and step-relationships/live-in partners. Perhaps I should say they are 'stereotypes of stereotypes'. In other words, those with complaints about their treatment seemed to be a selected sample of a selected sample. The question then becomes one of the extent to which the stereotype itself leads to the error. We have already discussed this possibility, mainly based on the general research evidence in Chapter 4. However, there is more to be said in connection with my cases.

The indirect evidence on this is reasonably strong. If we look at the social class, unemployment and other factors in the research sample of twenty cases we find the following:

Working class	100%
Single-parent family history	45%
Step-relationship/live-in partner	40%

It might be argued that some of these factors *are* typical of abusers. This is generally true, although the trends in my data seem stronger than the statistical evidence would warrant. Furthermore, as we saw in Chapter 3, the demographic characteristics of sexual abusers are somewhat different – there is no class bias, for example. To find that all or virtually all of the sample were working class by conventional criteria, irrespective of the type of abuse, raises questions about class biases in judgements which might lead to error. Of course, it is not being suggested that a doctor or social worker decides that abuse has occurred on the basis of knowledge of the parents' social background. It would have to be a more subtle process than that. For example, one theory which might explain why a child is battered is that abuse is a consequence of stress due to unemployment or money problems. A working-class person is more likely to fit this theory about who batters and why because unemployment or money problems might be deemed more common in such people.

An alternative explanation might be that the working class are less able to press their case and deal effectively with middle-class professionals. Certainly, one of the suggestions made about the Cleveland crisis and the Orkney's satanic abuse case is that the families involved tended to be middle class and better able to voice their complaints. As a consequence, it might be that the middle class are less likely to be wrongly accused because of their better knowledge of how to deal with professionals and create a favourable impression with them. None of this is to suggest that middle-class families are not involved in false allegations of abuse. In the course of the research I heard of a number of instances in which professionals had been on the receiving end of child protection errors. But these were seen as exceptions by informants rather than as typical. Certainly, if they exist in any great proportions, they did not volunteer for my research. Although many of my families had sought the assistance of law firms, this was too late to prevent the precipitating wrong decisions from occurring in the first place.

But raw figures, at best, are only suggestive evidence of the processes involved. Perhaps the more important question is: how do such factors explain the overrepresentation of such families? It is not possible, in every case, to document the thinking of the professionals involved, but in some cases the families told of things said to them by professionals which explained why it was believed that the allegations were well founded. These are the justificatory theories which we have already discussed (Chapters 6 to 8). Furthermore, a number of oddities suggest that such processes are at work: for example, the tendency for the blame to be addressed to the stepfather where the injuries could just as easily have been inflicted by the mother. Chapters 6 and 7 included at least two examples where the suspicion of abuse fell on the stepfather rather than the mother. Furthermore, one might suggest that the tendency to blame the parents in cases in which the babysitter was an alternative culprit can be seen as a further instance where the characteristics of stereotypical abusers might be influencing decisions.

The issue then becomes a rather worrying one. If part of the process by which families become involved in unjust child protection activities involves social characteristics other than the alleged abuse, then one has to question also the extent to which similar processes are involved in true cases of child abuse. This might not make sense at first sight, but one has to consider that there is no fixed social act which has been defined as 'abuse'. Abuse is typically defined in terms of (a) certain relationships; (b) certain types of act (though other acts thought by some to be harmful are excluded, as in the case of a sexually repressive upbringing which denies the child access to sex education); (c) the historic period (the caning of children being not uncommon in schools until fairly recently) and (d) the age of the perpetrator (so an older sibling repeatedly assaulting a younger one is unlikely to be seen as child abuse despite the repeated and extensive nature of the injuries). Consequently, child abuse has to be regarded as a fuzzy concept with indistinct boundaries.

Decisions about abuse may therefore be expected to have a degree of discretion built into them and to be prone to the influence of factors which are not properly concerned with child abuse decisions. In cases where there is a considerable degree of uncertainty, this discretion may be at its most likely to be exercised. We have discussed several example of this from experimental research in earlier chapters.

But, of course, it is not easy to be objective and to ignore non-evidential matters – after all, there is a long list of studies showing that judicial decision making may be influenced by non-relevant or extra-evidential factors. Carrying out the fieldwork for the research brought me into contact with a wide variety of home-settings – much the same as the social workers and other profesionals would have been exposed to. Many of the homes were well kept, cared for and very habitable. However, some were not. For example, entering a house with bare floorboards, walls with no wallpaper or paint, and just a couple of seats creates an uncomfortable feeling no matter how welcoming the people. It is very difficult not to succumb to irrational judgements about the veracity of the case being made by the parent. One is tempted to wonder, irrespective of whether abuse or neglect had occurred, whether a child in these circumstances might not have been better off fostered as the social workers may have decided. Social prejudices may affect all of us and in ways which we do not really like in ourselves. But it is a complex matter whether such circumstantial factors are appropriate to this sort of decision making. After all, we do not routinely take children away from parents who fail a routine quality control check on their dwellings or other circumstances. Such a routine quality check would be seen as a gross infringement of privacy. What then would be the ethics of being influenced by such factors in other decision making?

The variety of errors

While the public's perception of the errors made in child protection is probably significantly influenced by the national child abuse scandals, these probably do not reflect the typical error at all well. For example, in the public criticisms of child protection the primary focuses of concern have been the failure to act in the face of evidence that action was necessary (the Maria Colwell case is a classic example of this) or the failure to diagnose properly either through faulty medical evidence (the Cleveland case) or through apparent failures to decipher the reports of children adequately (Rochdale and Orkney's satanic abuse cases). Quite different emphases emerged in my research. While there were examples of misdiagnosis and examples where it was felt that intervention was needed but was not happening, the sorts of complaint made about interventions stretched the notion of error much further than this. Including all my case studies, I can tentatively suggest that a classification of types of error would need to incorporate some of the following categories:

1. Serious or moderate injuries to the child misdiagnosed as physical abuse when they were accidental.
2. Serious or moderate injuries to the child which are accepted by their families as being abuse but where the perpetrator was a baby sitter or similar such person, the dispute then being over the identity of the perpetrator of the abuse.
3. Very minor injuries being considered abuse.
4. Serious or moderate injuries, inflicted accidentally, being attributed to a parent when brittle-bone disease or some other innocent cause is responsible.
5. Abuse and neglect by an ex-partner leading to the innocent father or mother also being deprived of access to the children. It is notable that the cases involving the mother as the guilty party were ones of neglect. This reflects gender differences in the types of abuse most commonly perpetrated.
6. False allegations, possibly maliciously made, about physical or sexual abuse.
7. Unintended sexual contact being treated as deliberate sexual abuse.
8. Reporting of child sexual abuse by a partner leading to long-term injustice to the reporting mother.

9. Self-reported abuse leading to no help with a domestic difficulty, but rather to more draconian measures against the parent, such as attempts to remove a new baby at birth.
10. False intimations of physical or sexual abuse made by a child.
11. Asymmetry in the taking-into-care and releasing-from-care criteria. This leads to a child voluntarily placed in care not being released from care when circumstances change for the family.
12. Failure to acknowledge or act on concerns about the safety of a child, especially when communicated by a relative.

Doubtless there are other types of error which emerge from time to time. But even these twelve categories present a fairly complex picture of the range of things that can happen in child protection. It needs to be stressed that many of these categories are connected and sometimes more than one type of error will occur in any one case. This is important and underlines the fact that sequential processes are often involved which do not stem solely from a single misdiagnosis. Errors, it would appear, can emerge at a number of different stages:

1. Errors of reporting.
2. Errors in the diagnosis of abuse.
3. Errors in the identification of the perpetrator.
4. Errors in the actions taken – support, therapy, etc.

Cases could involve more than one of these stages.

Who is responsible for errors?

One thing that seems to emerge is that the responsibility for an error may involve any of a number of different professionals. Certainly, it did not universally emerge that social workers themselves were responsible for creating the difficulties which they had to resolve. So, for example, among the professions which were involved in creating errors were medical doctors, health visitors, and teachers, whose knowledge and experience of abuse may be inferior by far to that of social workers. In addition, we might mention that culpability, if that is an appropriate term to be used in all cases, also involved the psychological profession.

The police, however, were something of a curiosity in so far as they were criticised relatively rarely by the parents despite their universal involvement. Perhaps this may reflect the different standards of evidence required in police work compared to that of other professions. That is not to say that they were not sometimes criticised for violence or for unacceptable methods of trying to collect evidence. But that is not quite the same as suggesting that they contributed to errors of commission in the child protection system on anything other than a very temporary investigative basis. Given the nature of the complaints made by my sample, the police were probably unlikely to be a major focus, although, of course, we have seen some examples of very suspect police activity in the case studies.

It is not realistic to quantify the proportion of cases in which social workers were responsible for creating the errors. Because of the complexity of the cases, it is not easy precisely to identify the extent of each profession's involvement. The case studies of Chapters 6, 7 and 8 give an insight into the processes involved which is much more important. There is little point in trying to create a league table of blame – it would probably be fruitless given the range of things that can go wrong at any stage. Much more important for anyone concerned about child abuse errors is that difficulties may be the result of the input of a full range of professions. While social work should not escape censure through the spreading of blame, it is perhaps sufficient to suggest that all professions should be aware of their potential contribution to errors.

The effects of intervention on the family

It goes almost without saying that the effects on the families involved in these child protection interventions are traumatic. Quite simply, these are people who care about their children. Allegations cannot be dismissed as neutral. The issue of the effects of errors on the accused families is complex and varied. At this stage, it is difficult, perhaps impossible, to differentiate between the effects of an intervention (justified or not) that involves much disruption and the effects of a *false* allegation. A consequence of experiencing injustice may be a fundamental shock to the individual's beliefs about the nature of a world which allows such injustice to happen. But equally, part of the effect of the allegation is that an outright attack is made on the individual's self-image as a good parent. Attempts at suicide occurred in my sample as well as severe depression.

One outcome of the disruption of an individual's view of a just world is a substantial disjunction between attitudes towards the police and towards social workers. The police's involvement often helped partially to re-establish a person's self-image as a decent and adequate parent. Police and social workers have radically different requirements about proof of allegations. The police merely need to decide whether or not there is enough evidence of a sufficiently serious nature to bring criminal charges. A social worker's role is rather different and is not necessarily concerned with legalistic proof. Worries and concerns about the child's well-being and safety come into a social worker's ambit. The police, on the other hand, do not normally have to decide whether a child is at risk. It has to be stressed that it is the parents' perceptions of the professions that are under consideration here. I am not claiming that the police always get it right in other respects, or that no complaints were made against them. But central to the feelings of injustice is the nature of the social worker's task.

The police can, in some circumstances, provide the vindication of the parent that he or she desperately seeks. Proving that one has not abused a child is far from easy to do – many forms of sexual abuse leave no physical signs, and bruises are not always clearly labelled with their cause. However, while a decision by the police not to prosecute is frequently taken by the parents as evidence of their innocence, the same decision may well be read, perfectly reasonably, by child protection workers merely as evidence that a prosecution was not appropriate or was likely to fail due to the lack of evidence. It does not mean that there is no cause for concern. The lack of a prosecution does not equate for the social worker with innocence and the lack of risk. Typical of the comfort provided by the police response to abuse allegations is the following:

> I think [the policewoman] believed us, to be honest . . . [S]he interviewed Jim first, and he came downstairs and he was actually smiling . . . You could tell from her attitude, you know what I mean, she was a lot more sympathetic than any of the social workers.

The police also, from time to time, bring to the situation a perspective which is shared by the parent. This might be particularly in relation to corporal punishment and the matter of how children should be reared. So not only will the police be a lifeline in regard to subjective beliefs of innocence, but they will also provide validation of a view of parenting which is unlikely to be fashionable amongst social workers with a more child-centred ideology:

> And [the police inspector] said this is bloody stupid, because . . . if he'd been my kid . . . I'd have killed the bastard before now . . . because of the hell he's put you through . . . [H]e said the social workers are overreacting . . . they've got this little hobby horse that they're riding at the bloody moment, and it's causing us far too much work . . .

The failure of social work organisations to express regret that an error or a misjudgement has been made is psychologically damaging. Apologies are rare even in those cases in which there seems to be very good reason to apologise. While this may be a self-protecting strategy (serving, for example, to reduce the risk of legal action), it is also a consequence of the assessment of risk rather than proof. Whatever the reason, families often do not feel that justice has been done. Consequently attempts to obtain justice tend never to cease. Participating in my research often served the need to protest further. Involvement in parents' support groups may serve a similar function. The following comment, by a parent who had experienced a false accusation of child abuse, expresses something of this straw clutching:

> A subsequent visit by the child psychologist at our invitation was helpful in a way. His most valid contribution was when he was moved to say simply 'I'm sorry'. The gap between those with direct human experience and those from the ivory tower . . . had manifested itself again. The power of the social services is devastating and the unpreparedness and ignorance of ordinary people is total. Their strength and our problem is that *nobody* wants to know about *this* unsavoury business unless and until they are hit. (Anon, 1989, p. 19)

Of course, in the minds of some of the parents was a belief that some social workers were 'all right'. Not surprisingly, these were typically those who gave the parents some degree of support. One of the remarkable features of abuse interventions is the lack of support made available to most members of the family going through such a crisis. While, naturally, attention may be given to the 'abused' child's emotional and other needs by the workers involved, the parents and other members of the family are left to fend, psychologically, for themselves. Other members of the family or friends may give some support, but this is not always the case. Hostility can sometimes be the response of close relatives, neighbours and friends. Partners also provide support, but this is obviously prob-lematic given that the partner might be under suspicion of abuse. In the confusion and uncertainty surrounding false allegations, some partners inevitably begin to wonder if they are not actually true. This is especially likely when, say, one partner was not at home when an accidental injury occurred. Perhaps professional counselling ought to be available to all families facing allegations.

Effects on the children

The extent to which the effects of interventions on children can be distin-guished from those on their parents is obviously severely limited. Only a proportion of the children involved in my research were so young that they would be oblivious to the situation and to the distress that intervention caused to members of their family. Consequently, the dichotomy between the effects of intervention on parents and children is very flimsy in these circumstances. The range of possible effects is obviously enormous. Given that the circumstances of interventions will vary widely, even for the children of the family, it would be foolish to identify prematurely a few major effects. Furthermore, the effects of the intervention might well vary because of the range of actions taken concerning the children. They might be interviewed briefly or extensively or not at all. Their day-to-day routine might be virtually unaffected or they might be taken into care, temporarily or permanently. Many other parameters might be involved which produce different impacts on the children – the quality of the counselling received being one.

I explored with the parents this very question of the effects of the intervention on their children. There were some difficulties with this, since in a substantial number of cases the parents no longer had contact with their children. Some of them were being permanently fostered without parental access. In such circumstances the effects on the children and notions about the importance of the family still emerge quite forcibly. Sometimes the parents seemed very concerned about the current safety of their children. In one example, and this was not an isolated case, photographs of the child obtained at the early stages of fostering were seen as demonstrating abuse. It was impossible for me to confirm this given the poor quality of the photographs and other obvious reasons. The concern about this possible abuse in foster care reflects a commitment to an ideology about the special protection afforded by the natural family.

It is doubtful whether residential care of children would be seen as a satisfactory environment by many in the child protection field. More likely it would be regarded as the least bad of the available options. Fostering is seen as much the preferred alternative. There are good reasons for this, including the risks to children in residential settings. For example, a recent study of one authority's residential facilities for children found that sexual abuse was common. There were 380 children in residential care of this sort. Of 79 youngsters who had been taken into care because of sexual abuse, 26 were further sexually abused in the residential home. And 48 children who had not previously been sexually abused were sexually abused for the first time in residential care (Lunn, 1991). This amounts to almost one in five children – a figure which exceeds typical British figures outside of the institutional setting. Physical abuse appears not to be uncommon in organisations involved in the care of children. For example, Blatt and Brown (1986) found that excessive corporal punishment accounted for many of the complaints to the New York State Office of Mental Health concerning children in their residential care.

Lacerations, bruises, welts, fractures and burns accounted for about a quarter of these complaints.

Parents who did not lose their children to fostering or residential care tended to suggest that the children had become 'clingy' as a consequence of temporary separation, perhaps anxious about possible future interventions. Sometimes there emerged discipline problems because of the parent's perceived lack of sanctions, caused by the fear of future allegations which might follow the use of physical punishment.

Decision making

It would be a reasonable expectation of an equitable child protection system for there to be regularities in the decision-making processes involved. To the extent that judgements are not made on a consistent and rational basis the risk of errors and biases emerging will inevitably be increased. There are few good studies of decision making in child protection: however, the ones there are scarcely inspire confidence in the system.

An American study by Pellegrin and Wagner (1990) examined the factors affecting the child's removal from home in cases of child sexual abuse. She took 43 cases of child sexual abuse of girls and looked at the correlates of whether the child was allowed to remain at home or was removed. Independent raters scored the severity of the abuse on a four-point scale from fondling, to digital penetration, to oral–genital contact, to penile penetration. The child protection worker involved in the particular case assessed the mother's belief in what the child had to say and the degree of co-operation that the mother demonstrated with the child protection service's recommendations. Other data were available from the records. In some ways, the decision-making process seems quite rational. For example, the frequency and severity of the abuse were among the factors which actually increased the likelihood of the child's removal. Other predictors seem rather less equitable and, perhaps, reflect ideological biases. Mothers who were *not* in paid employment, for example, were the most likely to have their children taken away. Mothers who did not behave like model mothers of abused children were also in danger of having their child removed, since the case worker's judgements about the extent to which the mother accepted the child's account of events and the extent to which she co-operated with the child protection service recommendations affected the outcome. The significance of this for errors in child protection is, of course, that those who feel that injustice is being done are the most likely to express support for their partners and disbelief or criticism of the child, and are also probably the most likely to appear non-co-operative. Perhaps this is further evidence of the view that errors are the consequence of normal child protection processes.

Researchers who have observed child protection decision making in action also provide little which would encourage confidence. Dingwall *et al.* (1983) give examples of what they describe as 'total denunciation' of some parents at case conferences. Other researchers (Corby and Mills, 1986) are largely critical of the tendency for the decision about placing the child on a central child abuse register to dominate the proceedings:

> The registration issue was not the only one which diverted attention from focussing more explicitly on risks and resources. In the case conferences observed there was a general resistance to predicting outcomes too specifically which was without doubt fuelled by the climate of fear surrounding child abuse work and the difficulty of choosing between the apparently conflicting demands of child protection and preserving the integrity of the family. (p. 535)

Bad as this appears, the following confirms the unsystematic nature of the decision-making process: 'It was found that there were few explicit criteria used for making decisions' (p. 531). In the end, however, the authors defend the system on the following grounds:

> It should be noted here that although this paper is largely critical of the system observed it should not be thought that it did not operate without some degree of success. Of the 55 cases 69% had not been the subject of further case conferences two years later and a further 7% had been subject to only one further conference, suggesting that in ¾ of the cases the system had made good decisions (using the admittedly rough guide of further reported injury as a criterion of success). (p. 535)

Of course, to make such a statement assumes that the cases of abuse had been serious and sustained before registration of the child. But this is not shown in the report. After all, one might argue that the 24 per cent of cases which were subject to further case conferences, apparently because of further reported injury, are strong evidence of the failure of the system to protect these children.

An American study by Kienberger Jaudes and Morris (1990) raises further questions about the decision-making processes in child sexual abuse cases. They were interested in those factors which determined whether sexually abused children were fostered or remained with their original caretakers. They examined the outcomes of 180 cases admitted to a Chicago hospital for possible sex abuse. Virtually nothing they included in their study predicted the outcome – sex, age, presence of a sexually transmitted disease, developmental delay, whether or not the

perpetrator was identified, the relationship of t.
child, whether the child lived in the home or the perp
the child, the presence or absence of physical abuse
child had been sexually abused in the past all failed to
disposal of the child.

The one factor which made any difference was if the
statement about abuse in the early stages. This seemed
fostering-type decisions and seems to reflect what happened   of
the contested cases discussed in Chapters 7 and 8.

The costs and the benefits

Financially, the cost of child abuse work is hefty. Roberts (1989) mentions
survey evidence collected from local authorities in Britain which demonstrates a dramatic increase in sex abuse cases of nearly 60 per cent over a
three-year period. Almost 80 per cent of social services departments said
that they had insufficient resources to cope. It is dubious that even the
emotive nature of the issue of child abuse would lead to the provision of
sufficient funding to meet what the child protection services see as the
need. This is likely to be true of many countries. Indeed, in some parts of
the world, child protection work cannot be placed properly on the agenda
for social action given the extent of the problems caused by poverty in the
first place.

So, value for money considerations cannot be ignored in child protection work. There simply are not the resources available to do what ideally
we feel should be done. There are obvious savings to be made if false
reports and error can be eliminated. Many of the errors cost as much
to handle as serious cases of child abuse. Spreading resources too thinly
over too many cases is not conducive to best practice or preventing further errors. Large numbers of reports about abuse are made and, based
on the American evidence that many are unsubstantiated (Besharov,
1988), there is enormous potential for wasteful investigations. Seriousness criteria, which filter out trivial cases, would more probably be a
feature of organisations not acting defensively to fend off possible public
criticism.

It might be expected that this sort of interventionist social work would
be substantially effective in reducing abuse. But we have already seen
that many children escape the net and do not come to the attention of
child protection workers until serious injury or a fatality occurs. We have
also seen that many children are abused again despite receiving attention
from social workers or others. Whether or not intervention does reduce

risk of harm is a difficult issue for which to glean evidence. Geach (1983), concentrating on child abuse registration procedures, was able to suggest 'there is little evidence to show the success of registers or their associated procedures' (p. 51). Infanticide rates had remained stable for a ten-year period despite the introduction of registration. But Besharov claims that 'Increased reporting and specialized child protective agencies have saved many thousands of children from death and serious injury. The best estimate is that, over these twenty years, child abuse deaths are down from 2–3,000 a year to about 1,000 a year' (Besharov, 1988, p. 3). If accurate, this is a remarkable figure. But, of course, one needs to know precisely what such statistics refer to. The disparity could imply that some systems of child protection are more effective than others.

The other available forms of social work intervention, in general, have not proved to be particularly successful. For example, Goldberg (1987) suggested:

> Methods deliberately aimed at problem solving seem to enable clients to tackle some of their problems and bring about partial – sometimes very partial – resolutions, but they can rarely if ever achieve personality changes, personal growth or changes in basic behaviour patterns. (p. 609)

Garbarino (1986) asked a similar question about preventing child abuse. He is enthusiastic about the research into a number of 'model' programmes in which, for example, extensive home health visiting is provided to disadvantaged single teenage mothers. But such interventions are expensive and not at all typical in child abuse work. Furthermore, agency statistics show no clear indication that the number of cases involving severe injury or the proportion of reported cases involving serious abuse have decreased.

Four major US evaluation studies of child abuse treatment programmes were surveyed by Cohn and Daro (1987). Nearly 90 such programmes were studied, involving over three thousand families:

> The studies . . . provide some cause for concern. Treatment effects in general are not very successful. Child abuse and neglect continue despite early, thoughtful, and often costly intervention. Treatment programs have been relatively ineffective in initially halting abusive and neglectful behaviour or in reducing the future likelihood of maltreatment. One-third or more of the parents served by these intensive efforts maltreated their children while in treatment, and over one-half of the families serviced continued to be judged by staff as likely to mistreat their children following termination. Whether one views this level of success as notable or disappointing is largely a function of personal perspective and professional choice. (p. 440)

Of course, this does not mean that individual, limited-goal programmes will fail to succeed. For example, Fryer *et al.* (1987) demonstrated that a child's personal safety training programme increased participants' unwillingness to go with a stranger in an experimental test. But sometimes what appears as a success may have its own limitations. For example, Zimrim (1984) provides evidence that mere human contact given by professionals may help improve parenting behaviour – unfortunately, however, things rapidly return to normal once this support is taken away.

Can errors be prevented?

A precise definition of 'errors' has been avoided so far. The reasons for this have already been partially discussed. The difficulty is that the word 'error', with its connotations of a mistake or wrongful conduct or judgement, does not reflect very accurately the nature of many child abuse 'errors'. In other words, many of the events that might be seen as errors may not involve any clearly identifiable errant behaviour on the part of individuals. It is particularly difficult to use the term to refer to events which are constrained by time and place. While by common consensus the errors might refer to circumstances in which things have gone wrong, that is quite different from being able to say that any individual did something analogous to a musician playing sour notes in the band. Furthermore, concepts such as 'bad decisions' would also imply that good decisions are possible in these cases – itself a dubious proposition. What can be a good decision in circumstances in which all options are vexed?

One definition which seems helpful is provided by MacDonald (1990). However, she does not try to define 'errors' as such. Instead she casts light on what should be regarded as proper practice:

> Correctly taken decisions are those for which appropriate information is sought from diverse sources, appropriately weighted against available knowledge, and whose outcomes are fed back into that knowledge base (both in terms of future organizational practice and, where pertinent, a research base) to inform future practice. (p. 539)

Among the minimal requirements to meet this definition of 'correctly taken decisions', MacDonald lists a more rigorous 'empirically-based' practice, which emphasises task-oriented record keeping that differentiates fact and opinion. Furthermore, she suggests that social work training is 'all too often cluttered by unsubstantiated ideas of dubious utility' (p. 539). Unfortunately, she does not say what these unsubstantiated ideas are. Perhaps she means the sort of theories about abusers which seemed to be involved in some of the case studies we have discussed. She might mean some of the notions spread by the professional literature concerned with abuse, such as we have identified in earlier chapters. Certainly, she could extend her comments to the other professions primarily involved in child protection – such as teachers and medical people.

But the underlying idea of an organisational structure which encourages learning and accommodation to the deficiencies identified is a good one. A big difficulty, though, is how such knowledge is to be structured. The danger, as we have seen repeatedly, is turning the evidence of research into formulae of dubious applicability. But to a degree much also depends upon how the knowledge developed empirically is treated. That is, it depends on the broader framework within which it is interpreted and used. So, for example, if in-house research identified a geographical bias in the numbers of abuse cases, such that a particular area was overrepresented in numbers, what should be concluded? The temptation is, of course, to feel that this was a 'problem area' with 'problem people', since we tend to adopt an organisation-down viewpoint. However, the data may, in fact, have identified a problem with the organisation rather than with the population it serves.

In many ways, MacDonald gets close to suggesting the need for a brand new organisational ethos which regards errors not as catastrophes but as endemic to professional activity. To regard things that go wrong as anything other than integral to the work of organisations is to risk a pressure to sweep them under the carpet; in effect, not to learn from them. Regarding errors as part and parcel of professional involvement in child protection does not imply any complacency. It means that the topic of errors can be given a continuously high profile rather than being whispered about in corridors or bars. Errors can be seen as providing vital stimulus to progress and improvement. They offer data on which to build. By reducing the 'culpability' factor of errors, it might be possible to build procedures which are not so dependent on stultifying rules. (Evans, 1989, deals with ways of correcting 'cognitive' errors for those interested in a more individual-centred approach.)

Mills and Vine (1990) borrow from the way in which errors (near misses and the like) are dealt with in a field distantly removed from child protection – the aviation industry. They recommend to social workers the adoption of 'critical incident reporting'. This involves a lot more than dealing with disasters:

> Central to this approach is the recognition that critical errors do not necessarily result in bad outcomes and that error is a normal part of professional practice. Aircraft accidents . . . seldom result from isolated mistakes but rather from a combination of errors some of which may occur relatively frequently in normal operation . . .
> Central to the critical incident approach is the acceptance that errors

committed by individuals and agencies should be reported irrespective of outcome. (pp. 26, 218).

They suggest that such incidents should be reported to some sort of central body – perhaps the department in which the incident takes place. But the change in organisational ethos required to enable such a re-orientation is fundamental. It cannot be achieved by the circulation of a memo.

Other approaches to the reduction of error would have to include ways of altering which child abuse 'fish' enter the child abuse 'net'. It cannot be good that rather insignificant and, perhaps, one-off instances of abuse have to be dealt with while other children who are killed or seriously injured or subject to persistent sexual abuse go unnoticed by protection services. The trapping of trivial abuse or unfounded cases in the net uses up finite resources. Public inquiries are even more costly. Consequently, critical examination of notions about what abuse is, what effects it has, how extensive it is, who can be helped and a multitude of other questions may involve resources well spent. Accepting the need to understand errors is part of this. Moral outrage posing as justification for social policy is a costly luxury.

REFERENCES

Abbot, A. (1988) *The System of Professions: An essay on the division of expert labor*, Chicago, Ill.: University of Chicago Press.

Ackland, P. R. (1987) 'Child abuse and osteogenesis imperfecta', *British Medical Journal*, 295 (21 November), 1346.

Addison, C. (1982) 'A defence against the public? Aspects of intake in a social services department', *British Journal of Social Work*, 12, 605–18.

Alexander, P. C., and Lupfer, S. L. (1987) 'Family characteristics and long-term consequences associated with sexual abuse', *Archives of Sexual Behavior*, 16 (3), 235–45.

Alfaro, J. D. (1988) 'What can we learn from child abuse fatalities? A synthesis of nine studies', in D. J. Besharov (ed.), *Protecting Children from Abuse and Neglect: Policy and practice*, Springfield, Ill.: Charles C. Thomas.

Altemeier, W., O'Connor, S., Vietze, P., Sandler, H., and Sherrod, K. (1984) 'Prediction of child abuse: a prospective study of feasibility', *Child Abuse and Neglect*, 8, 393–400.

Anon. (1989) 'Case history', *PAIN Newsletter*, 6 August, 19.

Anon. (1991) 'Report's findings', *Social Work Today*, 22 (38), 4–9.

Avison, W. R., Turner, R. J., and Noh, S. (1986) 'Screening for problem parents: preliminary evidence on a promising instrument', *Child Abuse and Neglect*, 10, 157–70.

Baartman, H. E. M. (1990) 'The credibility of children as witnesses and the social denial of the incestuous abuse of children', paper presented at the 2nd European Congress on Law and Psychology, Nuremberg, 13–15 September.

Bain, O., and Sanders, M. (1991) *Out in the Open: A guide for young people who have been sexually abused*, London: Virago.

Baker, A. W., and Duncan, S. P. (1985) 'Child sexual abuse: a study of prevalence in Great Britain', *Child Abuse and Neglect*, 9, 457–67.

Bartlett, F. (1932) *Remembering: A study in experimental and social psychology*, Cambridge: Cambridge University Press.

Barton, C., and Alexander, J. F. (1981) 'Functional family therapy', in A. S. Gurman and D. P. Kniskern (eds), *Handbook of Family Therapy*, New York: Brunner Maze.

Barwick, S. (1991) 'Not men only', *The Spectator*, 1 June, 8–9.

Bayer, T., and Connors, R. (1988) 'The emergence of child sexual abuse from the shadow of sexism', *Response*, 11 (4), 12–15.

Bean, P. (1974) *The Social Control of Drugs*, London: Martin Robertson.

Bedford, A., and Bedford, J. (1985) 'Personality and personal disturbance in social workers: a research note', *British Journal of Social Work*, 15, 87–90.

Bekerian, D. A., and Dennett, J. L. (1990) 'The truth in content analyses of a child's testimony', unpublished paper presented to the European Conference on Law and Psychology, Nuremberg, 13–15 September.

Bell, S. (1988) *When Salem came to the Boro*, London: Pan.

Berger, A. M. (1981) 'An examination of the relationship between harsh discipline in childhood, later punitiveness towards children and later ratings of adjustment', unpublished doctoral dissertation, University of Iowa.

Berger, A. M., Knutson, J. F., Mehm, J. G., and Perkins, K. A. (1988) 'The self-report of punitive childhood experiences of young adults and adolescents', *Child Abuse and Neglect*, 12, 251–62.

Berliner, L., and Conte, V. R. (1990) 'The process of victimization: the victim's perspective', *Child Abuse and Neglect*, 14, 29–40.

Bernard, F. (1979) 'Pedophilia: the consequences for the child', in M. Cook and G. Wilson (eds), *Love and Attraction: An international conference*. Oxford: Pergamon.

Berridge, V. (1984) 'Drugs and social policy: the establishment of drug controls in Britain 1900–1930', *British Journal of Addictions*, 79, 17–28.

Besharov, D. (1988) 'The need to narrow the grounds for state intervention', in D. Besharov (ed.), *Protecting Children from Abuse and Neglect: Policy and practice*, Springfield, Ill.: Charles C. Thomas.

Bevan, W. (1980) 'On getting in bed with a lion', *American Psychologist*, 35 (9), 779–89.

Billig, M., Condor, S., Edwards, D., Gane, M., Middleton, D., and Radley, A. R. (1988) *Ideological Dilemmas*, London: Sage.

Blatt, E. R., and Brown, S. W. (1986) 'Environmental influences on incidents of alleged child abuse and neglect in New York State psychiatric facilities: towards an etiology of institutional child maltreatment', *Child Abuse and Neglect*, 10, 171–80.

Blume, E. S. (1990) *Secret Survivors: Incest and its effects in women*, New York: John Wiley.

Boat, B. W., and Everson, M. D. (1988) 'Use of anatomical dolls among professionals in sexual abuse evaluations', *Child Abuse and Neglect*, 12, 171–9.

Bowlby, J. (1952) *Maternal Care and the Mental Health*, Geneva: World Health Organisation.

Bowlby, J. (1973) *Attachment and Loss Vol. II: Separation: Anxiety and anger*. London: Hogarth Press and the Institute of Psychoanalysis.

Bradshaw, T. L., and Marks, A. E. (1990) 'Beyond a reasonable doubt: factors that influence the legal disposition of child sexual abuse cases', *Crime and Delinquency*, 36 (2), 276–85.

British Psychological Society (1990) 'Psychologists and child sexual abuse', *The Psychologist: Bulletin of the British Psychological Society*, 8, 344–8.

Browne, K., and Saqi, S. (1988) 'Approaches to screening for child abuse and neglect', in K. Brown, C. Davies, and P. Stratton (eds), *Early Prediction and Prevention of Child Abuse*, Chichester: John Wiley.

Brownmiller, S. (1975) *Against Our Will: Men, women and rape*, New York: Simon and Schuster.

Bull, R., and Clifford, B. (1979) 'Eyewitness memory', in M. M. Gruneberg and P. E. Morris (eds), *Applied Problems in Memory*, London: Academic Press.

Burgess, A. W., and Holmstrom, L. L. (1979) *Rape: Crisis and recovery*, Bowie, Md: Robert J. Brody.

Burke, P. (1991) 'Risk factors', *Social Work Today*, 22 (32), 28–9.

Burnham, J. B. (1986) *Family Therapy: First steps towards a systemic approach*, London: Tavistock.

Burnstein, P., and Pitchford, S. (1990) 'Social-scientific and legal challenges to education and test requirements in employment', *Social Problems*, 37 (2), 243–57.

Burt, M. R. (1980) 'Cultural myths and supports for rape', *Journal of Personality and Social Psychology*, 38, 217–30.

Butler-Sloss, E. (1988). *Report of the Inquiry into Child Abuse in Cleveland 1987*, London: Her Majesty's Stationery Office, Cm 412.

Campbell, B. (1988) *Unofficial Secrets*, London: Virago.

Campbell, B. (1989) 'Cleveland's dilemma', *New Statesman and Society*, 24 February, 14–15.

Campbell, M. (1991) 'Children at risk: how different are children on child abuse registers?' *British Journal of Social Work*, 21, 259–75.

Cavaiola, A. A., and Schiff, M. (1988) 'Behavioral sequelae of physical and/or sexual abuse in adolescents', *Child Abuse and Neglect*, 12, 181–8.

Cherniss, C. (1980) *Staff Burnout: Job stress in the human services*, Beverly Hills, Calif.: Sage.

Chesney, J. (1991) 'Us rapists', *Changes: An International Journal of Psychology and Psychotherapy*, 9 (1), 2–9.

Clark, A. (1987) *Women's Silence Men's Violence*, London: Pandora.

Cochrane, S. (1989) 'Abused by the experts', *New Statesman and Society*, 2 June, 28–30.

Cohen, S. (1972) *Folk Devils and Moral Panics*, London: McGibbon and Kee.

Cohn, A. H., and Daro, D. (1987) 'Is treatment too late?: what ten years of evaluative research tell us', *Child Abuse and Neglect*, 11, 433–522.

Community Care (1991) 'Live issue: pindown', *Community Care*, 6 June, 14–17.

Constantine, L. L. (1979) 'The sexual rights of children: implications of a radical perspective', in M. Cook and G. Wilson (eds), *Love and Attraction: An international conference*, Oxford: Pergamon.

Conte, J. R., and Schuerman, J. R. (1987) 'Factors associated with an increased impact of child sexual abuse', *Child Abuse and Neglect*, 11, 201–11.

Corby, B. (1987) 'Why ignoring the rights of parents in child abuse cases should be avoided', *Social Work Today*, 19 (13), 23 November, 8–9.

Corby, B., and Mills, C. (1986) 'Child abuse: risks and resources', *British Journal of Social Work*, 16, 531–42.

Cornwell, N. (1989) 'Decision making and justice: do they register?', *Social Work Today*, 20 (47), 3 August, 22–3.

Corse, S. J., Schmid, K., and Trickett, P. K. (1990) 'Social network characteristics of mothers in abusing and non abusing families and their relationships to parenting beliefs', *Journal of Community Psychology*, 18, 44–59.

Cotter, L. P., and Kuehnle, K. (in press) 'Sexual abuse within the family', in S. A. Garcia and R. Batey (eds), *Current Perspectives in Psychological, Legal and Ethical Issues*, Greenwick, Conn.: JAI Press.

Cowburn, M. (1990) 'Assumptions about sex offenders', *Probation Journal*, 37 (1), 4–9.

Creighton, S. J. (1985) 'An epidemiological study of abused children and their families in the United Kingdom between 1977 and 1982', *Child Abuse and Neglect*, 9, 411–48.

Cresswell, H. (1982) *The Secret World of Polly Flint*, London: Faber.

Criville, A. (1990) 'Child physical and sexual abuse: the roles of sadism and sexuality', *Child Abuse and Neglect*, 14, 121–7.

Cumberbatch, G., and Howitt, D. (1991) Unpublished.

Cupoli, J. M., and Sewell, P. M. (1988) 'One thousand fifty nine children with a chief complaint of sexual abuse', *Child Abuse and Neglect*, 12, 151–62.

Dale, P., Waters, J., Davies, M., Roberts, W., and Morrison, T. (1986) 'The towers of silence: creative and destructive issues for therapeutic teams dealing with sexual abuse', *Journal of Family Therapy*, 8, 1–25.

Daly, M., and Wilson, M. (1988) *Homicide*, New York: Aldine de Gruyter.

Dareer, A. (1982) *Woman, Why do you Weep?*, London: Zed.

Davies, G. (1991) 'Research on children's testimony: implications for interviewing practice', in C. R. Hollin and K. Howells (eds), *Clinical Approaches to Sex Offenders and their Victims*, Chichester: John Wiley.

de Jong, A. R., and Rose, M. (1989) 'Frequency and significance of physical evidence in legally proven cases of child sexual abuse', *Pediatrics*, 84 (6), 1022–5.

de Mause, L. (1976) *The History of Childhood: The evolution of parent–child relationships as a factor in history*, London: Souvenir.

Dembo, R., and Howitt, D. (1991) Unpublished.

Dembo, R., Dertke, M., La Voie, L., Borders, S., Washburn, M., and Schmeidler, J. (1987) 'Physical abuse, sexual victimization and illicit drug use: a structural analysis among high risk adolescents', *Journal of Adolescence*, 10, 13–33.

Dembo, R., Williams, L., La Voie, L., Berry, E., Getreu, A., Wish, E. D., Schmeidler, J. and Washburn, M. (1989) 'Physical abuse, sexual victimization, and illicit drug use: replication of a structural analysis among a new sample of high-risk youths', *Violence and Victims*, 4 (2), 121–38.

Dembo, R., Williams, L., Wothke, W., and Schmeidler, J. (1991) 'Examining a structural model of the role of family factors, physical abuse and sexual victimization experiences in a sample of high risk youth's alcohol/other drug use and delinquency/crime over time', unpublished manuscript, Department of Criminology, University of South Florida.

Department of Health (1991) *Child Abuse: A study of inquiry reports*, London: Her Majesty's Stationery Office.

Department of Health and Social Security (1974) *Report of the Committee of*

Inquiry into the Care and Supervision Provided in Relation to Maria Colwell, London: Her Majesty's Stationery Office.

Department of Health and Social Security (1982) *Child Abuse: A study of inquiry reports 1973–1981*, London: Her Majesty's Stationery Office.

Dingwall, R., Eekelaar, J., and Murray, T. (1983). *The Protection of Children: State intervention and family life*, Oxford: Basil Blackwell.

Doherty, M. E., Mynatt, C. R., Tweney, R. D., and Schiavo, M. D. (1979) 'Pseudodiagnosity', *Acta Psychologica*, 39 (2), 269–77.

Dominelli, L. (1986) 'Father–daughter incest: patriarchy's shameful secret', *Critical Social Policy*, 16, 8–22.

Dominelli, L. (1989) 'Betrayal of trust: a feminist analysis of power relationships in incest abuse and its relevance for social work practice', *British Journal of Social Work*, 19, 291–301.

Dominelli, L., and MacLeod, E. (1989) *Feminist Social Work*, London: Macmillan.

Downey, R. (1991) 'A child betrayed', *Social Work Today*, 22 (33), 2 May, 9.

Driver, E. (1989) 'Introduction', in E. Driver and A. Droisen (eds), *Child Sexual Abuse: Feminist perspectives*, London: Macmillan.

Droisen, A. (1989) 'Racism and anti-Semitism', in E. Driver and A. Droisen (eds), *Child Sexual Abuse: Feminist perspectives*, London: Macmillan.

Dykes, L. J. (1986) 'The whiplash shaken infant syndrome: what has been learned?' *Child Abuse and Neglect*, 10, 211–21.

Eaton, L. (1987) 'Kimberley report', *Social Work Today*, 19 (17), 21 December, 6–7.

Eaton, L. (1991) 'Ritual abuse: fantasy or reality', *Social Work Today*, 23 (5), 26 September, 8–11.

Edwards, C. A., and Forman, B. D. (1989) 'Effects of child interview method on accuracy and completeness of sexual abuse information recall', *Social Behavior and Personality*, 17 (2), 237–47.

Edwards, S. (1981) *Female Sexuality and the Law*, Oxford: Martin Robertson.

Eidelwich, J., and Brodsky, A. (1980) *Burn-out: Stages of disillusionment in the helping professions*, New York: Human Sciences Press.

Engelhardt, H. T. (1974) 'The disease of masturbation', *Bulletin of the History of Medicine*, 487, 234–48.

Evans, J. St. B. T. (1989a) 'Some causes of bias in expert opinion', *The Psychologist: Bulletin of the British Psychological Society*, 2 (3), 112–14.

Evans, J. St B. T. (1989b) *Bias in Human Reasoning: Causes and consequences*, London: Laurence Erlbaum.

Everson, M. D., and Boat, B. W. (1989) 'False allegations of sexual abuse by children and adolescents', *Journal of the American Academy of Child and Adolescent Psychiatry*, 28, 230–5.

Eysenck, H. J. (1985) *Decline and Fall of the Freudian Empire*, Harmondsworth: Viking.

Eysenck, H. J., and Wilson, G. D. (1973) *The Experimental Study of Freudian Theories*, London: Methuen.

Farber, E. A., and Egeland, B. (1987) 'Invulnerability among abused and neglected children', in E. J. AVNTHONY AND B. J. Cohler (eds), *The Invulnerabl* *Child*, New York: Guilford Press.

Farinatti, A. S., Fonsoca, N. M., Dondonis, M., and Brugger, E. (1990) 'Child abuse and neglect in a developing country', *Child Abuse and Neglect* 14, 133–4.

Fatout, M. F. (1990) 'Consequences of abuse on the relationships of children', *Families in Society: The Journal of Contemporary Human Services*, 71 (2), 76–81.

Fine, R. (1973) *The Development of Freud's Thought*, New York: Jason Aronson.

Finkelhor, D. (1984) *Child Sexual Abuse: New theory and research*, New York: The Free Press.

Finkelhor, D. (1990) 'Is child abuse over reported?: the data rebut arguments for less intervention', *Public Welfare*, Winter, 20–9.

Finkelhor, D., and Redfield, D. (1984) 'How the public defines sexual abuse', in D. Finkelhor, *Child Sexual Abuse: New theory and research*, New York: The Free Press.

Finkelhor, D., and Russell, D. (1984) 'Women as perpetrators: review of the evidence', in D. Finkelhor, *Child Sexual Abuse: New theory and research*, New York: The Free Press.

Finkelhor, D., and Williams, L. M. (1988) *Nursery Crimes: Sexual abuse in day care*, London: Sage.

Finkelhor, D., Gomes-Swart, B., and Horowitz, J. (1984) 'Professionals' responses', in D. Finkelhor, *Child Sexual Abuse: New theory and research*, New York: The Free Press.

Finkelhor, D., Hotaling, G. T., Lewis, I. A., and Smith, C. (1989) 'Sexual abuse and its relationship to later sexual satisfaction, marital status, religion, and attitudes', *Journal of Interpersonal Violence*, 4 (4), 379–99.

Finkelhor, D., Hotaling, G., Lewis, I. A., and Smith, C. (1990) 'Sexual abuse in a national survey of adult men and women: prevalence, characteristics, and risk factors', *Child Abuse and Neglect*, 14, 19–28.

Flin, R., and Boon, J. (1989) 'The child witness in court', in C. Wattam, J. Hughes, and H. Blagg (eds), *Child Sexual Abuse*, Harlow, Middlesex: Longman.

Fordyce, L. (1988) 'Sexual abuse of children', *The Psychologist: Bulletin of the British Psychological Society*, 12 (10), 443.

Foster, G. M., and Anderson, B. G. (1978) *Medical Anthropology*, New York: John Wiley.

Fournier, A. (1880/1986) 'Simulation of sexual attacks on young children', in J. M. Masson (ed./trans.), *A Dark Science: Women, sexuality and psychiatry in the nineteenth century*, New York: Farrar, Straus and Giroux.

Fox, L. M. (1982) 'Two value positions in recent child care law and practice', *British Journal of Social Work*, 12, 265–90.

Fox, S., and Dingwall, R. (1985) 'An exploratory study of variations in social workers' and health visitors' definitions of child mistreatment', *British Journal of Social Work*, 15, 467–77.

Freud, S. (1962) *Two Short Accounts of Psycho-Analysis*, Harmondsworth: Penguin.

Friedson, E. (1972) *Profession of Medicine: A study of the sociology of applied knowledge*, New York: Dodd, Mead and Company.

Frosh, S. (1987) 'Issues for men working with sexually abused children', *British Journal of Psychotherapy*, 3 (4), 332–9.

Froula, C. (1986) 'The daughter's seduction: sexual violence and literary history', *Signs: Journal of Women in Culture and Society*, 11 (4), 621–44.

Fryer, G. E., Kraizer, S. K., and Miyoshi, T. (1987) 'Measuring actual reductions of risk to child abuse: a new approach', *Child Abuse and Neglect*, 11, 173–9.

Garbarino, J. (1986) 'Can we measure success in preventing child abuse? Issues in policy programing and research', *Child Abuse and Neglect*, 10, 143–56.

Gale, A. (ed.) (1988) *The Polygraph Test, Lies Truth and Science*, London: Sage.

Gale, J., Thompson, R. J., Moran, T., and Sack, W. H. (1988) 'Sexual abuse in young children: its clinical presentation and characteristic patterns', *Child Abuse and Neglect*, 12, 163–70.

Gallop, J. (1982) *The Daughter's Seduction: Feminism and psychoanalysis*, Ithaca, NY: Cornell University Press.

Gardner, F. (1987) 'First steps towards a non-sexist child care practice', *Social Work Today*, 19 (8), 19 October, 12–13.

Geach, H. (1982) *Child Abuse Registers: A major threat to civil liberties*, London: Justice for Children.

Geach, H. (1983) 'Child abuse registers: a time for a change', in H. Geach and E. Szwed (eds), *Providing Civil Justice for Children*, London: Edward Arnold.

Gelles, R. J. (1979) *Family Violence*, Beverly Hills, Calif.: Sage.

Gelles, R. J., and Cornell, C. P. (1985) *Intimate Violence in Families*, Beverly Hills, Calif.: Sage.

Gerber, P. N. (1990) 'The assessment interview for young male victims', in M. Hunter (ed.), *The Sexually Abused Male*, vol. 1, Lexington, Mass.: Lexington Books.

Gerhardt, U. (1989) *Ideas about Illness: An intellectual and political history of medical sociology*, London: Macmillan.

Giovanni, J. M., and Becerra, R. M. (1979) *Defining Child Abuse*, New York: The Free Press.

Glick, I. D., and Hessler, D. R. (1974) *Marital and Family Therapy*, New York: Grune and Stratton.

Goldberg, E. M. (1987) 'The effectiveness of social care: a selective exploration', *British Journal of Social Work*, 17, 595–614.

Goodman, G. S. (1984) 'Children's testimony in historical perspective', *Journal of Social Issues*, 40, 9–31.

Goodwin, J. M., Cheeves, K., and Connell, V. (1990) 'Borderline and other severe symptoms in adult survivors of incestuous abuse', *Psychiatric Annals*, 20 (1), 22–23.

Gordon, L. (1985) 'Child abuse, gender, and the myth of family independence: a historical critique', *Child Welfare*, 64 (3), 213–24.

Gray, J., Cutler, C., Dean, J., and Kempe C. (1977) 'Prediction of child abuse', *Child Abuse and Neglect*, 1, 45–58.

208   *Child abuse errors*

Grillo, R. (ed.) (1989) 'Social anthropology and the politics of language', *Sociological Review Monograph*, 36, London: Routledge.

Hall, C. S. (1954) *A Primer of Freudian Psychology*, New York: Mentor.

Hall, D. F., and Loftus, E. F. (1983) 'Research on eyewitness testimony: recent advances and current controversy', in D. J. Muller, D. E. Blackman, and A. J. Chapman (eds), *Psychology and the Law*, Chichester: John Wiley.

Haller, J. S. and Haller, R. M. (1974) *The Physician and Sexuality in Victorian America*, Urbana, Ill.: University of Illinois Press.

Hallet, C., and Stevenson, O. (1980) *Child Abuse: Aspects of interprofessional cooperation*, London: George Allen and Unwin.

Halmos, P. (ed.) (1973) 'Professionalisation and social change', *Sociological Review Monograph*, 20, University of Keele.

Hanks, H., Hobbs, C., and Wynne, J. (1988) 'Early signs and recognition of sexual abuse in the pre-school child', in K. Browne, C. Davies, and P. Stratton (eds), *Early Prediction and Prevention of Child Abuse*, Chichester: John Wiley.

Harris, N. (1987) 'Defensive socialwork', *British Journal of Social Work*, 17, 61–9.

Haugaard, J. J., and Tilly, C. (1988) 'Characteristics predicting children's responses to sexual encounters with other children', *Child Abuse and Neglect*, 12, 209–18.

Heath, K. C., Donnan, H., and Halpin, G. W. (1990) 'Attributions for blame and responsibility among female incest victims', *Social Behavior and Personality*, 18 (1), 157–68.

Hechler, D. (1988) *The Battle and the Backlash*, Lexington, Mass.: Lexington Books.

Helfer, R. E. (1982) 'Correspondence', *British Journal of Social Work*, 12, 669–70.

Hendricks, H. (1990) 'Constructions and reconstructions of British childhood: an interpretive survey, 1800 to the present', in A. James and A. Prout (eds), *Constructing and Reconstructing Childhood: Contemporary issues in the sociological study of childhood*, Basingstoke, Hampshire: Falmer.

Herbert, C. P. (1987) 'Expert medical assessment in determining probability of alleged child sexual abuse', *Child Abuse and Neglect*, 11, 213–21.

Higginson, S. (1989) 'Predicting abuse', *Social Work Today*, 20 (39), 8 June, 16–17.

Higginson, S. (1990) 'Under the influence', *Social Work Today*, 22 (14), 29 November, 20–1.

Hill, M. (1991) 'Bruised beyond understanding', *The Times Higher Educational Supplement*, 5 April, 5.

Hill, T. (1982) 'Rape and marital rape in the maintenance of male power', in S. Friedman and E. Sarah (eds), *On the Problem of Men: Two feminist conferences*, London: The Women's Press.

Hobbs, C. J., and Wynne, J. M. (1986) 'Buggery in childhood: a common syndrome of child abuse', *The Lancet*, 4 October, 792–6.

Holt, K. S. (1987) 'Child abuse and osteogenesis imperfecta', *British Medical Journal*, 295 (21 November), 1346.

Home Office (1969) *Criminal Statistics England and Wales*, London: Her Majesty's Stationery Office, Cmnd 4398.

Home Office (1972) *Criminal Statistics England and Wales*, London: Her Majesty's Stationery Office, Cmnd 5402.

Home Office (1975) *Criminal Statistics England and Wales*, London: Her Majesty's Stationery Office, Cmnd 6566.

Home Office (1982) *Criminal Statistics for England and Wales*, London: Her Majesty's Stationery Office, Cmnd 1322.

Home Office (1987) *Criminal Statistics England and Wales*, London: Her Majesty's Stationery Office, Cmnd 498.

Home Office (1989) *Criminal Statistics England and Wales*, London: Her Majesty's Stationery Office, Cmnd 9040.

Hong, G. K., and Hong, L. K. (1991) 'Comparative perspective on child abuse and neglect: Chinese versus Hispanics and whites', *Child Welfare*, LXX (4), 463–75.

Horowitz, S., and Chadwick, D. L. (1990) 'Syphilis as a sole indicator of sexual abuse: two cases with no intervention', *Child Abuse and Neglect*, 14, 129–32.

Howard, G. S. (1985) 'The role of values in the science of psychology', *American Psychologist*, 40 (3), 255–65.

Howitt, D. (1990a) 'Expert opinion: risky sexual abuse diagnosis', *The Psychologist: Bulletin of the British Psychological Society*, 3 (1), 15–17.

Howitt, D. (1990b) 'Injustice to children and families in child abuse cases', paper presented at the 2nd European Conference on Law and Psychology, Nuremberg 13–15 September.

Howitt, D. (1991a) *Concerning Psychology: Psychology applied to social issues*, Milton Keynes: Open University Press.

Howitt, D. (1991b) 'Britain's "substance abuse policy": realities and regulation in the United Kingdom', *International Journal of the Addictions*, 3, 1087–111.

Howitt, D., and Cumberbatch, G. (1990) *Pornography: Impacts and influences*, London: Home Office Research and Planning Unit.

Howitt, D., and Owusu–Bempah, J. (1990) 'The pragmatics of institutional racism', *Human Relations*, 43 (9), 885–9.

Howitt, D., Billig, M., Cramer, D., Edwards, D., Kniveton, B., Potter, J., and Radley, R. (1989) *Social Psychology: Conflicts and continuities*, Milton Keynes: Open University Press.

Hughes, R. A. (1990) 'Psychological perspectives of infanticide in a faith healing sect', *Psychotherapy*, 27 (1), 107–15.

Ingram, M. (1979) 'The participating victim: a study of sexual offences against pre-pubertal boys', in M. Cook and G. Wilson (eds), *Love and Attraction: An international conference*, Oxford: Pergamon.

Ivory, M. (1991) 'Tarred for life: the postpindown syndrome', *Community Care*, 13 June, 6–8.

James, A., and Prout, A. (eds) (1990) *Constructing and Reconstructing Childhood: Contemporary issues in the sociological study of childhood*, Basingstoke, Hampshire: Falmer.

Jampole, L., and Weber, M. K. (1987) 'An assessment of the behavior of sexually abused and nonsexually abused children with anatomically correct dolls', *Child Abuse and Neglect*, 11, 187–92.

Jervis, M. (1987) 'Paradox of child sexual abuse', *Social Work Today*, 19 (13), 23 November, 7.

Jervis, M. (1988a) 'The Cleveland Inquiry Report', *Social Work Today*, 19 (45), 14 July, 6–11.

Jervis, M. (1988b) 'Dealing with child abuse by a generic approach', *Social Work Today*, 19 (49), 11 August, 22–3.

Jervis, M. (1991a) 'Grey area', *Social Work Today*, 22 (30), 11 April, 13–15.

Jervis, M. (1991b) 'Judge and fury', *Social Work Today*, 22 (27), 21 March, 27–8.

Johnson, T. C. (1988) 'Child perpetrators: children who molest other children – preliminary findings', *Child Abuse and Neglect*, 12, 219–29.

Jones, D. P. H., and Krugman, R. D. (1986) 'Can a three-year-old child bear witness to her sexual assault and attempted murder?' *Child Abuse and Neglect*, 10, 253–8.

Kail, R. (1990) *The Development of Memory in Children*, New York: W. H. Freeman.

Kalichman, S. C., Craig, M. E., and Follingstad, D. R. (1990) 'Professionals' adherence to mandatory child abuse reporting laws: effects of responsibility attribution, confidence ratings, and situational factors', *Child Abuse and Neglect*, 14, 69–77.

Kaufman, J., and Zigler, E. (1987) 'Do abused parents become abusive parents?', *American Journal of Orthopsychiatry*, 57 (2), 186–92.

Kelleher, M. (1987) 'Sexual abuse at Charity House: a case study of social policies in action', *Journal of Sociology and Social Welfare*, 14 (4), 95–113.

Kelley, S. J. (1988) 'Ritualistic abuse of children: dynamics and impact', *Cultic Studies Journal*, 5 (2), 228–36.

Kelley, S. J. (1989) 'Stress responses of children to sexual abuse and ritualistic abuse in day care centers', *Journal of Interpersonal Violence*, 4 (4), 502–13.

Kelley, S. J. (1990) 'Responsibility and management strategies in child sexual abuse: a comparison of child protective workers, nurses, and police officers', *Child Welfare* LXIX (1), 43–51.

Kelly, L. (1988) *Surviving Sexual Violence*, Cambridge: Polity.

Kelly, L. (1989) 'What's in a name?: defining child sexual abuse', *Feminist Review*, 28, 65–73.

Kempe, C. H. (1969) 'The battered child and the hospital', *Hospital Practice* 4, 44–57.

Kempe, R. S., and Kempe, C. H. (1978) *Child Abuse*, London: Fontana.

Kendall-Tackett, K. A., and Simon, A. F. (1987) 'Perpetrators and their acts: data from 365 adults molested as children', *Child Abuse and Neglect*, 11, 237–48.

Kidd, L., and Pringle, K. (1988) 'The politics of child sexual abuse', *Social Work Today*, 20 (3), 15 September, 14–15.

Kienberger Jaudes, P,, and Morris, M. (1990) 'Child sexual abuse: who goes home?' *Child Abuse and Neglect*, 14, 61–8.

Kimble, G. A. (1984) 'Psychology's two cultures', *American Psychologist*, 39 (8), 833–9.

Kitzinger, J. (1988) 'Defending innocence: ideologies of childhood', *Feminist Review*, 28, 77–87.

Kitzinger, J. (1990) 'Children, power and the struggle against sexual abuse', in A. James and A. Prout (eds), *Constructing and Reconstructing Childhood: Contemporary issues in the sociological study of childhood*, Basingstoke, Hampshire: Falmer.

Korbin, J. E. (1982) *Child Abuse and Neglect: Cross cultural perspectives*. Berkeley, Calif.: University of California Press.

La Fontaine, J. (1990) *Child Sexual Abuse*, Cambridge: Polity.

Lealman, G., Haigh, D., Phillips, J., Stone, J., and Ord-Smith, C. (1983) 'Prediction and prevention of child abuse: an empty hope?' *The Lancet*, 1, 1423–4.

Levey, A. B. (1988) *Polygraphy: An evaluative review*, London: Her Majesty's Stationery Office.

Levitt, C. (1990) 'Sexual abuse of boys: a medical perspective', in M. Hunter (ed.), *The Sexually Abused Male* vol. 1, Lexington, Mass.: Lexington Books.

Lightcap, J. L., Kurland, J. A., and Burgess, R. L. (1982) 'Child abuse: a test of some predictions from evolutionary theory', *Ethology and Sociobiology*, 3, 61–7.

Lindberg, F. H., and Distad, L. J. (1985) 'Survival responses to incest: adolescents in crisis', *Child Abuse and Neglect*, 9, 521–6.

Lindholm, K. J., and Willey, R. (1986) 'Ethnic differences in child abuse and sexual abuse', *Hispanic Journal of Behavioral Sciences*, 8 (2), 111–25.

Lindzey, G. (1967) 'Some remarks concerning incest, the incest taboo, and psychoanalytic theory', *American Psychologist*, 22, 12 1051–9.

Lipovsky, J. A., Saunders, B. E. and Murphy, S. M. (1989) 'Depression, anxiety, and behavior problems among victims of father–child sexual assault and non-abused siblings', *Journal of Interpersonal Violence*, 4 (4), 452–68.

Loftus, E. (1980) *Memory: Surprising new insights into how we remember and how we forget*, Reading, Mass.: Addison-Wesley.

Lunn, T. (1991) 'Confronting disbelief', *Social Work Today*, 22 (34), 9 May, 18–19.

MacDonald, G. (1990) 'Allocating blame in social work', *The British Journal of Social Work*, 20 (6), 525–46.

MacLeod, E., and Saraga, E. (1988) 'Challenging the orthodoxy: towards a feminist theory and practice', *Feminist Review*, 28, 16–55.

MacPherson, S. C. (1987) *Five Hundred Million Children: Poverty and child welfare in the Third World*, Hemel Hempstead: Harvester Wheatsheaf.

McIntyre, K. (1981) 'Role of mothers in father–daughter incest: a feminist analysis', *Social Work*, 26 (6), 462–6.

McPherson, S. (1990) 'Some areas of interface between psychology and the guardian ad litem programs in juvenile and domestic relations settings', paper presented at the 2nd European Conference on Law and Psychology, Nuremberg, 13–15 September.

Mannarino, A. P., Cohen, J. A., and Gregor, M. (1989) 'Emotional and behavioural difficulties in sexually abused girls', *Journal of Interpersonal Violence*, 4 (4), 437–51.

Margolin, L. (1986) 'The effects of mother–son incest', *Lifestyles: A Journal of Changing Patterns*, 8 (2), 104–14.

Margolin, L. (1990) 'Fatal child neglect', *Child Welfare*, LXIX (4), 309–19.

Masson, J. M. (1985) *An Assault on Truth*, New York: Penguin.

Masson, J. M. (1986) *A Dark Science: Women, sexuality and psychiatry in the nineteenth century*, New York: Farrar, Straus and Giroux.

Menzies, I. E. P. (1970) *The Functioning of Social Systems as a Defence against Anxiety*, Centre for Applied Social Research, Tavistock Institute of Human Relations.

Meriwether, M. H. (1988) 'Child abuse reporting laws: time for a change', in D. J. Besharov (ed.), *Protecting Children From Abuse and Neglect: Policy and practice*, Springfield, Ill.: Charles C. Thomas.

Merrick, J. (1986) 'Personal punishment of children in Denmark: a historical perspective', *Child Abuse and Neglect*, 10, 263–4.

Miller, A. (1985) *Thou Shalt Not Be Aware: Society's betrayal of the child*, London: Pluto.

Mills, C., and Vine, P. (1990) 'Critical incident reporting: an approach to reviewing the instigation and management of child abuse', *British Journal of Social Work*, 20, 215–20.

Mills, M. E. (1990) 'The new heretics: men', *American Psychologist*, 45, 5, 675–6.

Milner, J., and Blyth, E. (1989) *Coping with Child Sexual Abuse: A guide for teachers*, Harlow, Middlesex: Longman.

Ming Yuan, L. (1990) 'Child sexual abuse in West China', *American Journal of Psychiatry*, 147 (2), 258.

Montgomery, S. (1982a) 'Problems in the perinatal prediction of child abuse', *British Journal of Social Work*, 12, 189–96.

Montgomery, S. (1982b) 'Reply to Professor Helfer', *British Journal of Social Work*, 12, 670–2.

Mould, D. E. (1990) 'Data base or data bias?', *American Psychologist*, 45, 5, 676.

Nash, C. L., and West, D. (1985) 'Sexual molestation of young girls: a retrospective survey', in D. West (ed.), *Sexual Victimization: Two recent researches into sex problems and their social effects*, Aldershot, Hampshire: Gower.

Nava, C. (1988) 'Cleveland and the press: outrage and anxiety in the reporting of child sexual abuse', *Feminist Review*, 28, 103–21.

Neisser, U. (ed.) (1982) *Memory Observed: Remembering in natural contexts*, San Francisco, Calif.: W. H. Freeman.

Nelson, B. J. (1982) *Making an Issue of Child Abuse: Political agenda setting for social problems*, Chicago, Ill.: University of Chicago Press.

Nightingale, N. N., and Walker, E. F. (1986) 'Identification and reporting of child maltreatment by Head Start personnel: attitudes and experience', *Child Abuse and Neglect*, 10, 191–9.

Norman, D. A. (1981) 'Categorization of action slips', *Psychological Review*, 88 (1), 1–15.

Office of Population Censuses and Surveys (1979) *1979 Mortality Statistics England and Wales: Childhood and maternity*, London: Her Majesty's Stationery Office, Series DH3.

Office of Population Censuses and Surveys (1990) *1986, 1987 Mortality Statistics England and Wales: Childhood*, London: Her Majesty's Stationery Office, Series DH6 N1.

Office of Population Censuses and Surveys (1991) *1988 Mortality Statistics England and Wales: Childhood*, London: Her Majesty's Stationery Office, Series DH6 N2.

Ojanuga, D. N. (1990) 'Kaduna beggar children', *Child Welfare*, LXIX (4), 371–80.

Pagelow, M. D. (1984) *Family Violence*, New York: Praeger.

PAIN (1990) 'Press release', Bishop's Stortford, Hertfordshire: Parents Against Injustice.

Parker, S. (1976) 'The precultural basis of the incest taboo: towards a biosocial theory', *American Anthropologist*, 788 (2), 285–305.

Parry, N., and Parry, J. (1976) *The Rise of the Medical Profession: A study of collective social mobility*, London: Croom Helm.

Parton, N. (1981) 'Child abuse, social anxiety and welfare', *British Journal of Social Work*, 11, 391–414.

Parton, N. (1985) *The Politics of Child Abuse*, London: Macmillan.

Parton, N. (1986) 'The Beckford Report: a critical appraisal', *British Journal of Social Work*, 16, 511–30.

Paterson, C. R. (1981) 'Case report: vitamin D deficiency rickets simulating child abuse', *Journal of Pediatric Orthopedics*, 1, 423–5.

Paterson, C. R. (1986) 'Unexplained fractures in childhood: differential diagnosis of osteogenesis imperfecta and other disorders from non-accidental injury', *Journal of Neurological and Orthopaedic Medicine and Surgery*, 7 (3), 253–5.

Paterson, C. R. (1988a) 'Bones of contention', *Community Care*, 16 June, 25–7.

Paterson, C. R. (1988b) 'Collagen chemistry and the brittle bone diseases', *Endeavour*, 12 (2), 56–9.

Paterson, C. R., and McAllion, S. J. (1987) 'Child abuse and osteogenesis imperfecta', *British Medical Journal*, 295 (12 December), 1561.

Paterson, C. R., and McAllion, S. J. (1988) 'Child abuse and osteogenesis imperfecta', *British Medical Journal*, 296 (27 February), 644.

Paulson, M. J., Schwemer, G. T., Afifi, A. A., and Bendel, R. B. (1977) 'Parent attitude research instrument (PARI): clinical vs statistical inferences in understanding abusive mothers', *Journal of Clinical Psychology*, 33 (3), 848–54.

Pellegrin, A., and Wagner, W. G. (1990) 'Child sexual abuse: factors affecting victims' removal from home', *Child Abuse and Neglect*, 14, 53–60.

Pfohl, S. J. (1976) 'The "discovery" of child abuse', *Social Problems*, 24, 310–23.

Piaget, J. (1952) *The Origins of Intelligence in Children*, New York: International Universities Press.

Pierce, R., and Pierce, L. H. (1985) 'The sexually abused child: a comparison of male and female victims', *Child Abuse and Neglect*, 9, 191–9.

Pinchbeck, I. and Hewitt, M. (1969) *Children in English Society Vol. I: From Tudor Times to the Eighteenth Century*, London: Routledge and Kegan Paul.

Pinchbeck, I. and Hewitt, M. (1973) *Children in English Society Vol. II: From the Eighteenth Century to the Children's Act 1948*, London: Routledge and Kegan Paul.

Pithers, D. (1990) 'Stranger than fiction', *Social Work Today*, 22 (6), 4 October, 20–1.

Pless, I. B., Sibald, A. D., Smith, M. A., and Russell, M. D. (1987) 'A reappraisal of the frequency of child abuse seen in pediatric emergency rooms', *Child Abuse and Neglect*, 11, 193–200.

Plotkin, R. C., Azar, S., Twentyman, C., and Perri, M. G. (1981) 'A critical evaluation of the research methodology employed in the investigation of causative factors in child abuse and neglect', *Child Abuse and Neglect*, 5, 449–55.

Powers, J. L., and Eckenrode, J. (1988) 'The maltreatment of adolescents', *Child Abuse and Neglect*, 12, 189–99.

Pride, M. (1987) *The Child Abuse Industry*, Winchester, Ill.: Crossway.

Raskin, D. C., and Steller, M. (1989) 'Assessing credibility of allegations of child sexual abuse: polygraph examinations and statement analysis', in H. Wegener, F. Losel and J. Haisch (eds), *Criminal Behavior and the Justice System*, New York: Springer-Verlag.

Reason, J. (1979) 'Actions not as planned: the price of automatization', in G. Underwood and R. Stevens (eds), *Aspects of Conciousness Vol. 1: Psychological Issues*, London: Academic Press.

Reason, J., and Lucas, D. (1984) 'Absent-mindedness in shops', *British Journal of Clinical Psychology*, 23, 121–31.

Regehr, C. (1990) 'Parental responses to extrafamilial child sexual assault', *Child Abuse and Neglect*, 14, 113–20.

Reinhart, M. A. (1987) 'Sexually abused boys', *Child Abuse and Neglect*, 11, 229–35.

Riggs, D. S., O'Leary, K. D., and Breslin, F. C. (1990) 'Multiple correlates of physical aggression in dating couples', *Journal of Interpersonal Violence*, 5 (1), 61–73.

Ringwalt, C., and Earp, J. (1988) 'Attributing responsibility in cases of father–daughter sexual abuse', *Child Abuse and Neglect*, 12, 273–81.

Roberts, Y. (1989) 'After Cleveland', *New Statesman and Society*, 2 June, 10–11.

Robinson, I. (1989) 'Seeing life from the other side of the fence', *PAIN Newsletter*, 7 December, 7–8.

Rogers, E. M. (1983) *Diffusion of Innovations*, New York: The Free Press.

Rose, L. (1986) *The Massacre of the Innocents: Infanticide in Britain 1800–1939*, London: Routledge.

Rosenthal, J. A. (1988) 'Patterns of reported child abuse and neglect', *Child Abuse and Neglect*, 12, 263–71.

Roth, S., Wayland, K., and Woolsey, M. (1990) 'Victimization history and victim–assailant relationship as factors in recovery from sexual assault', *Journal of Traumatic Stress*, 3 (1), 169–80.

Rowan, J. (1979) 'Possible early-warning signs of non-accidental injury to children', in *Abstracts of 2nd International Congress on Child Abuse and Neglect*, New York.

Rowan, E. L., Rowan, J. B., and Langelier, P. (1990) 'Women who molest children', *Bulletin of the American Academy of Psychiatry and the Law*, 18 (1), 79–83.

Russell, D. E. H. (1983) 'The incidence and prevalence of intrafamilial and extra-familial sexual abuse of female children', *Child Abuse and Neglect*, 7, 133–46.

Russell, D. E. H. (1986) *Secret Trauma: Incest in the lives of girls and women*, New York: Basic Books.

Russell, D. E. H. (1988) 'Pornography and rape: a causal model', *Journal of Political Psychology*, 9 (1), 41–73.

Rutherford, D. (1977) 'Personality in social work students', *Social Work Today*, 8, 20–22 February, 9–10.

Rycraft, J. R. (1990) 'Redefining abuse and neglect: a narrower focus could affect children at risk', *Public Welfare*, Winter, 14–21.

Ryder, R. (1989) 'Child abuse', *The Psychologist: Bulletin of the British Psychological Society*, 2 (8), 333.

Sandfort, Th. G. M. (1988) *The Meanings of Experience: On sexual contacts in early youth, and sexual behavior and experience in later life*, Utrecht: Homostudies.

Sandfort, Th. G. M. (1989) 'Studies into child sexual abuse: an overview and critical appraisal', paper presented at the 1st European Congress of Psychology, Amsterdam, 2–7 July.

Sapp, A. D., and Carter, D. L. (1978) *Child Abuse in Texas: A descriptive survey of Texas residents' attitudes*, Survey Research Program, College of Criminal Justice, Sam Houston State University, Texas.

Schaefer, M. R., Sobieraj, K., and Hollyfield, R. L. (1988) 'Prevalence of childhood physical abuse in male veteran alcoholics', *Child Abuse and Neglect*, 12, 141–9.

Schultz, L. G. (1982) 'Child sexual abuse in historical perspective', *Journal of Social Work and Human Sexuality*, 1 (1–2), 21–35.

Schwebel, M., and Raph, J. (eds) (1974) *Piaget in the Classroom*, London: Routledge and Kegan Paul.

Segal, U. M., and Schwartz, S. (1985) 'Factors affecting placement decisions of children following short-term emergency care', *Child Abuse and Neglect*, 9, 543–8.

Segner, L., and Collins, A. (1967) 'Cross-cultural study of incest myths', unpublished manuscript, University of Texas.

Shearer, S. L., Peters, C. P., Quaytman, M. S., and Ogden, R. L. (1990) 'Frequency and correlates of childhood sexual and physical abuse histories in adult female borderline inpatients', *American Journal of Psychiatry*, 147, 214–16.

Sheldon, J. E. (1991) 'Practice study: throughcare work with a child sex offender – assessment and intervention', unpublished.

Siegel, D. R., and Romig, C. A. (1988) 'Treatment of adult survivors of childhood sexual assault: imagery within a system framework', *American Journal of Family Therapy*, 16 (3), 229–42.

Siegel, L. S., and Brainerd, C. J. (eds) (1978) *Alternatives to Piaget: Critical essays on the theory*, New York: Academic Press.

Silas, F. A. (1985) 'Would a kid lie?' *Journal of the American Bar Association*, 71, 17.

Smith, J., and Hogan, B. (1983) *Criminal Law*, London: Butterworth.

Smith, P. M. (1985) *Language, the Sexes and Society*, Oxford: Basil Blackwell.

Sommerville, C. J. (1982) *The Rise and Fall of Childhood*, Beverly Hills, Calif.: Sage.

Spencer, J. R., and Flin, R. H. (1990) *The Evidence of Children*, London: Blackstone.

Spender, D. (1985) *Man Made Language*, London: Routledge and Kegan Paul.

Steedman, C., Urwin, C., and Walkerdine, V. (eds) (1985) *Language, Gender and Childhood*, London: Routledge and Kegan Paul.

Steiger, H., and Zanko, M. (1990) 'Sexual traumata among eating disordered, psychiatric, and normal female groups: comparisons of prevalence and defence styles', *Journal of Interpersonal Violence*, 5 (1), 74–80.

Straus, M. (1980) 'Stress and physical child abuse', *Child Abuse and Neglect*, 4, 75–88.

Stubbs, P. (1989) 'Developing anti-racist practice: problems and possibilities', in H. Blagg, J. A. Hughes, and C. Wattam (eds), *Child Sexual Abuse: Listening, hearing and validating the experiences of children*, Harlow, Middlesex: Longman.

Szasz, T. (1986) 'The case against suicide prevention', *American Psychologist*, 41 (7), 806–12.

Szasz, T. (1990) 'The theology of therapy: the breaking of the First Amendment through the medicalization of morals', *Changes*, 8 (1), 2–4.

Taitz, L. S. (1987) 'Child abuse and osteogenesis imperfecta', *British Medical Journal*, 295 (31 October), 1082–3.

Taitz, L. S. (1988) 'Child abuse and osteogenesis imperfecta', *British Medical Journal*, 296 (23 January), 292.

Taylor-Gooby, P. (1990) 'Social welfare: the unkindest cuts', in R. Jowell, S. Witherspoon and L. Brook (eds), *British Social Attitudes: The 7th report*, London: Sage.

Tedesco, J. F., and Schnell, S. V. (1987) 'Children's reactions to sex abuse investigation and litigation', *Child Abuse and Neglect*, 11, 267–72.

Thoeness, N., and Pearson, J. (1987) *'Sexual abuse allegations in domestic relations cases: the research perspective'*, American Bar Association.

Thoeness, N., and Pearson, J. (1988) 'A difficult dilemma: responding to sexual abuse allegations in custody and visitation disputes', in P. J. Besharov (ed.), *Protecting Children from Abuse and Neglect*, Springfield, Ill.: Charles C. Thomas.

Trankell, A. (1972) *Reliability of Evidence: Methods for analyzing and assessing witness statements*, Stockholm: Beckmans.

Tredinnik, A. W., and Fairbairn, A. C. (1980) 'Left holding the baby', *Community Care*, 10 April, 22–5.

Tuckett, D. (ed.) (1976) *An Introduction to Medical Sociology*, London: Tavistock.

Undeutsch, J. (1982) 'Statement reality analysis', in A. Trankell (ed.), *Reconstructing the Past*, Deventer, The Netherlands: Kluwer.

US National Incidence Study (1981) *Study Findings: National study of the incidence and severity of child abuse and neglect*, Washington, DC: DHSS.

Uzoka, A. F. (1979) 'The myth of the nuclear family', *American Psychologist*, 34 (11), 1095–106.

Vizard, E. (1991) 'Interviewing children suspected of being sexually abused: a review of theory and practice', in C. R. Hollin and K. Howells (eds), *Clinical Approaches to Sex Offenders and their Victims*, Chichester: John Wiley.

Walker, L. E. A. (1989) 'Psychology and violence against women', *American Psychologist*, 44 (4), 695–702.

Walker, L. E. A. (1990) 'Response to Mills and Mould', *American Psychologist*, 45, 5, 676–7.

Walters, D. R. (1975) *Physical and Sexual Abuse of Children: Causes and treatment*, Bloomington, Ind.: University of Indiana Press.

Watkins, C. E. (1990) 'Psychiatric epidemiology II: the prevalence and aftermath of sexual assault', *Journal of Counseling and Development*, 68, January/February, 341–3.

West, D. J. (ed.) (1985) *Sexual Victimisation: Two recent researches into sex problems and their social effects*, Aldershot, Hampshire: Gower.

West, D. J. (1991) 'The effects of sexual offences', in C. R. Hollin and K. Howells (eds), *Clinical Approaches to Sex Offenders and their Victims*, Chichester: John Wiley.

Whiting, J. W. M. and Child, I. L. (1953) *Child training and personality: a cross cultural study*, New Haven, Conn.: Yale University Press.

Winfield, I., George, L. K., Swartz, M., and Blazer, D. G. (1990) 'Sexual assault and psychiatric disorders among a community sample of women', *American Journal of Psychiatry*, 147 (3), 335–41.

Wolters, W. A. G., Zween, E. J., Wagener-Schwencke, P. M. and Deenen, T. A. M. (1985) 'A review of causes of sexually exploited children reported to the Netherlands state police', *Child Abuse and Neglect*, 9, 571–4.

Wood, H. (1990) 'Exposing the secret', *Social Work Today*, 22 (12), 15 November, 18–19.

Woodhead, M. (1990) 'Psychology and the cultural construction of children's needs', in A. James and A. Prout (eds), *Constructing and Reconstructing Childhood*, Basingstoke, Hampshire: Falmer.

Wooley, P. N., and Evans, W. A. (1955) 'Significant skeletal lesions in infants resembling those of traumatic origins' *Journal of the American Medical Association*, 158 (7), 539–543.

Wyatt, G. E., and Peters, S. D. (1986a) 'Issues in the definition of child sexual abuse in prevalence research', *Child Abuse and Neglect*, 10, 231–40.

Wyatt, G. E., and Peters, S. D. (1986b) 'Methodological considerations in research on the prevalence of child sexual abuse', *Child Abuse and Neglect*, 10, 241–51.

Wyatt, G. W. (1985) 'The sexual abuse of Afro-American and white American women in childhood', *Child Abuse and Neglect*, 9, 507–19.

Wyre, R. (1987) *Working with Sex Offenders*, Oxford: Perry.

Zambaco, D. A. (1882/1986) 'Masturbation and psychological problems in two little girls', in J. M. Masson (ed./trans.), *A Dark Science: Women, sexuality, and psychiatry in the nineteenth century*, New York: Farrar, Straus and Giroux.

Zastrow, C. (1984) 'Understanding and preventing burn-out', *British Journal of Social Work*, 14, 141–55.

Zellman, G. L. (1990) 'Child abuse reporting and failure to report among mandated reporters: prevalence, incidence, and reasons', *Journal of Interpersonal Violence*, 5 (1), 3–22.

Zellman, G. L. and Antler, S. (1990) 'Mandated reporters and CPS: a study in frustration', *Public Welfare*, Winter, 30–7.

Zimrim, H. (1984) 'Do nothng but do something: the effect of human contact with the parent on abusive behaviour', *British Journal of Social Work*, 14, 475–85.

NAME INDEX

219

SUBJECT INDEX